THE BEST OF NEWSPAPER 18 DESIGN

CONTENTS

THE SOCIETY OF NEWSPAPER DESIGN
129 Dyer Street • Providence, RI • 02903-3904
Judging takes place at The S.I. Newhouse School of Public Communications • Syracuse University • Syracuse, NY
ROCKPORT PUBLISHERS, INC.
GLOUCESTER, MASSACHUSETTS

Book Credits

Designer & Editor
C. Marshall Matlock
S.I. Newhouse School of Public Communications
Syracuse University

Associate Designer
Shamus Walker
Syracuse, NY

Associate Copy Editor
Barbara Hines
Howard University
Washington, D.C.

Cover Illustration
Michael Jantze
San Rafael, Calif.

Manufactured in China
Color Seperation by Primaz Production Ltd.

Special Thanks

S.I. Newhouse School of Public Communications
Syracuse University

Judging Assistants

Stephen Cavendish, page one designer, San Jose Mercury News
Rob Covey, design editor, U.S. News & World Report, Washington, D.C.
Elizabeth Cromer, SND membership assistant, Providence, R.I.
Steve Dorsey, presentation director, Lexington Herald-Leader
Carolyn Flynn, assistant managing editor/photo & design, Albuquerque Journal
Bill Gaspard, senior editor/visuals, San Diego Union-Tribune
Scott Goldman, assistant sports editor, Charlotte Observer, 18th edition coordinator
Dave Gray, SND executive director, Providence, R.I.
Barbara Hines, professor & Journalism Department chair, Howard University, Washington, D.C.
Jim Jennings, international consultant, Lexington, Ky.
Marshall Matlock, associate professor, S.I. Newhouse School of Public Communications, Competition Committee chair
Kenny Monteith, features designer, Nashville Banner
Harris Siegel, managing editor/design & photo, Asbury Park Press & The Home News & Tribune, Neptune, N.J.
Randy Stano, Knight Chair Professor, University of Miami
Tony Sutton, editor, SND's Design magazine, Mississauga, Canada
Shamus Walker, entry audit coordinator, Syracuse University

S.I. Newhouse School of Public Communications Students
— Brett Africk, Deepa Bharath, Sara Bines, Kristin Bojanowski, Cristina Breen, Gerard Cagayat, Shannon Casey, Nate Clory, Grant Gegwich, Timothy Grandinetti, Jennifer Gwee, Celeste Joseph, Laurie Kenyon, Marybeth Luczak, Mary Mertz, Jason Minor, Christa Neu, Lisa Pettitt, Andrew Phillips, Steve Post, Tom Price, Naomi Rabinowitz, Jonathan Rosman, Luce Rubio, Noelle Sakellaropoulos, Hope Schuessler, Cori Shaw, Rich Tsong, Gabrielle Varmette

The Society of Newspaper Design
129 Dyer Street
Providence, R.I. 02903-3904
Telephone: 401•276•2100
FAX: 401•276•2105
snd@snd.org
http://www.snd.org

First published in the United States of America by:
Rockport Publishers, Inc.
33 Commerical Street
Gloucester, MA 01960
Telephone: 508•282•9590

Other distribution by:
Rockport Publishers, Inc.
Gloucester, MA 01960

ISBN 1-56496-362-4 (Hardcover edition)
ISBN 1-878107-07-0 (Softcover edition)

There is a ritual of sorts that takes place each February in snowy Syracuse, New York.

Some of the finest publication editors, designers and educators from around the world descend upon this city and Syracuse University for a common purpose – to define the state of the art in newspaper design.

It is not an easy task.

This year, 21 judges from five countries spent more than a thousand collective hours pouring over 9,840 entries from 15 countries to arrive at what you see in this book.

They saw little but newsprint, little stickers, newsprint, colored chips, newsprint, colored cups, newsprint, team captains, newsprint, assistants, newsprint, hard-working SU students and more newsprint.

What they accomplished over that four-day period was precisely what we asked them to show us – "The Best of Newspaper Design" for 1996.

By the end of judging, when asked to look at the Gold Medal winners to see if there was a Best of Show candidate, all 16 judges wound up standing in front of one entry – The Scotsman's stunning, haunting, breaking news coverage of the tragic shooting at Dunblane Primary School. The judges honored the newspaper for its tasteful restraint with this coverage, which left many judges noting the power of the pages, even months after the event.

One hundred and twenty-seven newspapers were honored for their excellent work. Judges named 16 publications the "World's Best-Designed Newspapers." Also, they awarded 16 Gold Medals, 81 Silver Medals, 711 Awards of Excellence and six Judges' Special Recognition awards in addition to the Best of Show for The Scotsman.

The qualities for which the judges honored The Scotsman – simplicity, elegance and restraint – are a constant theme throughout the award winners.

For the ninth consecutive year, the S.I. Newhouse School of Public Communications at Syracuse University provided all the support and assistance needed for this massive undertaking. The tireless efforts of Marshall Matlock, Shamus Walker and the students at Syracuse ensured that everything would run smoothly from the time the entries started to pour in to the time this book was completed. They have my sincere appreciation for everything they do, year-in and year-out, for this competition.

Thanks also to the judging team captains – Carolyn Flynn, Jim Jennings, Harris Siegel and Randy Stano – and assistants Steve Cavendish, Steve Dorsey and Kenny Monteith. I could not, and I would not, want to work at the competition every year without the guidance, help and dedication from the many assistants.

My co-workers and editors at The Charlotte Observer also get my thanks for their support as I juggled the responsibilities of this position with my daily duties at the paper.

And finally, this contest was my second baby this year. The first was my son, Andrew, who was born June 22. Thanks, Drew, for understanding while Daddy helped with this contest.

Scott Goldman, 18th Edition Coordinator

Thanks, Drew

Todos los meses de febrero en la nevada Syracuse, estado de Nueva York, tiene lugar una especie de ritual.

Algunos de los editores, diseñadores y educadores de las mejores publicaciones mundiales llegan a esta ciudad y a la Universidad de Syracuse con un propósito en común – definir lo que es la vanguardia en el diseño de periódicos.

No es una tarea fácil.

Este año, 21 jueces provenientes de cinco países se pasaron más de mil horas colectivas examinando el trabajo de más de 9.840 concursantes de 15 países, para llegar a las conclusiones que Ud. puede observar en este libro.

No vieron mucho más que papel periódico, pequeñas etiquetas engomadas, papel periódico, fichas de colores, papel periódico, tazas de colores, papel periódico, capitanes de equipos, papel periódico, asistentes, papel periódico, laboriosos estudiantes de la Universidad de Syracuse y más papel periódico.

Lo que lograron en ese período de cuatro días fue exactamente lo que les pedimos que nos mostraran: "El Mejor Diseño de Periódico" de 1996.

Hacia el final de las deliberaciones del concurso, cuando se les pidió que examinaran a los ganadores de Medallas de Oro para ver si había algún candidato para el premio Mejor de la Exhibición, los dieciséis jueces terminaron en frente del trabajo de The Scotsman, en su extraordinaria y perturbadora cobertura de la primicia del trágico tiroteo en la Escuela Primaria de Dunblane. Los jueces dieron reconocimiento al periódico por su buen gusto y moderación en esta cobertura, que dejó a mucho jueces comentando acerca del poder de estas páginas, aun varios meses después del acontecimiento.

Ciento veintisiete periódicos recibieron reconocimiento por su excelente trabajo. Los jueces designaron a 16 publicaciones como "Periódicos Mejor Diseñados del Mundo". Otorgaron, asimismo, 16 Medallas de Oro, 81 Medallas de Plata, 711 Premios de Excelencia y seis premios de Reconocimiento Especial de los Jueces, además del premio de Mejor de la Exhibición que se llevó el periódico The Scotsman.

Las calidades por las cuales los jueces dieron reconocimiento al periódico The Scotsman – simplicidad, elegancia y moderación – son una constante entre todos los ganadores de premios.

Por noveno año consecutivo, S.I. Newhouse School of Public Communications de la Universidad de Syracuse han proporcionado todo el apoyo y asistencia necesarios para este esfuerzo masivo. El trabajo incesante de Marshall Marlock, Shamus Walker y los estudiantes de Syracuse han hecho posible que todo funcione sin tropiezos desde el momento en que comenzaron a llegar los trabajos concursantes hasta el momento que se completó este libro. Cuentan con mi más sincero aprecio de todo lo que hacen, al comenzar y terminar cada año, para hacer posible esta competencia.

También quiero extender mi sincero agradecimiento a los capitanes de los equipos de jueces – Carolyn Flynn, Jim Jennings, Harris Siegel y Randy Stano – y a los asistentes Steve Cavendish, Steve Dorsey y Kenny Monteith. Yo no podría ni querría hacer todo el trabajo para la competencia todos los años sin la orientación y ayuda de todos los asistentes.

A mis compañeros de trabajo y editores de The Charlotte Observer también les quiero extender mi profundo agradecimiento por su apoyo, en momentos que tenía que ocuparme tanto de las responsabilidades de esta posición como de mis responsabilidades cotidianas en el periódico.

Finalmente, este concurso ha sido mi segundo bebé este año. El primero fue mi hijo, Andrew, que nació el 22 de junio. Gracias, Drew, por tu comprensión mientras que tu Papá ayudó a preparar este concurso.

Scott Goldman, Coordinador, Décimoctava Edición

It took five days, 21 judges and more than 45 assistants to sift through 9,840 entries from around the world to decide the winners in the 18th Best of Newspaper Design competition.

And after 230 hours of preparation and more than a thousand collective hours of judging, 127 newspapers from 15 countries received 831 awards. Sixteen newspapers were named the "World's Best-Designed Newspapers."

Many of the winners are displayed in this book.

Judges use a complex system to decide winners. Balloting is secret; the system uses cups and chips so a judge does not know how others are voting until all votes are cast.

Almost as complex is the system to guard against conflicts of interest during the judging. Conflicts occur when a judge encounters an entry from his or her publication, a publication for which he or she has done recent consulting work (within an 18-month period immediately prior to judging) or a publication with which he or she directly competes. In these cases a "floating" judge is used to vote for or against the entry. A number of qualified "floating" judges were available on the judging floor to perform this duty.

Each panel consisted of five judges. At least three of them had to vote "yes" to grant an award. Entries receiving fewer than three votes were removed from the competition.
- Entries receiving three votes received an Award of Excellence.
- Entries receiving four or more votes in the first round advanced to the medal round.
- Entries receiving four votes during the medal round were awarded a Silver Medal.
- Entries receiving five votes (unanimous vote of the judging panel) earned a Gold Medal.
- At the end of competition judging, all judging panels came together to re-examine all Silver and Gold medal winners. Sometimes, when confronted with the entire body of medal winners (rather than winners from just one or two categories), judges will re-vote on the worthiness of some of their choices. Only the judges can move an entry up or down the awards scale.

SND presented three levels of awards:

An Award of Excellence was granted for work that was truly excellent. This award goes beyond mere technical or aesthetic competency. These entries need not be "perfect." It is appropriate to honor entries for such things as being daring and innovative if the entry is outstanding but less than 100 percent in every respect. This award went to 711 entries.

A Silver Medal was granted for work that went beyond excellence. The technical proficiency of the Silver Medal should stretch the limits of the medium. These entries are judged outstanding. Eighty-one Silver Medals were awarded.

A Gold Medal was granted for work that defines the state of the art. Such an entry should stretch the limits of creativity. It should be impossible to find anything deficient in a gold-winning entry. It should be near perfect. Sixteen Gold Medals were awarded.

In addition to the Award of Excellence, Silver and Gold medals, two special honors are possible: the Judges' Special Recognition and the Best of Show. These honors are given only when specific, special circumstances warrant the awards.

A Judges' Special Recognition can be awarded by a team of judges or by all judges for work that is outstanding in an area not necessarily singled out by the Award of Excellence, Silver or Gold award structure. This recognition has been granted for such things as use of photography, use of informational graphics and the use of typography throughout a body of work. This body of work may be a particular publication, section or sections by an individual or staff. The special recognition does not supplant any Award of Excellence, Silver or Gold and should be seen as an adjunct. Six JSRs were awarded.

Best of Show is the best of the Gold Medal winners. Discussion for this award takes place at the conclusion of the judging. Judges have an opportunity to view all Silver and Gold winners at the same time. There is no limit as to the number of Best of Show awards that may be presented in one or more categories; however, in the past such awards were non-existent or very few in number. One Best of Show was given.

Se requirió cinco días, 21 jueces y más de 45 asistentes para procesar a más de 9.840 trabajos de concursantes de todo el mundo y decidir quiénes fueron los ganadores de la Décimoctava Competencia del Mejor Diseño Periodístico.

Y, después de 230 horas de preparación y más de mil horas colectivas de deliberaciones, los jueces otorgaron 831 premios a 127 periódicos de 15 países. En la presente se incluyen 16 periódicos denominados por los jueces como "Los Periódicos Mejor Diseñados del Mundo".

Muchos de estos ganadores aparecen en este libro.

Los jueces usan un sistema complejo para decidir quiénes son los ganadores. El voto es secreto; el sistema usa tazas y fichas, de tal manera que un juez no sabe cómo están votando los otros hasta que todos han terminado de votar.

Casi igual de complejo es el sistema para evitar conflictos de interés durante las deliberaciones. Se presentan conflictos cuando un juez tiene que juzgar a un concursante de su propia publicación, a una publicación para la cual recientemente ha hecho trabajo de consultoría (y reciente se define como un periódo de 18 meses inmediatamente anterior al concurso) o a una publicación que es su competidor directo. En estos casos se usa un "juez flotante" para echar el voto a favor o en contra. Para desempeñar esta función hubo varios "jueces flotantes" calificados disponibles en la sala de deliberaciones.

Cada panel estuvo compuesto por cinco jueces. Por lo menos tres de ellos tuvo que votar "sí" para otorgar un premio. Los concursante que recibieron menos de tres votos quedaron excluidos del resto de la competencia.

- Los concursantes con tres votos se ganaron un Premio de Excelencia.
- Los concursantes con cuatro votos o más en la primera ronda avanzaron a la ronda de medallas.

- Los concursantes con cuatro votos durante la ronda de meda las recibieron una Medalla de Plata.
- Los concursantes que recibieron cinco votos (el voto unánime del panel de jueces) se ganaron una Medalla de Oro.
- Al final de las deliberaciones de la competencia, todos los pa eles de jueces se reunieron para re-examinar todos lo ganadores de Medallas de Plata y de Oro. A veces, al ver frente a la totalidad de ganadores de medallas (en lugar de ganadores sólo de una o dos categorías), los jueces votan de nuevo con respecto al valor de algunas de sus selecciones. Sólo los jueces pueden mover a un concursante hacia arriba o hacia abajo en la escala de premios.

SND presentó tres niveles de premios:

Un Premio de Excelencia por trabajo verdaderamente excelente. Este premio trasciende la mera competencia técnica o estética. Pero para recibir uno de estos premios los concursantes no tienen que ser "perfectos". Es apropiado dar reconocimiento a trabajos por ser audaces e innovadores, si la presentación es sobresaliente aunque no 100% perfecta en todo sentido. Este premio lo recibieron 711 concursantes.

Una Medalla de Plata por trabajo más que excelente. El dominio técnico de la Medalla de Plata debe estar muy por encima del promedio. Estos concursantes son sobresalientes. Se otorgó Medallas de Plata a 81 concursantes.

Se otorgó una medalla de Oro por trabajo que define la vanguardia. Un concursante a este nivel eleva los límites de la creatividad y es imposible encontrar puntos deficientes en su trabajo, el cual es prácticamente perfecto. Se otorgó 16 Medallas de Oro.

Además del Premio de Excelencia y las Medallas de Plata y Oro, es posible ganarse dos honores especiales: el premio de Reconocimiento Especial de los Jueces y el premio Mejor de la Exhibición. Estos honores sólo se otorgan cuando circunstancias específicas y especiales ameritan estos premios.

Un premio de Reconocimiento Especial de los Jueces puede ser otorgado por un equipo de jueces o por todos los jueces, por trabajo sobresaliente en un área que no necesariamente ha sido reconocida por la estructura del Premio de Excelencia o las Medallas de Plata u Oro. Este reconocimiento se da por méritos en uso de fotografía, uso de gráficas informativas y uso de tipografía en todo el cuerpo de trabajo. Este cuerpo de trabajo puede ser una publicación particular, o una sección o secciones de un individuo o del personal de un periódico. El reconocimiento especial no suplanta a ningún Premio de Excelencia o Medalla de Plata u Oro, y debe considerarse como un premio adjunto. Se otorgaron seis premios de Reconomimiento Especial de los Jueces.

El premio de Mejor de la Exhibición se otorga al ganador de los ganadores de Medallas de Oro. Las deliberaciones de este premio se llevan a cabo después de todas las otras deliberaciones. Los jueces tienen la oportunidad de ver a todos los ganadores de Medallas de Plata y de Oro al mismo tiempo. No hay un límite en cuanto al número de premiosde Mejor de la Exhibición que pueden otorgarse en una o más categorías, aunque en el pasado o no se han otorgado o han sido muy escasos. Se ha otorgado un premio de Mejor de la Exhibición.

It took just over 25 hours for five judges to select the 16 winning newspapers from the 239 entries in the World's Best-Designed Newspaper category. "It's all about content," one judge explained. "All the technology – all the Macintoshes in the world – cannot make up for weak content."

Judges found the winning entries presented a design that was a part of the total package. It was often invisible, yet always supportive of the content. The best designs organized and provided consistency for the winners, while not drawing attention to themselves. The judges stressed the need to keep things focused on the reason for the newspaper – the reader. The winning publications selected from the many tools of design including typography, illustration, infographics and photography to determine the most effective way to tell their stories.

The winners used design to enhance their content while establishing their identity within the community they serve. They clearly knew who they were and who their readers were. They worked to help the readers navigate through the paper, using design to identify and prioritize material for them. They were easily accessible and presented a sense of personality of the newspaper and its community.

The winning designs were innovative and displayed variety. They reflected a willingness to take creative risks, while integrating the entire package. They showed restraint in what they presented the reader. The excesses of color, typography and computer-assisted imaging found little favor with the judges. The winners were, in short, fresh, lively and engaging mirrors of their communities and not simply "stamped-out" copies of yesterday's editions.

> " Remember, we're doing this for the reader. "

They were consistent in their approach from the first page to the last. Attention to detail was as apparent inside the paper as it was on section fronts. They had well planned, and well executed, centerpieces. Their writing was engaging; the photography was compelling; the news judgment was decisive and clear.

The use of photography as a communications tool was highly praised in the winning entries. Many of the winning newspapers used photography well. The judges noted that photographs are editorial content and should be allowed to compete for space as such. Photography was seen as a storytelling tool. The power of black and white photography, in an increasingly color medium, was noted as was that of a well-edited picture story.

The judges lamented the overall lack of infographics in entries. They said there was a need for more and better simple graphics that were immediately understandable and content-strong like locator maps, bar graphics and pie charts. Infographics should advance the story, not restate it. They are an underutilized resource at the storyteller's disposal, the judges said.

The advice of this year's judges for the future is best summarized by a comment made by the last judge leaving the room. "Remember, we're doing this for the reader."

"World's Best-Designed Newspapers" copy was written by Jim Jennings, judging team captain

A cinco jueces les tomó un poco más de 25 horas para sel
cionar a los 16 periódicos ganadores de los 239 concursantes en la categoría Periódico Mejor Diseñado del Mundo. "Lo esencial es el contenido", explicó uno de los jueces. "Toda la tecnología – todas las computadoras Macintosh del mundo – no pueden contrarrestar una debilidad en el contenido".

Los jueces determinaron que los concursantes ganadores habían presentado un diseño que formaba parte integral de la presentación completa. Con frecuencia el diseño era invisible, pero siempre daba apoyo al contenido. Los mejores diseños organizaban y les proporcionaban consistencia a los ganadores, sin atraer atención excesiva a sus técnicas. Los jueces hicieron énfasis en la necesidad de mantener el enfoque sobre la razón de ser del periódico – el lector. Las publicaciones ganadoras escogieron las herramientas del diseño – tipografía, ilustraciones, infografía, fotografía, etc. – para determinar la manera más eficaz de relatar sus notas.

Los ganadores usaron el diseño para realzar el contenido de la nota, a la vez de establecer su identidad dentro de la comunidad que sirven. Estaban plenamente conscientes de su propia identidad y la de sus lectores. Trabajaron para ayudar a sus lectores a navegar por el periódico, usando el diseño para identificar y dar prioridad a los materiales presentados. Fueron fácilmente accesibles y presentaron un sentido de personalidad del periódico y de su comunidad.

Los diseños ganadores fueron innovadores y ofrecieron variedad. Reflejaron el hecho de que estaban dispuestos a tomar riesgos, a la vez de integrar la presentación completa. Mostraron moderación lo que le presentaban al lector. Los excesos en color, tipografía e imágenes generadas por la computadora nunca resultaron favoritos de los jueces. En resumen, los ganadores fueron reflejos frescos, vibrantes y cautivadores de sus comunidades y no simples copias de ediciones previas producidas en masa.

Se caracterizaron por ser consistentes en cuanto a su enfoque, desde la primera página hasta la última. La atención a los detalles era evidente tanto al interior del periódico como en las carátulas de secciones. Sus páginas centrales habían sido bien planeadas y ejecutadas. Su redacción era cautivante; la fotografía apremiante; el criterio noticioso decisivo y claro.

El uso de la fotografía como herramienta de comunicación recibió muchos elogios en los trabajos ganadores. Muchos de los periódicos ganadores hicieron un excelente uso de la fotografía. Los jueces notaron que las fotografías vienen a ser contenido editorial y que se les debe permitir competir por el espacio como tal. Se consideró a la fotografía como una herramienta narrativa. El poder de la fotografía en blanco y negro, en un medio que cada vez usa más color, se notó tanto como el de una nota de imágenes bien editada.

Los jueces lamentaron la falta general de concursantes en infografía. Recalcaron que hacía falta una mayor cantidad de gráficas sencillas y mejores, que fueran inmediatamente comprensibles y de contenido fuerte – mapas localizadores gráficas de barra, gráficas de sectores, etc. La infografía debe acentuar la nota periodística, no volverla a expresar. Es un recurso poco utilizado a disposición del relator, según opinión de los jueces.

El consejo de los jueces de este año para el futuro se resume en un comentario que hizo el último juez en salir de la sala: "Recuerden, estamos haciendo esto por el lector".

THE WORLD'S BEST-DESIGNED NEWSPAPERS

The World's Best-Designed Newspapers excel at presenting the news. Judges were asked to evaluate, compare and discuss the papers entered in this category. Newspapers were evaluated on the quality of the writing, storytelling, execution, photography, headlines and design.

[WORLD'S BEST-DESIGNED NEWSPAPERS]

[BEST OF SHOW]

[JUDGES' SPECIAL RECOGNITION]

The American
Westhampton Beach, NY

"This is a newspaper that screams 'READ ME!' It was one of the more fully integrated packages we saw in any of the circulation divisions. It knows its audience and deals with the relevant 'talk stories' of the day. The design is extremely consistent from page to page. On inside pages nothing is left half done. They have wonderful finishing touches to their pages. They make great use of their art. It's a great piece of work."

"Éste es un periódico que reclama lectura. Fue una de las presentaciones más plenamente integradas que vimos entre todas las divisiones de circulación. El periódico conoce a su audiencia y toca los sucesos del día de mayor interés para ellos. Su diseño siempre es consistente, de página en página; y en las páginas interiores nada se ha dejado a medio hacer: todas las páginas tienen sus broches de oro. El periódico hace uso óptimo de sus artes gráficas y el resultado es una verdadera obra".

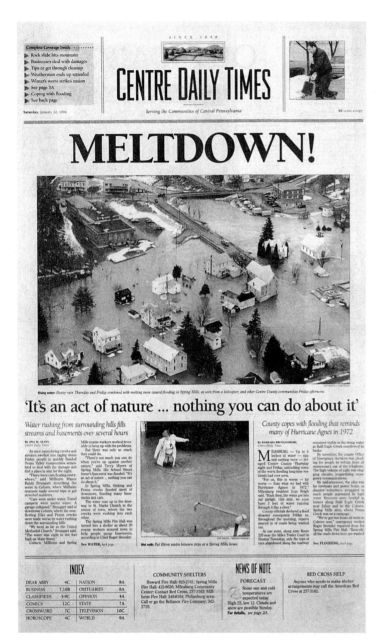

Centre Daily Times
State College, PA

"This is a very solid newspaper. One of the most organized, reader-friendly papers we've seen. It is extremely local in its approach to its story selection and play. It makes excellent use of its resources to tell its stories. It has a very refined look about it. Its typography is elegant. It has great local photography and isn't afraid to use it well. The inside pages really have a sense of where the paper lives and whom it is writing for."

"Éste es un periódico muy sólido. Uno de los periódicos mejor organizados y accesibles a sus lectores que vimos. Es extremadamente local en cuanto a su enfoque para seleccionar eventos noticiosos y entretenimiento. Hace un uso excelente de sus recursos para presentar sus notas periodísticas y tiene un aspecto muy refinado. Su tipografía es elegante, tiene una magnífica fotografía local y no tiene miedo de usarla bien. Las páginas interiores reflejan un conocimiento íntimo del lugar y de aquellos para quienes han sido redactadas".

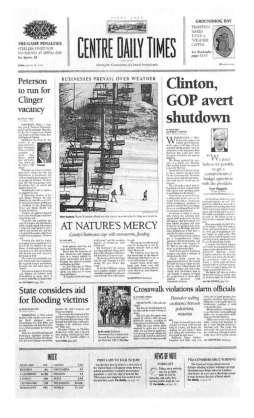

Daily Times-Call
Longmont, CO

"There is a strong sense of community about this newspaper. It seems to cover the entire range of life in the area. It has an attitude about it – it seems to be having fun, while trying to stretch or reach beyond the basics to localize national or international stories for its readers. It knows how to tell a story. It has a very consistent design that capitalizes on the use of great story selection, strong photography and good headline writing. It has incredible depth for a paper of this size."

"A este periódico lo distingue un fuerte sentido de comunidad. Parece cubrir la gama entera de la vida en el área. Se caracteriza por su actitud – a la vez de divertirse, se esfuerza por ofrecer más que simplemente lo básico, localizando eventos noticiosos nacionales e internacionales de interés para sus lectores. El periódico sabe cómo relatar un evento. Tiene un diseño muy consistente que se fundamenta en el uso de una excelente selección de notas periodísticas, buena fotografía y buena redacción de titulares. Ofrece una profundidad increíble para un periódico de este tamaño.

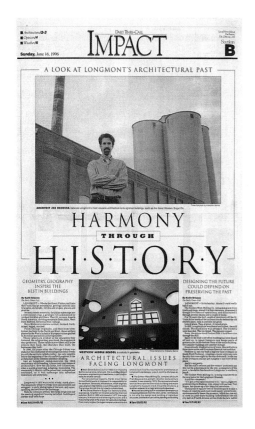

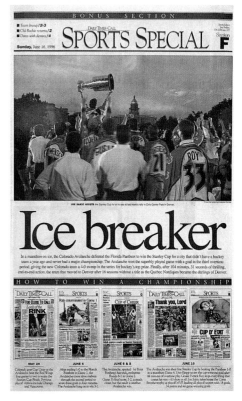

Diario de Noticias
Pamplona, Spain

"This is how a paper should look – lots of quick signals to the reader on what is really important. It is one of the few tabloids we saw where everything had a sense of scale about it. It doesn't fight with itself. Every page is packed with information with lots of entry points for the reader. It has a great sense of size and proportion about it. Yet, it is willing to take risks with its packaging. The design varies from day to day. The picture editing is very well done. It seems to work to find the best crop available from every image. The typography is handled very nicely."

"Es así como debe verse un periódico – muchas señales claras para el lector de lo que verdaderamente es importante. Es uno de los pocos pasquines que vimos en el cual todo cuenta con un excelente sentido de escala y proporción. No es en absoluto auto-contradictorio. Cada página está llena de información con muchos puntos de acceso a la misma para el lector. Y no por eso deja de tomarse ciertos riesgos en su presentación. El diseño varía a diario. La compaginación de imágenes está muy bien hecha. Se esfuerza por encontrar la mejor óptica disponible para cada imagen y la tipografía está muy bien hecha".

Le Devoir
Montreal, Canada

"This is an elegant and wonderfully charming paper. Its simplicity is its strong point. There is a lot of text here, but it isn't overwhelming. The paper has a very modern, stylish and sophisticated feel to it. This is not a newspaper that is stamped out every day. A great deal of thought goes into the organization of this paper. Its main virtue is its restraint in its use of color, photography and design. This is a clear winner."

"Éste es un periódico elegante y encantador. Su simplicidad es su punto fuerte. Contiene bastante texto, pero no en proporciones abrumadoras. El periódico tiene un efecto muy moderno, sofisticado y de moda. No es un periódico ordinario producido en masa, sino uno en el que la organización ha sido bien pensada. Su principal virtud es su moderación en el uso de color, fotografía y diseño. Es un verdadero ganador".

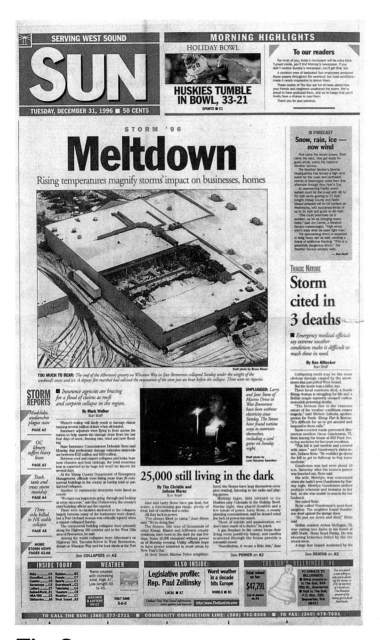

The Sun

Bremerton, WA

"This is a very well organized package with a very strong sense of place about it. It has a design that uses all of its resources to make it easy for the reader to navigate its pages. It works hard to integrate the entire package – words, illustrations, graphics and pictures – effectively. It makes great use of lists to keep the reader informed. This was a clear winner."

"Este periódico tiene una presentación muy bien organizada, con un fuerte sentido de lugar. Cuenta con un diseño que usa todos sus recursos para hacer que sea fácil para el lector navegar por sus páginas. Pone un gran esfuerzo para integrar de manera eficaz el paquete entero – palabras, ilustraciones, gráficas e imágenes. Hace un excelente uso de listas para mantener a sus lectores informados. Es un verdadero ganador".

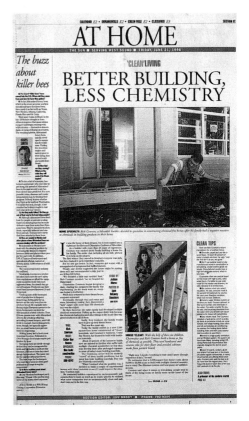

Dayton Daily News
Dayton, OH

"This paper is packed with information presented in a very orderly fashion. It pays a lot of attention to the little details that kept many of the papers in this division from making the grade. The inside pages are very well thought out. The 'Info Plus' and 'Close-up' features and the 'Start-Up,' which begins on the front and carries onto page 2, are especially well done. The section fronts are in a class by themselves. This is a paper that shows that it cares about its readers by making it easy for them to navigate their way through the paper. The section flags are extremely active. They are filled with information to make it easy for the reader."

"Este periódico está repleto de información presentada de una manera muy ordenada. Le presta mucha atención a los detalles pequeños, lo cual no hacen muchos de los periódicos en esta categoría. Las páginas interiores están bien pensadas. Las crónicas "Info Plus" (información adicional) y "Close Up" (de cerca), así como "Start-Up" (inicio), que comienza en la primera plana y va a la página 2, están especialmente bien hechas. Los frentes de sección son únicos en su género. Este periódico demuestra que está interesado en ser fácil de navegar para sus lectores. Los banderines de sección son extremadamente activos. Están llenos de información para facilitarle la labor al lector".

Die Woche
Hamburg, Germany

"Everything this paper does works toward one goal – reaching the reader. It is very well packaged. It shows what is possible with technology, without letting it get in the way. It has a sophisticated approach to every element in its design – color, typography, visuals. It is really trying to move into a new direction. It is innovative in its approach toward its presentation. It is absolutely beautiful."

"Todo lo que hace este periódico tiene un objetivo central: llegar al lector. Está muy bien presentado. Demuestra lo que es posible hacer con la tecnología, sin que ésta se ponga en primera plana. Tiene un enfoque sofisticado hacia todos los elementos de su diseño – color, tipografía, imágenes. Realmente se está tratando de encaminar hacia una nueva dirección. Su enfoque hacia la presentación es totalmente nuevo y absolutamente hermoso".

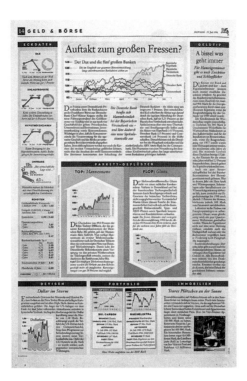

San Francisco Examiner
San Francisco, CA

"This is a paper that is full of energy. It knows who it is and who its readers are. It gives the reader the feel of the community it serves. It's 'earthy,' yet elegant in its presentation. The mix of typography is wonderful. It has lots of entry points for the reader. It has something for the reader on every page. It's trying to do something different every day. It isn't afraid to take risks. It wins more often than it loses."

"Éste es un periódico lleno de energía. Conoce su propia identidad y sabe quiénes son sus lectores. Le da al lector el sentido de comunidad a la cual sirve. Tiene "los pies sobre la tierra" y, sin embargo, es elegante en su presentación. La combinación de tipografía es maravillosa. Tiene muchos puntos de acceso para el lector. Tiene algo para el lector en cada página. Se esfuerza por hacer algo nuevo y diferente todos los días. No tiene miedo de arriesgarse; y gana más veces que pierde".

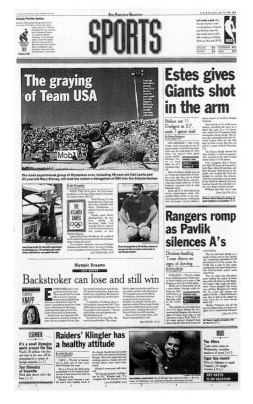

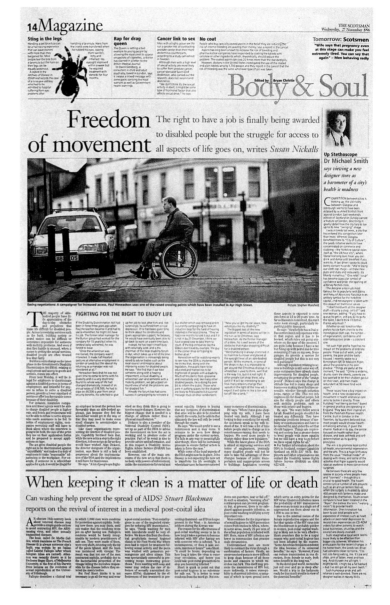

The Scotsman
Edinburgh, Scotland

"This is a complete newspaper. It has an incredible sense of place about it. It knows its readers and writes for them. It seems to do everything well. Its writing is wonderful. Look at the coverage of the shooting at Dunblane (note pages 40-43). Its pages have impact from the first to the last. Its typography is brilliant. Its photography is vibrant. Its use of color is restrained. In a word it is 'elegant.' It is a standard for the industry."

"Éste es un periódico completo. Tiene un sentido de lugar increíble. Conoce a sus lectores y escribe para ellos. Parece hacer todo bien. Su redacción es maravillosa. Fíjese en la cobertura del incidente en Dunblane (note las páginas Mejor de la Exhibición). Sus páginas tienen un impacto de comienzo a fin. Su tipografía es brillante, su fotografía vibrante, su uso del color moderado. En una sola palabra es "elegante". Ofrece un estándar para la industria".

The Spokesman-Review
Spokane, WA

"This is a very reader-oriented paper. It has a lot of personality. Everything it does seems to be done with the reader in mind. There are lots of entry points on every page. The design is really easy on your eyes. It avoids the gimmicks and relies on good use of photography, elegant typography, well thought-out white space and great packaging on the inside pages. Its design doesn't get in the way to the stories. It's a joy to read."

"Éste es un periódico muy orientado a sus lectores. Tiene una gran personalidad. Todo lo que hace lo parece hacer con sus lectores en mente. Todas las páginas tienen muchos puntos de acceso. Tiene un diseño muy abordable que evita las artimañas y se basa sobre el buen uso de la fotografía, una tipografía elegante, espacios en blanco bien pensados y una muy buena presentación en las páginas interiores. Su diseño no obstaculiza las notas periodísticas. Es un placer de leer".

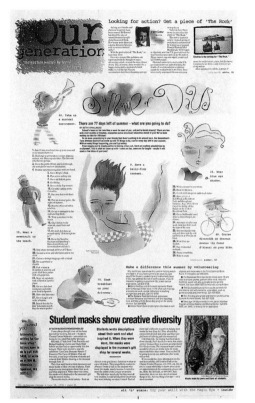

Boston Globe
Boston, MA

"This paper shows you can have a high story count and not be gray or ugly. It uses its space very effectively. It has a well organized, substantive and authoritative feel about it. Yet, it has fun with its coverage. It doesn't take itself too seriously. There are lots of entry points for the reader. It has great photography. The design is well organized. The design exists to guide the reader through the paper. It has an elegant feel about it. The typography is beautiful. The color is subtle and used only when it is needed. There is just the right amount of white space. It is just what one would expect from a paper from Boston."

"Este periódico demuestra que es posible tener una gran cantidad de notas y no ser gris o feo. Usa su espacio de manera muy eficaz. Da la sensación de estar muy bien organizado, así como de ser substantivo y autoritativo. Y, sin embargo, su cobertura es creativa. No se toma demasiado en serio. Ofrece muchos puntos de acceso para sus lectores. Tiene una fotografía muy buena, el diseño está bien organizado y su razón de ser es guiar al lector a través del periódico. Además, es elegante: la tipografía es hermosa, el color sutil y éste sólo se usa cuando es necesario. Tiene la proporción correcta de espacios en blanco. Es justo lo que puede esperarse de un periódico de Boston.

The Globe and Mail
Toronto, Canada

"This paper shows what you can do in black and white. It uses its creative resources for the reader. It has a clear sense of identity. Its presentation is serious, without being stuffy, and fits its readership. It is a newspaper for people who want to read. It has superb organization throughout the paper. It makes excellent use of its photography. Every picture is edited for maximum impact. It is one of the best we've seen."

"Este periódico demuestra lo que se puede hacer en blanco y negro. Usa sus recursos creativos teniendo como mira al lector. Tiene un sentido claro de identidad. Su presentación es seria sin ser pomposa y se adecúa a sus lectores. Es un periódico para gente que quiere leer. Tiene una organización exquisita de comienzo a fin. Hace un uso excelente de la fotografía: cada imagen es editada para lograr su mayor impacto. Es uno de los mejores periódicos que vimos".

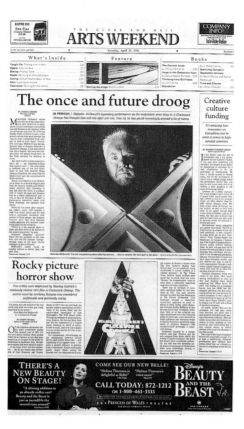

The Orange County Register
Santa Ana, CA

"This is the ultimate reader-conscious newspaper. Everything they do is done with the reader in mind. It is packaged very well. They never miss an opportunity to help the reader. It is well organized. There are lots of breakouts and entry points which makes it easy to access. The page 2 digest package is one of the best of its type out there. All of this supports the content. They know their community and the content reflects that knowledge."

"Éste es el periódico más consumido en cuanto a estar pendiente de sus lectores. Todo lo que hace es con el lector en mente, y tiene una muy buena presentación. Nunca se pierde ni una sola oportunidad para facilitarle la labor al lector. Está muy bien organizado. Tiene muchos puntos de entrada que le dan al lector fácil acceso a la información. La presentación en resumen de la página 2 es una de las mejores de su tipo. Todo esto está en apoyo del contenido. Este periódico conoce a su comunidad y el contenido lo refleja".

The Oregonian
Portland, OR

"This is a newspaper where everything is planned to the last detail. You just get that feel throughout the whole paper and the reader is the beneficiary of that. It is the perfect mix of dynamic presentation and great writing. It has a real local feel about it. The organization of the pages is excellent. The centerpieces are thought out and well executed. The design flexibility shows it isn't a daily formula. It has contrast, wonderful typography, great use of photography and lots of entry points. The color usage is well done. The planning that goes into putting out a newspaper like this is very evident in the coordination that has to take place on any story, whether it's big or small. Impressive job."

"En este periódico todo está planificado hasta el último detalle. Y esto se detecta desde la primera hasta la última página, siendo el beneficiario el lector. Es la combinación perfecta de presentación dinámica y excelente redacción. Además, tiene un sabor local. La organización de sus páginas es excelente. Las páginas centrales están bien pensadas y bien ejecutadas. La flexibilidad del diseño demuestra que no se trata de una fórmula. Tiene contraste, una maravillosa tipografía, excelente uso de la fotografía y muchos puntos de acceso. El uso del color está bien hecho. La planificación necesaria para un periódico como éste se hace evidente en la coordinación que tiene que haber para cualquier nota periodística, así sea grande o pequeña. Hace una labor impresionante".

The Oregonian

LIVING

Fashion • Entertainment • Television • Advice

Closet Cash

Savvy shoppers can turn their used clothing into money and earn plenty on the things they buy

SELLING

BUYING

Tracey Ullman shows a lot of character

Will the blame game never Cease?

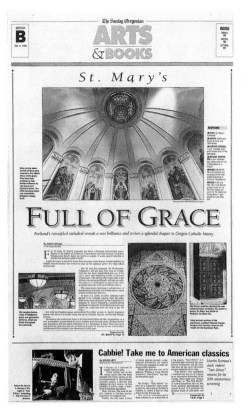

The Sunday Oregonian

ARTS & BOOKS

St. Mary's

FULL OF GRACE

Portland's remodeled cathedral reveals a new brilliance and revives a splendid chapter in Oregon Catholic history

Cabbie! Take me to American classics

The Sunday Oregonian

SPORTS

Stock goes up for Oregon's All-Stars

Dunk contest becomes Barry's coming-out party

ON THE Sidelines

" There has been a steady decline over the past 15 years. "

No bowlers to spare

Bowling is struggling to recapture the popularity it had in the 1960s and '70s by focusing on a new generation

Ducks feel like Wile E. Coyote after loss at WSU

The Sunday Oregonian

FORUM

YOUNG BLOOD

Violence by children and teens isn't new, but its randomness and senselessness are

I hope I might be able to change things. It seems like every other week, someone you know gets into a terrible fight or gets shot or stabbed. After a while, it becomes this pain that always stays inside you.

The same neighborhood, but an entirely different world

The Sunday Oregonian

TRAVEL

Visiting The Rock • Papua New Guinea's Huli wigmen • A Croatian vacation

GREECE: WHERE THE GAMES BEGAN

10 Atlanta icons

If you're traveling to Atlanta, here are 10 sites in the city you don't want to miss

Myths & marathons

Following in the footsteps of ancient athletes on the road from Olympia to Athens

Quiet, picturesque Lake County resort a home on the Ridge

The Sunday Oregonian

BUSINESS

"We believe the silicon age is just starting."

In the Northwest:

Taiwan's chip city

Booming Hsinchu is overcrowded with chip-makers and is spilling over into the Northwest with Taiwan Semiconductor's next big factory going up in Camas, Wash.

The key players:

Vice president brings a hard edge to Microsoft

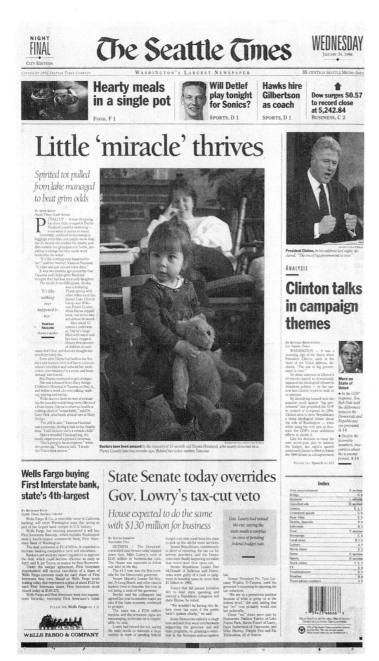

The Seattle Times
Seattle, WA

"This is a paper that draws the reader into it. Its coverage is well planned and very substantive. There are a lot of surprises as the reader goes through the paper in terms of how it uses its fronts, how it uses color and how all that works together to help the reader discover what's going on. It makes excellent use of its photography and illustration. This is an excellent read."

"Éste es un periódico que absorbe al lector. Su cobertura está bien planeada y es muy substantiva. A medida que va pasando las páginas, el lector encuentra varias sorpresas, en cuanto a cómo el periódico usa sus frentes, el color, y cómo todo se compagina para ayudar al lector a descubrir los sucesos del día. Hace un uso excelente de su fotografía e ilustraciones. Ofrece una excelente lectura".

Gold
- **for Breaking News Editors Choice National**
- **Also an Award of Excellence for News Page**

The Scotsman
Edinburgh, Scotland
Staff

The Scotsman won a Best of Show for demonstrating the awesome power of pictures and words when presented without gimmicks and tricks.

THE SCOTSMAN
◆ SCOTLAND'S NATIONAL NEWSPAPER ◆

THURSDAY 14 MARCH 1996   PRICE 42p

THE DUNBLANE PRIMARY SCHOOL TRAGEDY: A town devastated and a nation numbed after the murder of 16 children and their teacher

Gunman who brought horror to the classroom

JOHN SMITH, STEPHEN BREEN, JIM McBETH and JAMES ROUGVIE

THE man who shot dead 16 children along with their teacher in a Dunblane primary school believed he had been the victim of a smear campaign over allegations of child sex abuse.

Thomas Hamilton, 43, from Stirling, a gun club member with firearms certificates, also wounded a further 12 children and two other teachers before turning one of his four guns on himself.

It has emerged that Hamilton, who also ran youth clubs and summer camps, had been investigated by four Scottish police forces over a number of years after allegations of inappropriate sexual behaviour, but was never prosecuted. He was known to think himself a victim of smear campaigns and resent what he saw as harassment.

The 29 five-year-old children of Class P1 were in the gymnasium at Dunblane Primary,

Perthshire, when Hamilton – who police say had no history of mental illness – burst in at about 9.15am and opened fire.

Fifteen children died in the hail of bullets. Another died in hospital. Only one child escaped injury which police described as "sheer luck". Two children were off sick.

Last night, the injured children and teachers were being treated in hospitals in Stirling, Falkirk and Glasgow.

Ambulancemen who were among the first on the scene told how they found teachers trying to help and protect the injured children. "They were lying over the children and I got the impression they were trying to gather them in when they were shot," said John McEwen, the divisional manager of the Forth Valley Scottish Ambulance Service.

"We found them embracing and comforting, nursing individual children, some of whom were in a very poor way and doing their best with school first aid kits and bits and pieces.

"They were kneeling on the floor, covered in blood and cradling the heads and bodies of these wee souls with bullet holes in them. It wasn't so much the dying, it was five-year-old children looking unbelievingly at bullet holes in their arms and

Profile of a lone killer, Page 2

Chronicle of the shootings, Page 3

Caution over school security, Page 4

The arms control debate, Page 5

Editorial comment, Page 12

The place we call home, Page 13

Hamilton: investigated by four police forces

legs and who couldn't comprehend what was happening to them."

The class teacher, Gwen Mayor, 44, was also killed. The two other teachers, Mary Blake and Eileen Harild, were understood to have been injured as

Hamilton went to the gym. A third adult was injured but later released from hospital.

News of the shooting spread rapidly through the town, which has a population of about 7,300 and parents rushed to the school in Old Doune Road.

Police had sealed off the school and faced the awful task of giving the news to the parents of the children who had died and allowing others to take their children home. Last night, grieving families were receiving counselling.

The Scottish Secretary, Michael Forsyth, whose Stirling constituency includes Dunblane, and his Labour shadow, George Robertson, whose home is in Dunblane and whose children went to the school, visited the town.

Mr Forsyth said: "I cannot find words to express the horror at what has happened in Dunblane here today." Mr Robertson said: "We saw parents in grief and I think that's the abiding impression ... and I don't think I'll ever forget it."

Borders Police 18 months ago. Officers had spotted him with his trousers down in a compromising position with a young man in Edinburgh's Calton Hill area.

Last night, a spokesman for the procurator-fiscal service would not comment on reports that police investigations into Hamilton had not proceeded to court.

The incident brought messages of sympathy from all over the world and again raised the issues of school security and gun control.

He had been forced to resign as a Scout leader more than 20 years ago after allegations of improper behaviour – and it also emerged yesterday that he had taken photographs of semi-naked boys.

No fewer than four police forces investigated Hamilton after allegations from parents about bullying by Hamilton at clubs he ran in Dunblane, Falkirk, Linlithgow and Alva.

Hamilton, who had no convictions for any sexual offences, was cautioned by Lothian and

Hamilton, who lived in Stirling, about four miles from Dunblane, was a member of one local gun club and, only a month ago, was told he was not fit to join Callander Rifle and Pistol Club because his behaviour had been dangerous at a trial for would-be members. The club secretary, Raymond Reid, said: "He was not safe with a gun."

Just five days ago, Hamilton wrote to Buckingham Palace accusing the Scout Association of mounting a campaign to vilify his reputation.

The Queen, in a message to Mr Forsyth, said: "I was deeply shocked by the appalling news from Dunblane. In asking you to pass my deepest and most heartfelt sympathy to the families of all those who were killed or injured, and to the injured themselves, I am sure I share in the grief and horror of the whole country."

The Prime Minister, John Major, who was informed of the incident as he attended the anti-terrorism summit in Egypt, de-

scribed the massacre as a "mad and evil act", and added: "It is beyond belief that so many young lives can have been so brutally ended in this way."

The Labour leader, Tony Blair, said: "These are little children who at the weekend would have been playing with their brothers and sisters and mothers and fathers. They went to school today with the whole of their lives in front of them – now, nothing."

Alex Salmond, the leader of the Scottish National Party, said: "For so many young lives to have been ended in such a cruel and senseless manner is horrific and deeply shocking. Words cannot convey the deep horror that everyone will feel.

The Liberal Democrat leader, Paddy Ashdown, said: "At times like this, it is impossible to find words to express how you feel."

The Moderator of the General Assembly of the Church of Scotland, the Rt Rev James Harkness, said the slaughter left all civilised people "numbed and bewildered"

'It's a massacre, a massacre ... we'll never get over it'

LYNN COCHRANE

A SMALL boy with hair the colour of ripened wheat walked from the school into the arms of his parents.

At that moment he was, more than ever, their most precious being. He had just survived Britain's worst massacre. Behind him in Dunblane Primary School lay the tiny bodies of school companions mown down a before they had begun to live.

Other parents had run there too, abandoning ironing, workbenches,

accounts, after rumours of a terrible happening swept through the town.

For those with children in his Primary 1 class there would be none of the relief experienced by the parents of the boy with flaxen hair.

They gathered outside the large detached house at the school entrance for news of the children they had waved off scarcely two hours earlier. They were ushered in by a policeman. They were so hushed that you could hear the chirping of sparrows and the rush of a nearby river.

Moments later everything

was drowned by anguished screams and the walls of mothers calling their children's names. One woman was screaming, "Victoria, Victoria".

They told those waiting outside the worst.

It was hard for those still waiting, unsure whether there was worse yet to come. Some drank hot tea from flasks and stamped their feet to keep warm on a bitingly cold March morning.

"Everyone with Primary 5 children come in," shouted a policeman as he opened the gates to the next batch of

relatives. For the Primary 5 parents the news of their children was good.

They came out, subdued but thanking God that their children had been spared.

Sheila Nairn left with her arm around her daughter, Laura, and said: "If this had been on television, I would have thought it far-fetched."

Tucked at the back of quiet Old Doune Road, the ugly 1970s-built school looked out of place among surrounding handsome stone villas and their well tended gardens. Reporters asked to enter and

see the gymnasium where the atrocity occurred. "You wouldn't want to," Supt Louis Munn of Strathclyde Police replied solemnly as he announced that the gym was strictly out of bounds.

The detached properties around the school are home to scores of commuters who make the daily trek to Glasgow and Stirling. Usually the closest they get to violence is when they rent a video from the High Street shop. That shop, like most others in Dunblane, was closed yesterday as a mark of respect.

The streets emptied as the dark day went on, except for a few locals who gathered outside the Victoria Halls where a makeshift press centre had been set up.

Richard Kelly, 53, sobbed openly. Summing up the feelings of the whole community, he muttered: "I know some of the families. It's a massacre, a massacre. We'll never get over it.

"What can we do? Put armed guards at school gates? You worry when they're not home by four, but you think they're safe in school."

A few yards up the road next to Dunblane's ancient cathedral local people intent on marking the tragedy called out the fire brigade to help erect a flag at half mast outside the Burgh Chambers.

A woman rushed past me and said she was heading for the cathedral – "I just had to get out, I felt the walls closing in on me, so I'm going to say a prayer."

A stream of villagers made their way to the cathedral throughout the day. "They have sat quietly grieving, praying and comforting one another," said church officer

Bill Saichney. "We are devastated. It all started off so quietly this morning. It was really a trickle of news that something was happening that became a tidal wave which has swept over all of us."

No.47,568

4 NEWS

THE SCOTSMAN
Thursday, 14 March 1996

DUNBLANE PRIMARY SCHOOL TRAGEDY

Classroom safety: *There is a need to introduce more control over who enters school buildings, but teachers, parents and council leaders are determined not to rush into any knee-jerk decisions*

Caution urged over security

GRAEME WILSON
Education Correspondent

Tribute

'She was always smiling, always laughing'

GWEN Mayor, who died in yesterday's attack, was remembered last night as a committed and enthusiastic teacher who was always smiling.

Anxious parents hurry towards one of the entrances of Dunblane Primary School after news of the killings began to spread through the town.   Picture: Ian Rutherford

The school

An ordinary primary where a community must now learn how to cope with tragedy

GRAEME WILSON

Bullet holes puncture a window.   Picture: Ian Rutherford

A quiet family town finds itself engulfed by torment

Residents mourn: *Close-knit community left to wonder why*

AILEEN EASTON

THE SCOTSMAN
Thursday, 14 March 1996

DUNBLANE PRIMARY SCHOOL TRAGEDY

NEWS 5

Gun laws: *The fact that Thomas Hamilton met tough post-Hungerford restrictions on private firearms ownership will reopen the row over how to legislate on who can be licensed to carry weapons in Britain*

Experts split on arms curbs

NIC OUTTERSIDE

One of the children is led away from the school. Hundreds of distraught parents and relatives who had flocked there within an hour of the incident.   Picture: Ian Rutherford

Surviving the trauma

Mental scars will take long time to heal

BRYAN CHRISTIE
Health Correspondent

William Wilson, Central's chief constable, at the scene   Picture: Ian Rutherford

Flashback

Shooting stirs tragic memories

DANI GARAVELLI

Killer's motives

Lone gunmen baffle psychologists

Dani Garavelli

The Scotsman ganó un premio de Mejor de la Exhibición por demostrar el asombroso poder de las imágenes y palabras cuando se presentan sin artimañas y trucos.

Gold
• for News Front Page & Breaking News
The Scotsman
Edinburgh, Scotland
Staff

THE SCOTSMAN

◆ SCOTLAND'S NATIONAL NEWSPAPER ◆

FRIDAY 15 MARCH 1996   PRICE 42p

Ian Bell: *"Call it madness or evil, sickness or sin: those are just the words we use to give a name to our incomprehension. Thomas Hamilton was one of us, part of the species. There is horror in the suffering he inflicted but a deeper horror, a terror, in the fact that we cannot explain how one of us became what Thomas Hamilton became."* **Page 19**

Now the questions begin

JOHN SMITH, EWEN MacASKILL, LYNN COCHRANE and STEPHEN BREEN

A PUBLIC inquiry was ordered by the Scottish Secretary, Michael Forsyth, yesterday to carry out a full investigation into the Dunblane massacre, ranging from security in schools to why Thomas Hamilton – the subject of at least 12 separate complaints to the police and local authorities – was granted firearms certificates.

The inquiry is to be headed by Lord Cullen, who is widely respected for his report into the Piper Alpha disaster.

"In general terms it will be to look into the circumstances surrounding the murder of these children and the teacher at Dunblane Primary School," said Mr Forsyth.

"I have no doubt the issues surrounding the licensing of guns

weapons and the nature of the individual will be addressed. Lord Cullen will look at all aspects of children's safety and schools and any other matters arising from this incident."

Much of the focus will be on how Hamilton had a firearms certificate not only for the four handguns he had taken to the school – two 9mm pistols and two .357 revolvers – but a 7.36 rifle and a .22 rifle.

In the Commons, the Prime Minister, John Major, said: "There will be many questions which now have to be addressed." Ministers would have to consider the implications of the incident "for any future changes in firearms control".

He said he had an open mind on the tightening of gun laws.

The police are under statutory obligation to make thorough checks on everyone who applies for a firearms certificate to ensure they are a "fit and proper person".

The longest day of their lives, Pages 2 and 3
A human timebomb, Pages 4 and 5
Letters of grievance, Pages 4 and 5
Editorial Comment, Page 18
Lesley Riddoch, Page 19
The mind of a murderer, Page 20

Hamilton, a loner, described yesterday as a "timebomb ticking away", was considered by Central Scotland Police to be fit for a certificate.

Hamilton, 43, was investigated by four police forces over allegations of sex abuse involving children over a number of years. He was never charged or convicted of any offence. However, he was cautioned by Lothian and Borders Police 18 months ago after officers had spotted him with his trousers down in a compromising position with a young man in

Edinburgh's Calton Hill area.

Although police refused to discuss Hamilton's firearms certificate, a senior police source was last night reported as saying there was no question of revoking the certificate as he had never been charged with an offence, far less convicted.

Mr Major travelled to Scotland with Mr Forsyth last night and will visit some of the injured children in hospital in Stirling today, before going on to the primary school in Dunblane. Mr Major will be accompanied by the Labour leader, Tony Blair.

The Queen and the Princess Royal are to visit Dunblane on Monday.

It was disclosed yesterday that the school may be demolished if experts decide it would be too traumatic for survivors to return to the scene.

The struggle of the whole country to come to terms with the tragedy was reflected in the Commons, which heard in silence comments delivered by ministers and MPs, many close to tears.

No-one could recall any event over the last 30 years which has so moved MPs. Mr Blair, barely able to get his words out because of the emotion, said: "Politics is silent today."

The shadow Scottish secretary, George Robertson, who sounded as if he might break down, said: "I have to say that Dunblane today is worse than yesterday in its mourning and tomorrow will probably be worse still as the enormity of the

massacre comes home in the shape of real children gone, real families afflicted and a whole community scarred and tortured."

Part of the explanation as to why the event has brought such a response not only throughout Britain but the world was given by Mr Forsyth when he said: "The cold-blooded slaughter of tiny children is beyond atrocity."

He said the inquiry will begin work as quickly as possible. Lord Cullen is to meet the Lord Advocate and the Lord President of the Court of Session today to discuss the terms of the inquiry.

A final accident inquiry will also be held.

Mr Forsyth also revealed that a Scottish Office proposal that would have relaxed the regulations on playgroups and holiday activities for under-eights is to be put on hold until after the inquiry. At present, any such

activity lasting more than six days is subject to police checks on suitability of staff. The Scottish Office proposal would have extended this to 60 days.

A message of sympathy from the Pope was read out to the people of Dunblane last night at the first of a series of church services to mourn those killed in the massacre.

Pope John Paul said he was

"profoundly sad" about what he described as the "senseless violence". He offered prayers and blessings.

More than 200 residents of all faiths packed the Roman Catholic Church of the Holy Family.

There was standing room only at the 45-minute service which was led by Canon Basil O'Sullivan.

Head tells of the day evil visited his school

STEPHEN BREEN and MICHAEL PATERSON

"WE tried to identify those who were still alive and those whose wounds could be treated, but there were so many of them."

The words of Ron Taylor, the headmaster of Dunblane primary, brought home the full horror of Wednesday morning's outrage at his school.

"Evil visited us yesterday. We don't know why, we don't understand it and I guess we never will." He said he would never forget the carnage which left 16 of his pupils and their teacher dead.

He described the teacher Gwen Mayor as a "super col-

league and friend. She was a highly respected and very experienced, lovely lady."

Mr Taylor, his voice filled with emotion, told of the moment he opened the gym doors to be confronted with the extent of the massacre. "The scene that met us in the hall was just utterly appalling and is one's worst nightmare. I just cannot get the images out my head."

In the Commons, Michael Forsyth praised Mr Taylor's "heroic efforts" to save the lives of dying pupils.

But Mr Taylor, 45, who lives in Stirling and has two daughters aged 13 and 17, denied he had been a hero coping with the aftermath. "That's unjustified, we all did the best we could together. I got my strength from them, and we got our strength from each other."

Mr Taylor, head for just over two years, added: "During the course of the day we talked and comforted one another in the appalling circumstances. I telephoned most of my staff today and I hope we'll get together

Ron Taylor: "I can't get the images out of my head"

and talk tomorrow morning. The staff were just magnificent and we did everything we could, but it was a terrible sight and there was really little we could do.

"I think the school will recover but we are going to need lots of help to heal the scars.

"We will recover. There is a strong team spirit in the staff and it is a close-knit community. I know we will recover."

Killer's letter of last resort to the Queen

JOHN SMITH

IN ONE of his last acts before killing 16 children and a teacher in Dunblane Primary School on Wednesday morning, Thomas Hamilton posted details of his 20-year grievance against the authorities to *The Scotsman*.

The copies of the seven letters arrived yesterday morning, almost exactly 24 hours after the tragedy was reported to unfold. Other newspapers and television and radio stations received the same letters.

They included one he wrote a week ago to the Queen in which he states he is contacting her "as a last resort".

The letter to the Queen, patron of the Scout Association, contains a litany of hate for the movement's leadership. The others feature yet more complaints about Central Scotland Police and Central Region.

Hamilton, 43, also included letters to his local MP Michael Forsyth, the Scottish Secretary. One, dated March 1993, and headed "Juvenile Crime", refers

to the "horrific murder" of James Bulger by two ten-year-old boys.

"The work of my group in providing sporting and leisure-time activities for young boys has the effect of channelling young energies into creative and worthwhile pursuits," he wrote.

Hamilton said it was "ironic" that the closure of two Dunfermline Boys Sports Clubs in 1992 had been caused by the "irresponsible actions of overzealous officers from Central Scotland Police". They had been "obsessed with child abuse in carrying out their failed pervert hunt".

He added: "Mr Forsyth, in twenty years of operation of our lawful activity, there has never been any lawbreaking or any suggestion of sexual child abuse against either myself or any of my leaders."

He claimed that by giving "sinister slants" to ordinary, everyday events to parents, police officers had caused serious and lasting damage to his work.

In the letter to the Queen, Hamilton said that he wanted to make her aware of his long-standing complaint against the Scout Association.

After being asked over 20 years ago to become a Scout leader, he had been offered a better position locally, but this had never been ratified. A former district commissioner had attempted to brand him as a pervert.

Hamilton claimed rumours had reached "epidemic proportions" across Central region.

"As well as my personal distress and loss of public standing, this situation has also resulted in loss of my business and ability to earn a living. Indeed, I cannot even walk the streets for fear of embarrassing ridicule."

In a final paragraph that signalled his desperation, Hamilton told the Queen: "I turn to you as a last resort and am appealing for some kind of intervention in the hope that I may be able to regain my self-esteem in society."

TV and Radio: 23 ● Bulletin and Weather: 24 ● Crosswords: 24, 42 ● Births, Marriages and Deaths: 17

No.47,569

The Scotsman won a Gold Medal for its vibrant pages. Twelve months after the massacre in Scotland the same pages are still vibrant. They have the power to recreate the moment. All design elements are strong – the content, size and placement of photos, the typographical treatment and the way headlines recreate emotion. Done the day after the massacre, the coverage is complete. There is nothing more The Scotsman needed to tell this chilling story better.

The Scotsman ganó una Medalla de Oro por sus páginas vibrantes. Doce meses después de la masacre en Escocia, las mismas páginas siguen vibrando. Tienen el poder de recrear el momento. Todos los elementos del diseño son fuertes – el contenido, tamaño y colocación de las fotos, el tratamiento tipográfico y la forma en que los titulares vuelven a crear la emoción del momento. La cobertura de la masacre es completa, al haber sido preparada el día siguiente de ocurrir. No hay nada más que The Scotsman hubiera podido hacer para presentar mejor esta nota deprimente.

Gold
• for Color Illustration
The New York Times Book Review
New York, NY
Steven Heller, Art Director; Mirko Ilic, Illustrator

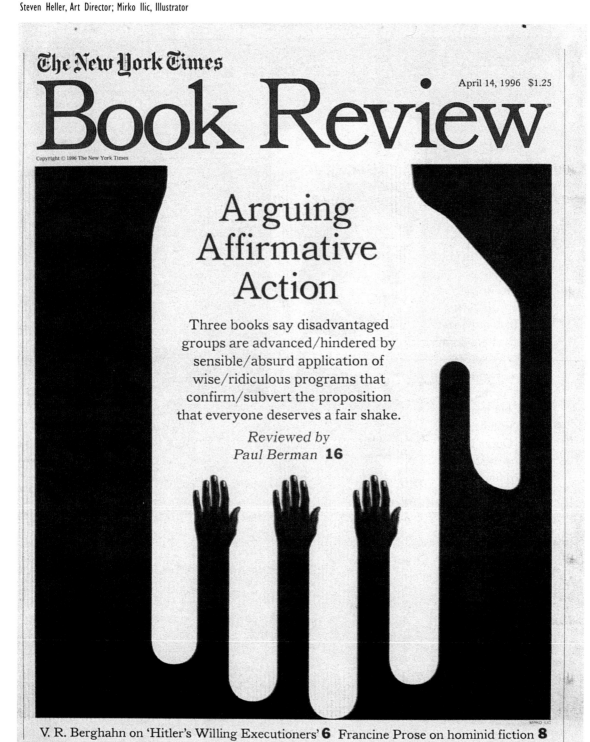

The New York Times Book Review was awarded a Gold Medal and a JSR for the merging of very different, yet essential, elements: movement, black, white, color and words. Realistic graphic elements convey the message behind this text.

El New York Times Book Review se ganó una Medalla de Oro y un premio de Reconocimiento Especial de los Jueces por combinar elementos muy diferentes aunque esenciales: movimiento, negro, blanco, color y palabras. Elementos gráficos de gran realismo comunican el mensaje que subyace este texto.

Gold
• for Sports Section
The Scotsman
Edinburgh, Scotland
Staff

The Scotsman won a Gold Medal and a JSR for its sports sections which have great consistency in presentation. The typography is elegant, especially for a sports section, and every page has the strength of a section cover. The Scotsman chooses good photos and uses them well, elevating the impact of the content. The size and selection of photos made the judges feel as though they were watching television rather than viewing newspaper photos.

The Scotsman se ganó una Medalla de Oro y un premio de Reconocimiento Especial de los Jueces por sus secciones de deportes, las cuales tienen una excelente consistencia de presentación. La tipografía es elegante, especialmente para una sección de deportes, y todas las páginas tienen la solidez de la primera plana de una sección. The Scotsman escoge buenas fotografías y las usa bien, acentuando el impacto del contenido. El tamaño y selección de fotos hizo sentir a los jueces como si estuvieran viendo televisión, en lugar de estar viendo fotos en un periódico.

A JSR was awarded to the staff of The Scotsman for storytelling through their design.

The Scotsman was awarded a Gold Medal for the innovative integration of type and image by using placement, contrast in color and graphic technique to create diversion.

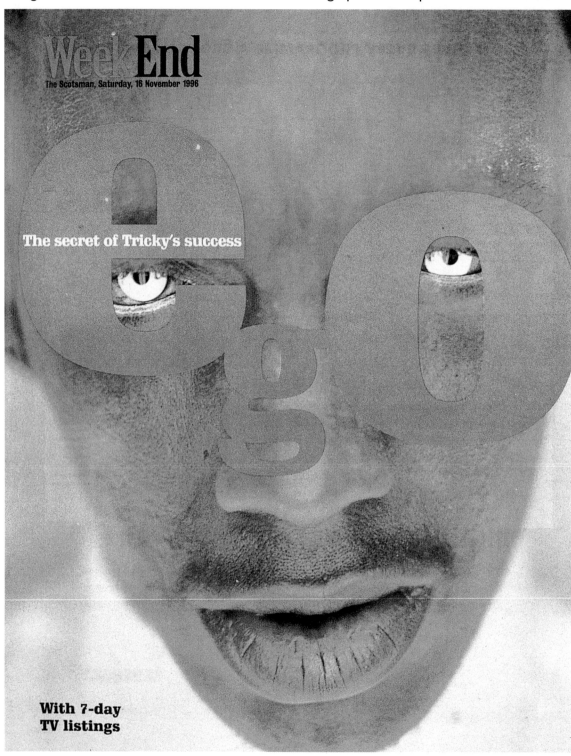

Gold
• for Magazine Cover Color
The Scotsman
Edinburgh, Scotland
Ally Palmer, Art Director; David Gray, Designer

The Scotsman se ganó una Medalla de Oro por su integración novedosa de tipo e imagen por medio del uso de la colocación, el contraste de colores y técnicas gráficas para crear diversiones.

Silver
• for Regularly Appearing Feature Section
El Pais
Madrid, Spain
Staff

12-13. Gabriel García Márquez, un premio Nobel de Literatura en EL PAÍS. 14. 7 de julio de 1982: concierto de los Rolling Stones en Madrid. 24. 23 de enero de 1990: inauguración de la Exposición Velázquez en el Museo del Prado.

Sábado 4 de mayo de 1996   EL PAIS 20 AÑOS   Número 236

El Pais received a JSR for the overall use of typography, carefully orchestrated use of color and elegance in design. The thought going into the organization, use of images and packaging is of the highest quality.

El País recibió un premio de Reconocimiento Especial de los Jueces por su uso general de tipografía y el uso cuidadosamente orquestado de color y elegancia en su diseño. Su organización bien pensada, uso de imágenes y presentación es de la más alta calidad.

Award of Excellence
• for Single-subject Series
The Atlanta Journal & Constitution
Atlanta, GA

Tony Deferia, AME News Art & Photography; Thomas Oliver, AME Olympics; Don Boykin, AME Sports;
D.W. Pine, Designer; Sheri Taylor, Designer; Moni Basu, Designer; Jonathan Newton, Photographer;
John Glenn, Photo Director; Glenn Hannigan, Ellen Voss, Robert Mashburn, News Editors

Judges recognized The Atlanta Journal & Constitution for 30 days of coverage surrounding the 1996 Olympic games. The judges recognized the magnitude of the project and the difficulty of creating a paper within a paper which covered a singular topic.

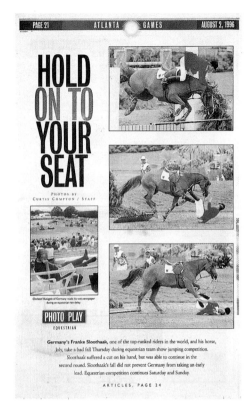

• **Also an Award of Excellence for News Page**

Los Jueces dieron reconocimiento a The Atlanta Journal & Constitution por 30 días de cobertura de los Juegos Olímpicos de 1996 por la magnitud del proyecto y la dificultad de crear un periódico dentro de un periódico, a cargo de cubrir un tópico singular.

Award of Excellence
• for News Inside Page
Expressen
Stockholm, Sweden
Lotta Magnusson, Designer; Marianne Lindberg

TIDSBILDER
EXPRESSEN

***
DET FINNS MÅNGA
förklaringar till våldet i Rio de Janeiro. Inget land har så dana klyftor mellan rika och fattiga som Brasilien. Och ingenstans är dessa så uppenbara som i det ljuvliga, magiska Rio med sitt Copacabana, sina skyskrapor och sina stränder, och det brutala, mörka Rio med sina favelor, sin korrupta polis och sin narkotika.

Brasilien är också ett land uppvuxet med våld. Här avskaffades slaveriet först för lite drygt 100 år sedan. Brasiliens befolkning är betydligt mer blandad än USA:s, men även här finns en utbredd rasism, och de svarta är hopplöst överrepresenterade i slummen och bland liken.

Här styrde en militärjunta mellan 1964 och 1985. Polisen uppträdde som milisära i kla med tortyr och avrättningar som vapen. Det är svårt att vänja dem av med det.

En stor del av brotten förblir dessutom ouppklarade. Åklagare Tania Salles Moreira berättar för mig att cirka 20 procent av morden i hennes distrikt kommer till åtmålet.

Då ska ni veta att hon är en av Rios modigaste åklagare, som renast bort dödspatrullerna i sitt område och som måste ha livvakt dygnet runt.

Och så är det knarket.

För drygt tio år sedan började de kokainbaronerna i Colombia, Peru och Bolivia använda Brasilien som genomfartsled. Rio de Janeiro blev den stora smuggelcentralen. Favelorna – slumområdena – deras lager och försäljningsplatser.

Det finns cirka 700 favelor i Rio. Så gott som alla är kontrollerade av lokala knarkmaffior. I många av dem är staten över huvud taget inte närvarande. Det är knarkbossen i favelan som styr.

Gängen slåss mot varandra och mot polisen. Det är en evig kamp, ett krig som förs varje dag, varje natt. Därav våldet, därav blodet, därav morden.

EN DÖD MAN – ingen överraskande syn. Barnen leker och pillar nyfiket på liket som på morgonen låg på deras gata i en förort till Rio de Janeiro. Han blev troligen ännu ett offer i kampen mellan stadens många narkotikagäng.

→Vänd...

Ingen skräms av liket. De har sett döda förr.

Expressen won a JSR for this spread which was part of a section about life on the streets in Rio de Janeiro. The headline reads "The dead body doesn't scare anybody. They have seen dead bodies before." Judges were taken by the brute strength of the photograph and the simplicity of the design. This is risk-taking journalism that transcends language barriers.

Expressen se ganó un premio de Reconocimiento Especial de los Jueces por esta doble página que formó parte de una sección acerca de la vida en las calles de Río de Janeiro. El titular dice "El muerto no asusta a nadie. Ya han visto muertos antes". Los Jueces se conmovieron por la fuerza bruta de la foto y la simplicidad del diseño. Este periodismo arriesgado es el que trasciende las barreras del idioma".

NEWS

In this chapter judges reco-
gized outstanding design for
front pages, local news pages,
sports pages, business pages,
inside pages and other news
pages. Breaking news pages
include local/regional,
national and international.
Special news topcis must represent one theme and are
divided into local/regional,
national and international.

[NEWS SECTIONS]

[NEWS PAGES]

[BREAKING NEWS PAGES]

[SPECIAL NEWS TOPICS]

Silver
The Scotsman
Edinburgh, Scotland
Staff

The Scotsman front page

THE SCOTSMAN
◆ SCOTLAND'S NATIONAL NEWSPAPER ◆
WEDNESDAY 4 SEPTEMBER 1996   NEWSPAPER OF THE YEAR   PRICE 42p

15 Education A three-page guide to selecting the right university

18 Chris Brand Is this man a racist?

Autumn Breaks Collect today's token on Page 4

Fear of Saddam reprisals

Operation Desert Strike: *Iraqi leader could hit at soft targets after Clinton's cruise missile attack*

War of words: President Clinton and Saddam Hussein address their nations after the US attacks on Iraq

EWEN MacASKILL
Political Editor

On the way: A Tomahawk missile is launched from the bow of the destroyer USS Laboon in the Gulf yesterday.

Inquiry call over jail suicides

Comton Vale: *Woman found hanged in cell takes toll to five*

JOHN SMITH

Bodies of abducted girls found buried

SUMMER SALE
OF FINEST QUALITY SCOTTISH
CASHMERE KNITWEAR

TV and Radio: 21 ● Bulletin and Weather: 22 ● Crosswords: 22, 34 ● Births, Marriages and Deaths: 14

The Scotsman inside pages

THE SCOTSMAN
Wednesday, 4 September 1996

10 EUROPE & WORLD

CRISIS IN IRAQ

Clinton's move brings political dividend

United States: *Dole is left struggling to catch up as his presidential rival takes the big decisions*

TIM CORNWELL
in Los Angeles

Bill Clinton: 'We must make it clear that reckless acts have consequences, or these acts will increase'

Saddam changes the rules

Analysis: *The battle the Iraqi leader is fighting has its own kind of logic*

JOHN ROBERTS

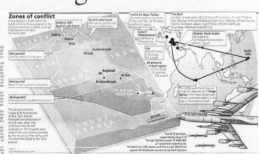

Zones of conflict

Kurds: Pawns in a complex regional game

FRED BRIDGLAND

Russia: Attacks condemned as unacceptable

Moscow brands strikes 'presidential election ploy'

ROBERT EVANS
in Berlin

France: A different tack from European allies

Concern as firms hope for easing of sanctions

JULIAN NUNDY
in Paris

Award of Excellence
Aberdeen American News
Aberdeen, SD
Staff

Award of Excellence
• Also an Award of Excellence for News Front Page & Breaking News
The Detroit News
Detroit, MI

Dale Peskin, Deputy ME; Chris Kozlowski, Design/Graphics Ed.; Chris Willis, Asst. Graphics Ed.; Shayne Bowman, Asst. Design Ed.; Michael Brown, Designer; Joe Greco, Designer; Gladys Rios; Designer; Daryl Swint, Designer; David Kordalski, Asst. Graphics Ed.; Theresa Badovich, Asst. News Ed.; Christy Bradford, ME; Frank Lovinski; Deputy ME News; Bill McMillan, News Ed.; Steve Fecht, Photo Ed.

Award of Excellence
The Detroit News
Detroit, MI

Chris Willis, Assistant Graphics Editor; Chris Kozlowski, Design/Graphics Editor; Dale Peskin, Deputy ME; Diana Thomas, Designer; Judy Diebolt, City Editor; George Bulluard, AME/Metro; Nancy Hanus, AME; Steve Fecht; Photo Editor; Karen Van Antwerp, Graphics Researcher; Shana Flowers, Asst. Metro Editor

The Detroit News ··
The Metro
SECTION C

Your local news section for Monday, June 17, 1996

City & Suburbs: Romney opposes Dole on abortion. 3C
MetroLife: Even pro golfers work to stay fit. 6C

In MetroLife
SUMMER

Slain mom reportedly feared son

He extorted money from her and threatened her, her sister says. Murder charges expected this week.

By Wayne Woolley
The Detroit News

Make sure your little camper has right gear

SPECIAL REPORT: MYSTERY MURDER

Doctor's slaying still a puzzle

By Judy DeHaven • The Detroit News

Dr. Robert Iverson will never forget the phone call.

Names in the case

Dr. Robert Iverson continues to help police in the investigation of his wife's death. "I think it's crucial for me to deal with this absolutely senseless act," he says. "They are going to catch these people."

First Arab International Festival declared a multicultural success

By David Shepardson
The Detroit News

Contact The News

Award of Excellence
Reforma
Mexico City, Mexico

Marco Antonio Roman, Gilberto Avila, Jose Luis Martinez, Heberto Monroy, Tadeo Guerrero, Designers; Jose Manuel Mendoza, Section Designer; Emilio Deheza, Art Director; Eduardo Danilo, Design Consultant; Salvador Camarena, Editor; Maria de Jesus Garcia, Editor

Award of Excellence
The Detroit News
Detroit, MI
Alan Whitt, Deputy Sports Editor; Chris Kozlowski,
Design/Graphics Editor; Annette Vasquez, Designer; Alan Lesig,
Photographer; David Kordalski, Assistant Graphics Editor; Rick
Epps, Designer

Award of Excellence
The New York Times
New York, NY
Wayne Kamidoi, Designer; Joe
Ward, Graphics Editor; Bedel
Saget, Graphics Editor;
Stephen Jesselli, Picture
Editor; Sarah Kass, Picture
Editor; Jay Schreiber, Assistant
Sports Editor; Sports Staff

Award of Excellence
Le Soleil
Quebec, Canada
Marcel Colbert, Designer; Desk Staff;
Jacques Samson, AME; Jean-Pascal
Beaupre, AME

Silver
The Seattle Times
Seattle, WA

Michael Kellams, Designer; Cathy McLain, Editor; David Miller, Art Director

Award of Excellence
The Albuquerque Tribune
Albuquerque, NM

David Carrillo, Designer

Award of Excellence
• Also an Award of Excellence for Sopt News Photography
The Atlanta Journal & Constitution
Atlanta, GA

Tony Deferia, AME News Art & Photography; D.W. Pine, Designer; Rich Addicks, Photographer; Glenn Hannigan, News Editor

Award of Excellence
The Atlanta Journal & Constitution
Atlanta, GA

John Caserta, Moni Basu, Designers; Rich Addicks, Photographer; Tony Deferia, AME News Art & Photography; Glenn Hannigan, News Editor

Award of Excellence
• Also an Award of Excellence for News Portfolio
The Atlanta Journal & Constitution
Atlanta, GA

D.W. Pine, Designer; Tony Deferia, AME News Art & Photography; Glenn Hannigan, News Editor

Award of Excellence
Ball State Daily News
Muncie, IN

Bill Webster, Editor/Art Director

Award of Excellence
Berlingske Tidende
Copenhagen, Denmark
Staff

Award of Excellence
Centre Daily Times
State College, PA
Curtis Chan, News Copy Editor

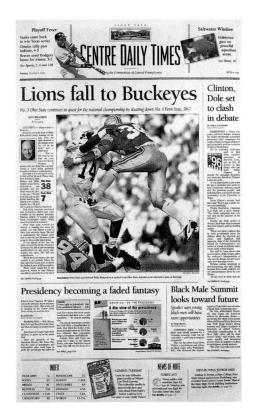

Award of Excellence
Chicago Tribune
Chicago, IL

Steve Layton, Graphic Artist; Therese Shechter, Associate Graphics Editor; Ken Marshall, Graphics Coordinator; Jeanie Adams, Assistant Picture Editor; Rich Anderson, Sunday News Editor

Award of Excellence
• Also an Award of Excellence for Breaking News
Chicago Tribune
Chicago, IL
Staff

Award of Excellence
The Courier-News
Elgin, IL
Jeff Boda, Designer

Award of Excellence
Detroit Free Press
Detroit, MI
Scott Albert, Designer; Todd Winge, Picture Editor; Alex Cruden, News Editor

Award of Excellence
Detroit Free Press
Detroit, MI
Scott Albert, Designer; Mike Smith, Picture Editor; Alex Cruden, News Editor

Award of Excellence
The Detroit News
Detroit, MI
Dale Peskin, Deputy ME; David Kordalski, Assistant Graphics Editor; Chris Willis, Assistant Graphics Editor; Shayne Bowman, Assistant Graphics Editor; Tim Summers, Graphic Artist

Award of Excellence
The Detroit News
Detroit, MI
Dale Peskin, Deputy ME; Diana Thomas, Page Designer; David Kordalski, Assistant Graphics Editor; Tim Summers, Graphic Artist

Award of Excellence
El Norte
Monterrey, Mexico

Perla Olmeda, Designer; Raul Braulio Martinez, Art Director;
Eduardo Danilo Ruiz, Design Consultant; Jorge Vidrio, Graphics
Editor; Alexandro Medrano, Graphics Editor

Award of Excellence
Diario de Noticias
Pamplona, Spain

Javier Errea, Art Director

Award of Excellence
El Pais
Madrid, Spain

Javier López, Designer

Award of Excellence
Folha de Sao Paulo
Sao Paulo, Brazil

Eleonora de Lucena, ME; Paula Cezarino, Deputy Front Page
Editor; Joana Brasileiro, Deputy Art Director; Joao Bittar,
Photo Editor; Moacir de Almeida Lima, Page Designer

Award of Excellence
• Also an Award of Excellence for Breaking News
The Greenville News
Greenville, SC

Scott Stoddard, Art Director & Designer; Ralph Jeffery, News
Editor; Phil Randall, Assistant News Editor; Alan Hawes,
Photographer; Suzie Riddle, News Artist; Kevin Walker, News
Artist

Award of Excellence
El Periodico de Catalunya
Barcelona, Spain

Olga Puig, Designer; Jaume Mor, Picture Editor; Ferran Sendra,
Digital Art; Jose Antonio Sorolla, Editor-in-Chief; Jose Luis
Martinez Ibanez, News Editor

Award of Excellence
The Home News & Tribune
East Brunswick, NJ

Harris Siegel, ME/Design & Photo/Designer; Teresa Klink, ME/News; Joe Lee Jr, Design Editor/Designer; Dick Hughes, Editor

Award of Excellence
The Idaho Statesman
Boise, ID

Randy Wright, Designer

Award of Excellence
Le Devoir
Montreal, Canada

Lise Bissonnette, Publisher; Bernard Descoteaux, Ed-in-Chief; Claude Bearuegard, News Editor; Roland-Yves Carignan, Art Director; Guy Taillefer, Deputy News Editor

Award of Excellence
Le Devoir
Montreal, Canada

Lise Bissonnette, Publisher; Bernard Descoteaux, Ed-in-Chief; Claude Bearuegard, News Editor; Roland-Yves Carignan, Art Director; Pierre Beaulieu, Deputy News Editor

Award of Excellence
Le Soleil
Quebec, Canada

Michel Samson, Designer

Award of Excellence
Le Soleil
Quebec, Canada

Michel Samson, Designer

Award of Excellence
Le Soleil
Quebec, Canada

Jacques Samson, Designer

Award of Excellence
The Miami Herald
Miami, FL

Herschel Kenner, News Editor; Hiram Henriquez, Graphic Artist

Award of Excellence
Newsday
Melville, NY

Joanne Utley, Assistant Art Director; John Paraskevas, Photographer; James Dooley, Director of Photography; Deanna Hutchison, News Editor

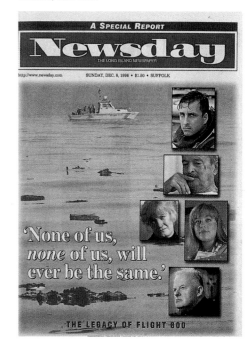

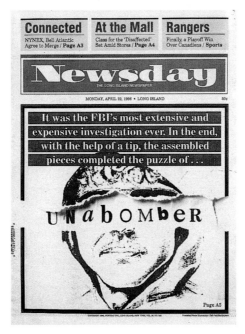

Award of Excellence
Newsday
Melville, NY

Dan van Benthuysen, Senior Art Director; Vince Antolini, Photo Editor; Judy Yuan, News Editor; Bob Brandt, ME; Tim Healy, Senior News Editor

Award of Excellence
Ole
Buenos Aires, Argentina

Martin Marotta, Art Editor; Jorge Doneiger, Art Director; Jorge Duran, Photo Editor; Ricardo Carcova, Photo Editor

Award of Excellence
Portland Press Herald
Portland, ME

Ken Jones, Slot Editor; Andrea Nemitz, AME Design; Bob Dixon, AME Operations; David A. Rodgers, Photographer; Doug Jones, Photographer

Award of Excellence
Reforma
Mexico City, Mexico

Jose Manuel Mendoza, Section Designer; Monica Solorzano, Photo Artist; Carlos Torio, Editor; Eduardo Danilo, Design Consultant; Emilio Deheza, Art Director

Award of Excellence
Reforma
Mexico City, Mexico

Marco Antonio Roman, Designer; Jose Manuel Mendoza, Section Designer; Luis Cortes, Photographer; Raymundo Rivapalacio, Ed.; Emilio Deheza, Art Director; Eduardo Danilo, Design Consultant

Award of Excellence
Reforma
Mexico City, Mexico

Carlos Torio, Editor; Jose Manuel Mendoza, Section Designer; Emilio Deheza, Art Director; Eduardo Danilo, Design Consultant

Award of Excellence
Reforma
Mexico City, Mexico

Marco Antonio Roman, Designer; Jose Manuel Mendoza, Section Designer; Israel Mejia, Illustrator; Francisco Vidal, Editor; Carlos Torio, Editor; Emilio Deheza, Art Director; Eduardo Danilo, Design Consultant

Award of Excellence
The Register-Guard
Eugene, OR

Staff

Award of Excellence
The San Diego Union-Tribune
San Diego, CA

Channon Seifert, Designer; Scott Linnett, Photographer; Paul Horn, Graphics Journalist; Bill Gaspard, Senior Editor/Visuals

Award of Excellence
San Francisco Examiner
San Francisco, CA

Jay Johnson, Executive News Editor; Staff; Kelly Frankeny, AME Design; Margorie Rice, Graphics Editor; Pam Dunston, Photo Editor; Richard Paoli, Director of Photography; Christina Koci Hernandez, Photographer

Award of Excellence
San Francisco Examiner
San Francisco, CA

Jay Johnson, Executive Editor; Staff; Kelly Frankeny, AME Design; Margorie Rice, Graphics Editor; Pam Dunston, Photo Editor; Richard Paoli, Director/Photography; Christina Koci Hernandez, Photographer

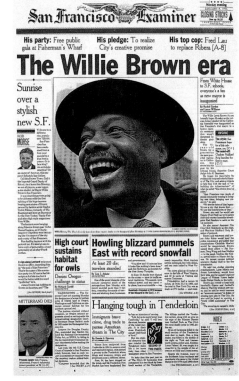

Award of Excellence
Savannah Morning News
Savannah, GA

J. Frank Lynch, News Planning & Design Editor; M. Daniel Suwyn, ME; Daniel Niblock, Design Intern

Award of Excellence
• Also an Award of Excellence for News Portfolio
The Seattle Times
Seattle, WA

Michael Kellams, Designer; Tom Reese, Photographer; Fred Nelson, Photo Editor; Cathy McLain, Editor; David Miller, Art Director

Award of Excellence
Star Tribune
Minneapolis, MN

Denise M. Reagan, Designer; Stormi Greener, Photographer; David Braunger, Graphics Artist; Bill Higgins, Weekend 1A Editor; Anders Ramberg, Design Director

Award of Excellence
The Stuart News
Stuart, FL

Jim Sergent, Chief Designer

Silver
The New York Times
New York, NY

Ken McFarlin, Art Director

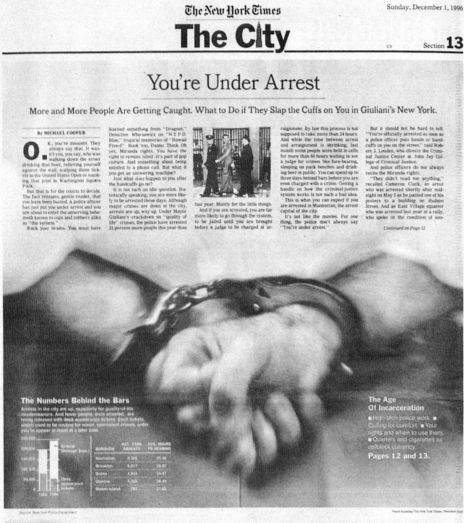

Award of Excellence
Times-News
Burlington, NC

John Pea, Managing Editor

Award of Excellence
The Times-Picayune
New Orleans, LA

Doug Parker, Photo Editor; Eliot Kamenitz, Photographer;
George Berke, Design Director; James O'Byrne, Sunday Editor;
Paul Fresty, Graphics Editor

Award of Excellence
El Pais
Madrid, Spain
Luis Mapáir, Photographer; Staff

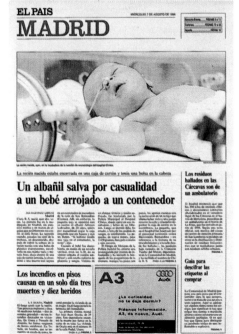

Award of Excellence
El Pais
Madrid, Spain
Morgana Vargas Llosa, Photographer; Staff

Silver
Reforma
Mexico City, Mexico
Daniel Esqueda Guadalajara, Section Designer; Ignacio Guerrero, Designer; Maria Luisa Diaz de Leon, Editor; Emilio Deheza, Art Director; Eduardo Danilo, Design Consultant; Alberto Cervantes, Illustrator

Award of Excellence
El Periodico de Catalunya
Barcelona, Spain

Mireis Armengol, Designer; Jaume Mor, Picture Editor; Javier Jubierre, Photo Editor; Losu de la Torre, News Editor

Award of Excellence
The New York Times
New York, NY

Joe Zeff, Designer; Newman Huh, Illustrator

Award of Excellence
• Also an Award of Excellence for News Portfolio
The New York Times
New York, NY

Joe Zeff, Designer

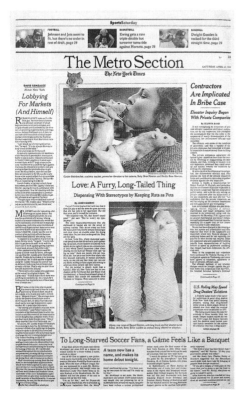

Award of Excellence
The New York Times
New York, NY

Joe Zeff, Designer

Award of Excellence
The New York Times
New York, NY

Anne Leigh, Art Director; Tiina Loite, Photo Editor; Fred Conrad, Photographer

Award of Excellence
The New York Times
New York, NY

Ken McFarlin, Art Director

Award of Excellence
• Also an Award of Excellence for News Portfolio
The New York Times
New York, NY

Ken McFarlin, Art Director

Award of Excellence
The New York Times
New York, NY

Joe Zeff, Designer

Award of Excellence
The New York Times
New York, NY

Joe Zeff, Designer

Award of Excellence
O Globo
Rio de Janeiro, Brazil

Tadeu de Aguiar, Editor; Andrei Bastos, Designer; Domingos Peixoto, Photographer

Award of Excellence
Reforma
Mexico City, Mexico

Daniel Esqueda Guadalajara, Section Designer; Luis Jorge Gallegos, Photographer; Gustavo Hernandez, Editor; Emilio Deheza, Art Director; Eduardo Danilo, Design Consultant

Award of Excellence
Newsday
Melville, NY

Ned Levine, Illustrator & Designer; Bob Eisner, Art Director; Jeff Massaro, Art Director & Designer; Howard Schneider, Editor; Tony Marro, Editor; Vince Antolini, Photo Editor

Award of Excellence
Reforma
Mexico City, Mexico
Daniel Esqueda Guadalajara, Section Designer; Ismael Garcia, Editor; Emilio Deheza, Art Director; Eduardo Danilo, Design Consultant

Award of Excellence
Reforma
Mexico City, Mexico
Daniel Esqueda Guadalajara, Section Designer; Luis Jorge Gallegos, Photographer; Adrian Rueda, Editor; Emilio Deheza, Art Director; Eduardo Danilo, Design Consultant

Award of Excellence
Reforma
Mexico City, Mexico
Ignacio Guerrero, Designer; Daniel Esqueda Guadalajara, Section Designer; Joel Merino, Photographer; Tomas Martinez, Photographer; Alejandro Ramos, Editor; Emilio Deheza, Art Director; Eduardo Danilo, Design Consultant

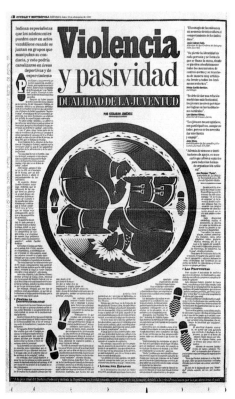

Award of Excellence
Reforma
Mexico City, Mexico
Ignacio Guerrero, Designer; Oscar Yanez, Designer; Daniel Esqueda, Section Designer; Alberto Nava, Photo Artist; Alejandro Ramos, Editor; Emilio Deheza, Art Director; Eduardo Danilo, Design Consultant

Award of Excellence
Reforma
Mexico City, Mexico
Oscar Yanez, Designer; Ignacio Guerrero, Section Designer; Israel Mejia, Illustrator; Gustavo Hernandez, Editor; Daniel Esqueda Guadalajara, Graphics Coordinator; Emilio Deheza, Art Director; Eduardo Danilo, Design Consultant

Award of Excellence
The San Diego Union-Tribune
San Diego, CA
Chris Ross, Designer; Nancee E. Lewis, Photographer; Michael Franklin, Photo Editor

Award of Excellence
San Francisco Examiner
San Francisco, CA

Richard Paoli, Director/Photography; Bernadette Fay, Sunday Editor; Margorie Rice, Graphics Editor; Kelly Frankeny, AME Design; Christina Koci Hernandez, Photographer

Award of Excellence
San Francisco Examiner
San Francisco, CA

Richard Paoli, Director/Photography; Bernadette Fay, Sunday Editor; Margorie Rice, Graphics Editor; Kelly Frankeny, AME Design

Award of Excellence
St. Paul Pioneer Press
St. Paul, MN

Doug Belden, Designer; Chris Polydoroff, Photographer

Award of Excellence
The Virginian-Pilot
Norfolk, VA

Julie Elman, Designer; Tamara Voniski, Picture Editor

Award of Excellence
The Albuquerque Tribune
Albuquerque, NM

David Carrillo, Designer

Award of Excellence
The Albuquerque Tribune
Albuquerque, NM

David Carrillo, Designer

Silver
Le Soleil
Quebec, Canada

Marcel Colbert, Designer; Desk Staff; Jacques Samson, AME; Jean-Pascal Beaupre, AME

Award of Excellence
The Albuquerque Tribune
Albuquerque, NM

Joan Carlin, Designer

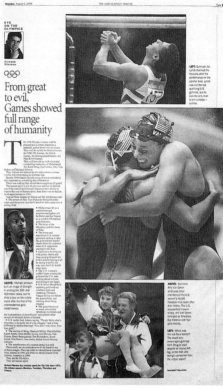

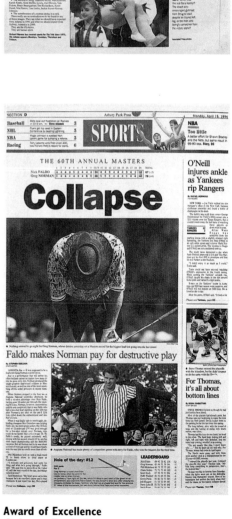

Award of Excellence
Asbury Park Press
Neptune, NJ

Stephen Cavendish, News Designer; John Quinn, ME/Sports; Harris Siegel, ME Design & Photography; Gary Potosky, Night Sports Slot

Award of Excellence
Asbury Park Press
Neptune, NJ

Stephen Cavendish, News Designer; Andrew Prendimano, Art & Photo Director; Harris Siegel, ME Design & Photography; John Quinn, ME Sports; Dan Weber, Assistant Sports Editor

Award of Excellence
Asbury Park Press
Neptune, NJ

John Quinn, ME/Sports; Andrew Prendimano, Art & Photo Director; Harris Siegel, ME Design & Photo/Designer

Award of Excellence
Asbury Park Press
Neptune, NJ

Christine A. Birch, Designer; Dan Weber, Assistant Sports Editor; John Quinn, ME Sports; Andrew Prendimano, Art & Photo Director; Harris Siegel, ME Design & Photography

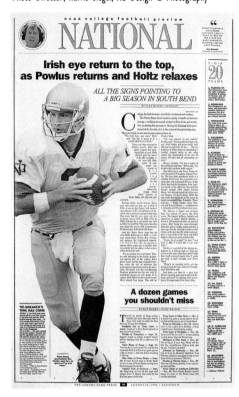

Award of Excellence
Asbury Park Press
Neptune, NJ

Stephen Cavendish, News Designer; Greig Henderson, Sports Slot Editor; Harris Siegel, ME Design & Photography; Celeste LaBrosse, Night Photo Editor; John Quinn, ME Sports; Janet Michaud, Night Layout Editor

Award of Excellence
The Boston Globe
Boston, MA

Janet L. Michaud, Designer

Award of Excellence
The Boston Globe
Boston, MA

Janet L. Michaud, Designer

Award of Excellence
The Boston Globe
Boston, MA

Keith A. Webb, Art Director & Designer

Award of Excellence
Centre Daily Times
State College, PA

Jon Tully, Sports Copy Desk Editor; Michele Guisewite, Photo/Graphics Editor; Pat Little, Photographer

Award of Excellence
The Detroit News
Detroit, MI

Dale Peskin, Deputy ME; Chris Kozlowski, Design/Graphics Director; Shayne Bowman, Assistant Graphics Editor; Rick Epps, Page Designer

Award of Excellence
Marca
Madrid, Spain

Jose Juan Gamez, Design Director; Mar Domingo, Graphic Artist; Diego Arambillet

Award of Excellence
The Detroit News
Detroit, MI

Dale Peskin, Deputy ME; Chris Kozlowski, Design/Graphics Editor; Annette Vazquez, Page Designer; Tim Summers, Graphic Artist; Jim Russ, Assistant Sports Editor; Todd McInturf, Photographer; Patrick Witty, Photographer; Heather Stone; Photographer

Award of Excellence
El Sol
Lima, Peru

Eduardo Danilo, Design Consultant; Miguel Gomez, Art Director; Marco Santibanez, Art Director; Gabriela Hernandez, Designer

Award of Excellence
The Idaho Statesman
Boise, ID

Chris Hopfensperger, Designer; Randy Wright, Design Director

Award of Excellence
Morgenavisen Jyllands-Posten
Viby, Denmark

Carsten Andreasen, Photographer; Ivan Philipsen, Journalist; Hans Thuesen Madsen, Sub-Editor/Sports

Award of Excellence
The New York Times
New York, NY

Wayne Kamidoi, Designer; J. Kyle Keener, Photographer

Award of Excellence
Marca
Madrid, Spain

Jose Juan Gamez, Design Director; Cesar Galera, Artist

Award of Excellence
Ole
Buenos Aires, Argentina

Martin Marotta, Art Editor; Jorge Doneiger, Art Editor; Jorge Duran, Photo Editor; Ricardo Carcova, Photo Editor

Award of Excellence
Ole
Buenos Aires, Argentina

Martin Marotta, Art Editor; Jorge Doneiger, Art Director; Jorge Duran, Photo Editor; Ricardo Carcova, Photo Editor

Award of Excellence
Providence Journal-Bulletin
Providence, RI

Lynn Rognsvoog, Picture Editor/Designer

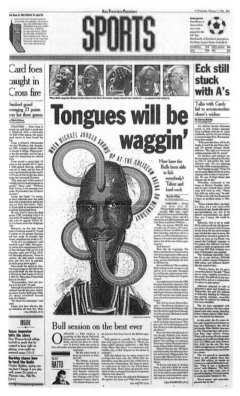

Award of Excellence
San Francisco Examiner
San Francisco, CA

Glenn Schwarz, Sports Editor; Sports Staff; Kelly Frankeny, AME Design; Don Asmussen, Illustrator

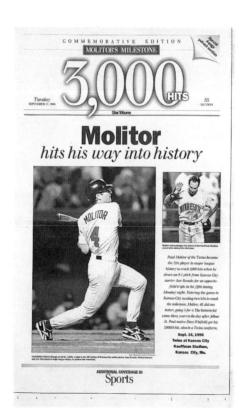

Award of Excellence
Star Tribune
Minneapolis, MN

Tim Wheatley, Sports Section Coordinator; Elida Witthoeft, Pro Sports Team Leader; Mark Wollemann, Sports Night Section Coordinator; Vickie Kettlewell, Photo Editor; Anders Ramberg, Design Director; Jeff Wheeler, Photographer

Award of Excellence
Star Tribune
Minneapolis, MN

Anders Ramberg, Design Director; Mike Blahnik, Outdoors/GA Team Leader; Dennis Anderson, Outdoors Columnist; Vickie Kettlewell, Photo Editor

Award of Excellence
The Sun
Bremerton, WA
Gale Engelke, Designer

Award of Excellence
Star Tribune
Minneapolis, MN
Tim Wheatley, Sports Section Coordinator; Sid Jablonski, Graphic Designer; Jerry Zgoda, Writer; Dennis Bracklin, Sports Team Leader; Anders Ramberg, Design Director; Ray Grumney, News Graphics Editor

Award of Excellence
The Virginian-Pilot
Norfolk, VA
Latane Jones, Designer; Jerry Reed, Olympic Section Editor; Bob Fleming, Sports Editor; Tracy Porter, Art Director; Bill Kelley, Picture Editor

Award of Excellence
The Sun
Bremerton, WA
Randy Mishler, Designer

Award of Excellence
The Virginian-Pilot
Norfolk, VA

Tracy Porter, Designer

Award of Excellence
The Virginian-Pilot
Norfolk, VA

Latane Jones, Designer; Denis Finley, News Editor; Bob Fleming, Sports Editor; Tracy Porter, Art Director; Bill Kelley, Picture Editor

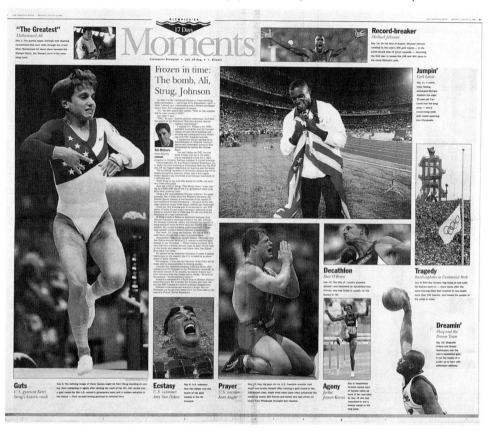

Award of Excellence
Chicago Tribune
Chicago, IL

Stephen Ravenscraft, Graphic Artist; Lara Weber, Graphics Coordinator

Award of Excellence
The Detroit News
Detroit, MI

Dale Peskin, Deputy ME; Chris Willis, Assistant Graphics Editor; Brad Stertz, Automotive Editor; Pat McFadden, Page Designer

Award of Excellence
La Gaceta
San Miguel de Tucuman, Argentina

Sergio Fernandez, Art Director; Mario Garcia, Design Consultant

Award of Excellence
La Gaceta
San Miguel de Tucuman, Argentina

Sergio Fernandez, Art Director; Mario Garcia, Design Consultant;
Oscar Ferronato, Designer; Guillermo Sobrino, Designer

Award of Excellence
Expansión
Madrid, Spain

Jose Juan Gamez, Design Director; Pablo Ma Ramirez, Graphic Artist; Blanca Serrano, Graphic Artist; Juan D. Ferreira, Graphic Artist

Award of Excellence
The Miami Herald
Miami, FL

Ana Lense Larrauri, Graphic Artist

Award of Excellence
The Los Angeles Times/Orange County Edition
Costa Mesa, CA

Val B. Mina, Artist/Designer; Kirk Christ, Designer

Award of Excellence
The Los Angeles Times/Orange County Edition
Costa Mesa, CA

Kirk Christ, Designer; Val B. Mina, Artist

Award of Excellence
The Miami Herald
Miami, FL

Ana Lense Larrauri, Graphic Artist

Award of Excellence
Nashville Banner
Nashville, TN

Brad Diller, Illustrator; Vince Troia, Page Designer; Tim Tanton, Business Editor; Mike McGehee, Design Editor

Award of Excellence
The New York Times
New York, NY

Tim Oliver, Presentation Editor; Dylan McClain, Graphics Editor

Award of Excellence
The New York Times
New York, NY

Tim Oliver, Presentation Editor; Dylan McClain, Graphics Editor; Carl A. Sharif, Photo Illustrator

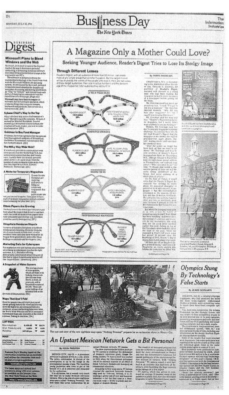

Award of Excellence
The New York Times
New York, NY

Tim Oliver, Presentation Editor; Kris Goodfellow, Graphics Editor

Award of Excellence
The New York Times
New York, NY

Tim Oliver, Presentation Editor; Kris Goodfellow, Graphics Editor

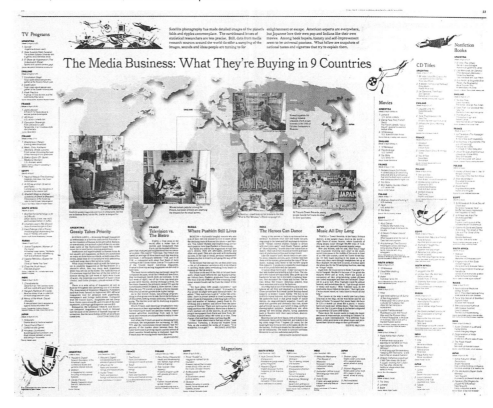

Award of Excellence
Reforma
Mexico City, Mexico

Ricardo Pena, Section Designer; Israel Mejia, Illustrator; Rossana Fuentes-Berain, Editor; Rene Sanchez, Editor; Emilio Deheza, Art Director; Eduardo Danilo, Design Consultant; Ernesto Carrillo, Graphics Editor

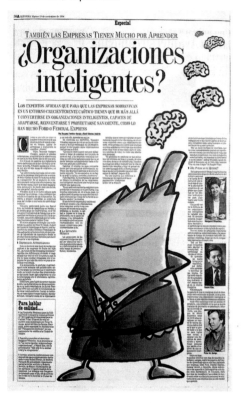

Award of Excellence
The San Diego Union-Tribune
San Diego, CA

Kris Lindblad, Designer; Roni Galgano, Photographer

Award of Excellence
San Francisco Examiner
San Francisco, CA

Kelly Frankeny, AME Design; Pat Sedlar, Illustrator; KT Rabin, Business Editor; Don McCartney, Designer

Award of Excellence
The Virginian-Pilot
Norfolk, VA

Courtney D. Murphy, Designer; John Corbitt, Graphic Artist; Ted Evanoff, Section Editor

Award of Excellence
The Washington Times
Washington, DC

Virginia Tinker Brace, Art Director; Cliff Owen, Photographer; Michael Wheatley, Assistant Business Editor; Joseph W Scopin, AME Graphics

Silver
La Gaceta
San Miguel de Tucuman, Argentina

Sergio Fernandez, Art Director; Mario Garcia, Design Consultant; Sebastian Rosso, Designer/Illustrator; Daniel Fontanarrosa, Illustrator

Award of Excellence
The Dallas Morning News
Dallas, TX

Alison Hamilton, Designer/Illustrator; Karel Holloway, Education Editor; Kathleen Vincent, Art Director

Award of Excellence
La Gaceta
San Miguel de Tucuman, Argentina

Sergio Fernandez, Art Director & Designer; Mario Garcia, Design Consultant

Award of Excellence
La Gaceta
San Miguel de Tucuman, Argentina

Sergio Fernandez, Art Director; Mario Garcia, Design Consultant; Daniel Fontanarrosa, Illustrator

Award of Excellence
La Gaceta
San Miguel de Tucuman, Argentina

Sergio Fernandez, Art Director; Garcia Mario, Design Consultant; Falci Ruben, Designer

Award of Excellence
La Gaceta
San Miguel de Tucuman, Argentina

Sergio Fernandez, Art Director & Designer; Garcia Mario, Design Consultant; Valverdi Raul, Illustrator; Abel Federico, Editor

Award of Excellence
The New York Times
New York, NY

Greg Ryan, Art Director

Award of Excellence
Le Soleil
Quebec, Canada

Louise Pepin, Designer; Raymond Giroux, AME

Award of Excellence
The Oregonian
Portland, OR

Steve Cowden, Artist/Illustrator; Mark Friesen, Designer

Award of Excellence
The Orlando Sentinel
Orlando, FL

John Corbitt, Artist

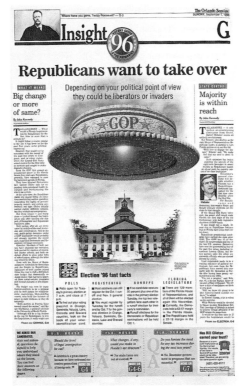

Award of Excellence
Reforma
Mexico City, Mexico

Alejo Najera, Section Designer; Israel Mejia, Illustrator; Hilda Garcia, Editor; Eduardo Danilo, Design Consultant; Ernesto Carrillo, Graphics Editor; Emilio Deheza, Art Director

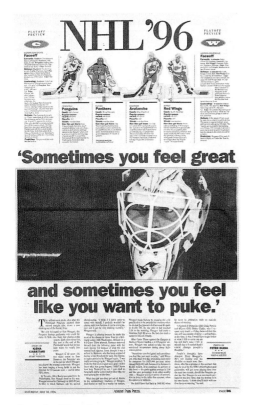

Award of Excellence
Asbury Park Press
Neptune, NJ

John Quinn, ME/Sports; Andrew Prendimano, Art & Photo Director; Harris Siegel, ME Design & Photo/Designer; Ed Gabel, Graphic Artist; Peter Diana, Photographer

Award of Excellence
• Also an Award of Excellence for News Portfolio
Asbury Park Press
Neptune, NJ

Andrew Prendimano, Art & Photo Director; Ed Gabel, Graphic Artist; Harris Siegel, ME Design & Photo/Designer; John Quinn, ME/Sports; David Bergman, Photographer

Award of Excellence
El Norte
Monterrey, Mexico

Hugo Malacara, Designer; Raul Braulio Martinez, Art Director; Eduardo Danilo Ruiz, Design Consultant; Jorge Vidrio, Graphics Editor; Alexandro Medrano, Graphics Editor

The Asbury Park Press received a Gold Medal for taking a wonderfully fresh approach to a common subject – hockey – that other papers have done with far less distinction, including an elegant use of page furniture and a subtle use of color to guide readers through hockey team summaries.

Gold
Asbury Park Press
Neptune, NJ

Andrew Prendimano, Art and Photo Director; Ed Gabel, Artist; Harris Siegel, ME Design & Photo/Designer; James J. Connolly, Photographer; John Quinn, ME/Sports; Dan Weber, Assistant Sports Editor; Joe Zedalis, Assistant Sports Editor

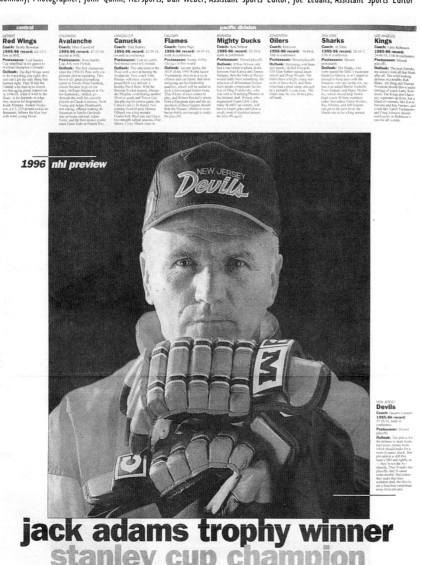

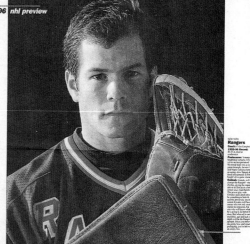

The Asbury Park Press recibió una Medalla de Oro por su enfoque maravillosamente fresco de un tema común y corriente – el hockey – tema que otros periódicos han abordado con mucho menos distinción. Hace un uso elegante de enseres de página y un uso sutil del color, para guiar a sus lectores por los resúmenes de los equipos de hockey.

Silver
Asbury Park Press
Neptune, NJ
Andrew Prendimano, Art and Photo Director; Ed Gabel, Artist; Harris Siegel, ME Design & Photo/Designer; John Quinn, ME/Sports

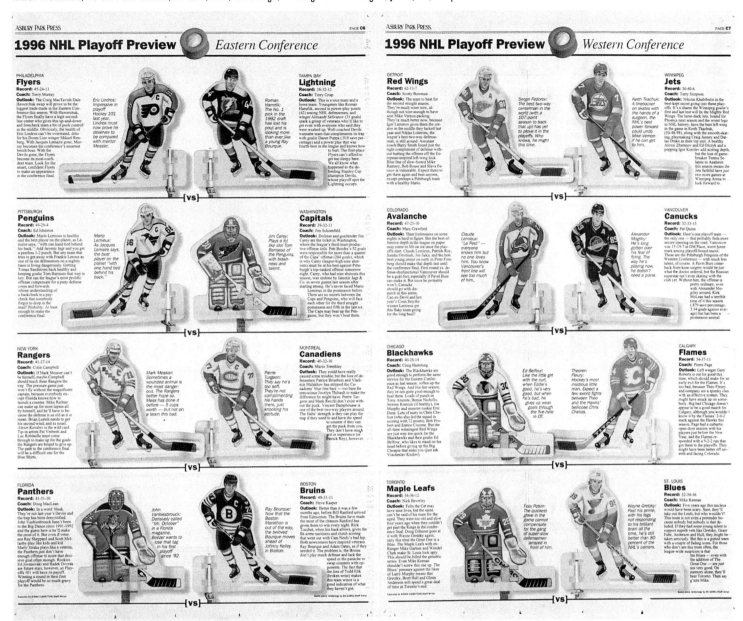

Award of Excellence
Expressen
Stockholm, Sweden
Lotta Magnusson, Designer

Vattnet rinner i en väldig pipeline genom slummen. Men bara de rika kan dricka av det.

Award of Excellence
El Norte
Monterrey, Mexico

Juan de Dios Garza, Designer; Raul Braulio Martinez, Art Director; Eduardo Danilo Ruiz, Design Consultant; Jorge Vidrio, Graphics Editor; Alexandro Medrano, Graphics Editor

Award of Excellence
The Oregonian
Portland, OR

Renee Byer, Assistant Director of Photo; Kathryn Scott, Photographer

Award of Excellence
The Idaho Statesman
Boise, ID

Randy Wright, Designer; Chris Hopfensperger, Designer; Patrick Davis, Graphic Artist

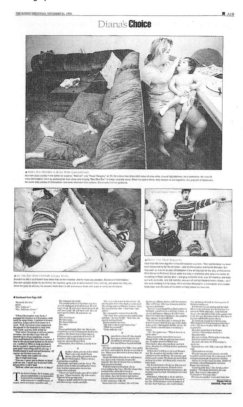

Award of Excellence
Expressen
Stockholm, Sweden

Lotta Magnusson, Designer

Award of Excellence
Reforma
Mexico City, Mexico

Gilberto Avila, Designer; Jose Manuel Mendoza, Section Designer; Juan Jesus Cortes, Illustrator; Eduardo Danilo, Design Consultant; Monica Solorzano, Photo Artist; Emilio Deheza, Art Director; Rossana Fuentes-Berain, Editor

Award of Excellence
The New York Times
New York, NY

Wayne Kamidoi, Designer; Joe Ward, Graphics Editor; Barton Silverman, Photographer; Stephen Jesselli, Picture Editor

Award of Excellence
The Virginian-Pilot
Norfolk, VA

Dan Janke, Designer; Denny Brack, Designer; Paul Nelson, Designer; Latane Jones, Designer; Denis Finley, News Editor; Eric Seidman, Art Director; Tracy Porter, Designer; Bill Kelley; Picture Editor; Bob Fleming, Sports Editor

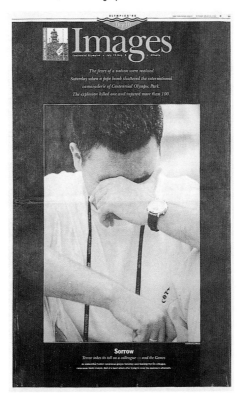

Award of Excellence
The Washington Times
Washington, DC

Geoffrey Lee Etnyre, News Editor

Award of Excellence
The Orange County Register
Santa Ana, CA

David Medzerian, Design Team Leader; John Fabris, Design Team Leader; Andrea Voight, Designer; Staff

Award of Excellence
The San Diego Union-Tribune
San Diego, CA

Bill Gaspard, Designer; Chris Ross, Designer; Channon Seifert, Designer; Gordon Murray, Designer; Michael Canepa, Designer; Michael Franklin, Photo Editor; Paul Horn, Graphics Journalist; Mark Nowlin; Graphics Journalist

Award of Excellence
Star Tribune
Minneapolis, MN

Roger Buoen, World/Nation Team Leader; Ray Grumney, News Graphic Director; Mike Pashalek, World/Nation Editor; Jim Kelly, A Section Coordinator; Anders Ramberg, Design Director; Greg Branson, Graphic Designer; Hal Sanders, 1A Layout Editor; Staff

Silver
• Also an Award of Excellence for Special News Topics
The New York Times
New York, NY
Staff; Tom Bodkin, AME Design; Margaret O'Connor, Deputy Design Director

---

"All the News That's Fit to Print"

The New York Times

Late Edition
New York: Today, limited sun, possible sprinkle. High 63. Tonight, mostly cloudy, mild. Low 55. Tomorrow, cloudy, showers late. High 64. Yesterday, high 59, low 45. Details, page B20.

VOL. CXLVI . No. 50,603   Copyright © 1996 The New York Times   NEW YORK, WEDNESDAY, NOVEMBER 6, 1996 $1 beyond the greater New York metropolitan area   **60 CENTS**

CLINTON ELECTED TO A 2D TERM
WITH SOLID MARGINS ACROSS U.S.;
G.O.P. KEEPS HOLD ON CONGRESS

Democrats Fail to Reverse Right's Capitol Hill Gains

By DAVID E. ROSENBAUM

With close races all across the country, Republicans retained control of the Senate and the House in yesterday's elections.

The votes in several states were still in doubt early today, but Republicans were guaranteed of having at least 51 Senate seats in the next Congress. And around 2 A.M., Speaker Newt Gingrich proclaimed that his party had retained control of the House. [Page B3.]

The Republicans won in the Senate by holding most of their own seats and picking up at least two seats in states where popular Democratic Senators are retiring.

In one of the most compelling political contests of the year, Senator John Kerry of Massachusetts was re-elected. All other Democratic incum-

bents who were running also won.

But only one Republican Senator lost, and Republican newcomers won in Nebraska and Alabama, replacing retiring Democrats.

Republicans began Election Day with a 53-to-47 advantage and thus could afford to lose a net of two seats and still have a majority in the 100-member Senate.

Among the Republican Senators who were re-elected were Jesse Helms of North Carolina and Strom Thurmond of South Carolina.

Senator Larry Pressler of South Dakota, a Republican, was the only Senator running for re-election who lost. He was defeated by Representative Tim Johnson, now the state's only Congressman.

Early last night, Senator Robert C. Smith of New Hampshire seemed likely to be defeated by his Democratic challenger, former Representative Dick Swett. But Mr. Smith gained as the night progressed, and shortly after midnight, Mr. Swett conceded defeat.

Among the other Republicans who were re-elected were Mitch McConnell of Kentucky, John W. Warner of Virginia, Thad Cochran of Mississippi, James M. Inhofe of Oklahoma, Fred Thompson of Tennessee and Phil Gramm of Texas.

In Nebraska, Chuck Hagel, a Republican investment banker who has never held elective office, defeated the state's Democratic Governor, Ben Nelson. Mr. Nelson began the year as the odds-on favorite to replace Senator Jim Exon, a Democrat who is retiring after three terms, but Mr. Hagel rallied in the last month.

In Alabama, Jeff Sessions, the Republican State Attorney General, defeated State Senator Roger Bedford.

In an interview on CNN, Senator Trent Lott of Mississippi, the Republican leader, said, "It looks like I will be majority leader."

Other Democrats who held their

Continued on Page B1, Column 1

Rail Victim's Widow
Captures House Seat

Carolyn McCarthy, whose husband was shot on a Long Island commuter train and who ran on a gun control platform, won a House seat by soundly defeating a freshman Republican.

In Connecticut, Representative Gary A. Franks, a black conservative considered a rising G.O.P. star, lost his seat, while voters in New York City rejected a plan to lengthen term limits for elected city officials.

Articles, Pages B14, B15 and B16.

TORRICELLI WINS
SENATE CONTEST

Defeats Zimmer for Open Seat in Bitter New Jersey Fight

By BRETT PULLEY

Representative Robert G. Torricelli, a Democrat who has served in Congress for seven terms, won election to New Jersey's open United States Senate seat yesterday.

Mr. Torricelli, known for throwing himself into the center of high-profile and volatile issues, defeated Representative Richard A. Zimmer after a race that had become a testament to the ever-increasing expense and negative nature of campaigning. In the end, the race was not as close as the polls had predicted. With 84 percent of precincts reporting at 12:52 A.M. today, Mr. Torricelli had 53 percent of the popular vote, compared with 42 percent for Mr. Zimmer.

In selecting Mr. Torricelli, 45, from Englewood in Bergen County, over Mr. Zimmer, a 52-year-old, three-term Congressman from Delaware Township in Hunterdon County, voters sided with the Democratic candidate's belief that government should play an active role in preserving Medicare, protecting the environment and strengthening education initiatives.

"You have given me the blessing of success, but the burden of being worthy of all that you have given," a somewhat daggedly Mr. Torricelli told a crowd of ebullient supporters gathered at a Woodbridge hotel shortly after 10 last night.

He then alluded to the nastiness of the race and his hope that it would not be repeated. "Let this campaign be remembered finally for this," he said, "that it was the beginning of a new civility in the public life of New Jersey."

About half an hour earlier, at 9:30, Mr. Zimmer had conceded defeat and credited Mr. Torricelli with run-

Continued on Page B12, Column 1

INSIDE

Wall St. Bets on Status Quo
Expectations of a Democratic White House and a Republican Congress drove stocks up yesterday. Page D8.

G.I.'s May Aid Africa Relief
The U.S. is considering sending troops to Central Africa to aid refugees caught in the conflict. Page A6.

News Summary	A2
Arts	C11-18
Business Day	D1-19
Editorial, Op-Ed	A3-27
International	A3-13
Living Section	C1-6
Metro	B17-20
National	A16-20
Sports Wednesday	B22-27

Education	B11	Real Estate	A21
Health	C10	TV Listings	C19
Obituaries	B18	Weather	B20
Classified	A25	Auto Exchange	B20

On the Internet: www.nytimes.com

The voters' message was to work together and put aside politics, President Clinton said in claiming victory in Little Rock with Hillary Rodham Clinton, their daughter Chelsea and Vice President Gore.

The Second Term: Promise and Peril

By TODD S. PURDUM

Four years ago Bill Clinton won the Presidency with an outsized agenda and an underwhelming mandate, and the gulf between the two left him struggling in the first half of his term simply to establish his legitimacy. By the midpoint, the President had been reduced to proclaiming his own relevance.

Last night Mr. Clinton won re-election with a larger margin but with a manifesto both smaller and less clear. And if the promise of achievement glistens, potential pitfalls abound, from the ancient feuds of Bosnia to the paper chase of special prosecutors at home.

Campaigning in El Paso last week, Mr. Clinton declared, "This is an election of enormous moment, with great consequences." But far more than a year the President has steadily strived to blur the traditional divisions of American ideology in a politics of pointillism, at once capturing the electorate's vital center and renewing questions about his own.

In this President's effective view, it is possible to both balance the budget

Many Goals Left for Clinton, and Many Pitfalls

and provide new tax breaks for college education, to force families off welfare and find new jobs for them, to expand the Federal role in everything from encouraging school uniforms to deterring violence on television — all the while declaring that "the era of big government is over."

Surveys of voters leaving the polls yesterday showed that 6 in 10 did not believe he could cut the deficit and pay for his programs at the same time, and that a like number did not

Continued on Page B5, Column 1

Bob Dole conceded defeat before supporters in Washington.

An Election Day For 2d Thoughts

More than half the voters yesterday spoke openly about having second thoughts. Those voting for President Clinton said they had confidence enough in the nation's economy to overcome doubts about their candidate's honesty. Bob Dole meanwhile pulled nearly half the wavering voters his way as the campaign ended.

Article, page B1.

PEROT A FAR THIRD

President's Success Lay in Ability to Co-opt Republican Issues

By RICHARD L. BERKE

William Jefferson Clinton was re-elected President of the United States yesterday, capping a yearlong political resurgence that made him the first Democrat since Franklin Delano Roosevelt to win a second term as President.

Mr. Clinton built a landslide in the Electoral College and won a decisive victory in the popular vote, overwhelming Bob Dole in all regions of the country except the South and the High Plains, where the Republican won several states. The President's sweep carried in California, where Mr. Dole, in an enormous gamble, diverted millions of dollars from other states and stumped daggedly in the final weeks of the campaign.

Ross Perot, the Texas billionaire who ran on the ticket of the Reform Party he had created, finished a distant third, drawing roughly half of the 19 percent he won in 1992.

With 64 percent of the popular vote tallied at 3 A.M. today, Mr. Clinton drew 49 percent; Mr. Dole 41 percent and Mr. Perot 8 percent. The President surpassed his showing of 43 percent of the popular vote in 1992.

A state-by-state breakdown of those returns gave Mr. Clinton more than the 370 electoral votes he won four years ago, a commanding showing in the Electoral College, which requires 270 votes for victory.

The support for Mr. Clinton did not run deep enough to allow Democrats to declare a reversal of the Republican tide that swept Congress two years ago. The Republicans retained control of the Senate, by nearly this morning, they appeared headed to keep a majority in the House.

With a Democrat still in the Oval Office and Republicans still dominant at least one chamber of Congress, the nation's political landscape remains competitive and unsettled.

Shortly after midnight, eastern time, Mr. Clinton and Vice President Al Gore and their families emerged before a joyous crowd jamming the streets in front of the Old State House in Little Rock, Ark., where they had their victory celebration four years ago.

"Today the American people have spoken," Mr. Clinton said, recognizing the power of the mixed message that voters seemed to be sending him and Congress.

"America has told every one of us — Democrats, Republicans and independents — loud and clear: It is time to put politics aside, join together

Continued on Page B4, Column 1

Economy Helps Again

Clinton Rode Wave of Discontent in 1992; With Times Better, He Gets to Ride Again

By R. W. APPLE Jr.

Four years ago, a faltering economy persuaded American voters to give Bill Clinton a chance as President. Yesterday, surveys of voters leaving the polls showed, a robust economy persuaded them that he deserved a second term.

News Analysis

Four years ago, only 39 percent of voters said they thought the country was headed in the right direction — a key indicator of the nation's mood. That figure grew this year to 53 percent.

But Mr. Clinton's success in occupying "the vital center," as he called it in his victory statement, in a phrase borrowed from the historian Arthur M. Schlesinger Jr., did not extend to Capitol Hill. He and his party failed in their quest to recapture control of the Senate, and they appeared headed for failure in the struggle for dominance of the House of Representatives. So he and his country face two more years at least of divided Government.

After a campaign filled with fundraising abuses on a grand scale, Mr.

Clinton pledged early action on campaign-finance reform. His Vice President, Al Gore, said he was ready to work with the Republicans, and the President himself said, "It is time to put country ahead of party."

But appeals to eschew partisanship may be lost in the clamor of investigations of alleged scandals in the first Clinton Administration.

The returns showed little diminution in the conservative trend that has coursed through the country since the 1970's. The new Senate will be more conservative than the old. In California, the most publicized initiative of the year, opposing affirmative action, was approved.

Bob Dole did everything he could to refocus the Presidential contest, the last of the 20th century, as Mr.

Continued on Page B4, Column 5

Yeltsin Has 7-Hour Heart Surgery
And Doctors Say It Was a Success

By LAWRENCE K. ALTMAN

MOSCOW, Wednesday, Nov. 6 — President Boris N. Yeltsin came out of a seven-hour, multiple-bypass heart operation in a hospital here on Tuesday with his doctors declaring the operation a success. They said they were optimistic about the 65-year-old Russian leader's chances of resuming a full workload.

At a news conference in the hospital an hour after the operation, the doctors said the surgery went without a hitch. Mr. Yeltsin's heart was stopped for 68 minutes during one phase of the operation.

Mr. Yeltsin signed a decree this morning reassuming his presidential powers, the Kremlin said. Sergei Yastrzhembsky, his press spokesman, said the President signed the document at 6 A.M. (10 P.M. Tuesday, Eastern time), 23 hours after he had delegated the powers to Prime Minister Viktor S. Chernomyrdin on Tuesday morning, minutes before undergoing anesthesia.

In the operation, surgeons sewed five grafts to restore blood flow to

coronary arteries. They had become constricted by the fatty deposits of atherosclerosis that had built up over a period of years and deprived the organ of vital nourishment, leading to two heart attacks.

Even if all goes well for Mr. Yeltsin, it may yet be months before he can run the country again. And when he does return to the Kremlin, many find it hard to imagine that he will be the same forceful leader who has for five years driven Russia away from Communism and toward a market economy. [News analysis, page A12.]

On Tuesday, Mr. Yeltsin was reported in stable condition in an intensive care unit, where he remained connected to an artificial respirator used during the operation. He opened his eyes early Tuesday evening but had not fully awakened from the anesthesia. Patients usually awaken from 6 to 18 hours after such surgery.

Mr. Yastrzhembsky said today

Continued on Page A12, Column 1

TIME WARNER COMMUNICATIONS — BLMI

THE NEW YORK TIMES is available for home or office delivery in most major U.S. cities. Call, toll-free, 1 800 NYTIMES. Ask about TimesTravel

Award of Excellence
Chicago Tribune
Chicago, IL

Stacy Sweat, Graphics Editor; Therese Shechter, Associate Graphics Editor; Celeste Bernard, Graphics Coordinator; Jim Prisching, Photographer

Award of Excellence
Chicago Tribune
Chicago, IL

Stacy Sweat, Graphics Editor; Therese Shechter, Associate Graphics Editor; Jim Prisching, Photographer; Celeste Bernard, Graphics Coordinator

Award of Excellence
The New York Times
New York, NY

Wayne Kamidoi, Designer; Sports Staff

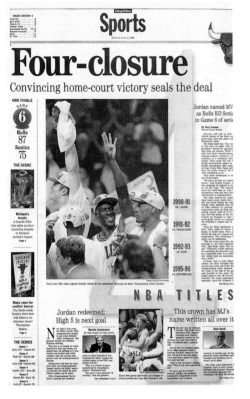

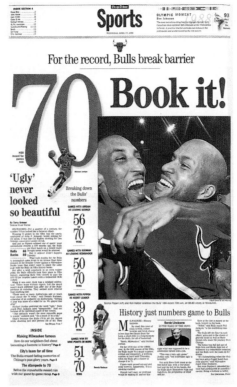

Award of Excellence
The New York Times
New York, NY

Sports Staff; Wayne Kamidoi, Designer

Award of Excellence
Diario de Noticias
Pamplona, Spain

Staff

The New York Times received a Gold Medal for the impressive comprehensiveness of these pages. The graphics, especially, play an important role in the paper's ability to communicate – each graphic having just enough information to communicate to readers in full without overtelling the story.

Gold
The New York Times
New York, NY

Staff; Tom Bodkin, Design Director; Charles M. Blow, Graphics Director; Margaret O'Connor, Deputy Design Director

The New York Times recibió una Medalla de Oro por la impresionante exhaustividad de sus páginas. Las gráficas en particular desempeñan un papel importante en la habilidad del periódico de comunicarse – cada gráfica contiene la información justa para ser comunicada a los lectores sin exagerar la nota.

Silver
Asbury Park Press
Neptune, NJ

Andrew Prendimano, Art and Photo Director; Janet Michaud, Designer; Harris Siegel, ME Design & Photography; James J. Connolly, Photographer; Celeste LaBrosse, Photo Editor; John Quinn, ME/Sports

Award of Excellence
The Atlanta Journal & Constitution
Atlanta, GA

Tony Deferia, AME News Art & Photography; D.W. Pine, Lead Designer; John Glenn, Photo Director; Moni Basu, Designer; Sheri Taylor, Lead Designer; Sara Franquet, Designer; Ellen Voss, News Editor; Glenn Hannigan; News Editor

Award of Excellence
The Virginian-Pilot
Norfolk, VA

Tracy Porter, Project Designer; Bob Fleming, Olympics Editor; Courtney Murphy, Designer; Latane Jones, Designer; Denny Brack, Designer; Katey Charles, Designer; Dan Janke, Designer; Bill Kelley; Photo Editor; Eric Seidman, Creative Director

Award of Excellence
The Boston Globe
Boston, MA

Don Skwar, Editor; Robin Romano, Designer; Staff

Silver
The New York Times
New York, NY

Joe Zeff, Designer; Archie Tse, Graphic Artist; C. B. Williams, Graphic Artist; Nancy Lee, Photo Editor; Rick Perry, Photo Editor; Keith Meyers, Photographer

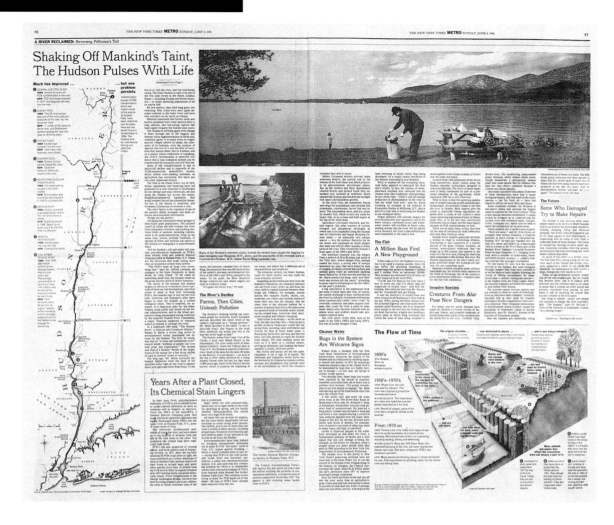

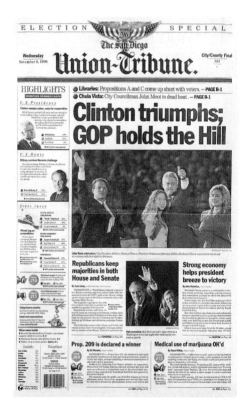

Award of Excellence
The San Diego Union-Tribune
San Diego, CA
Staff

Award of Excellence
Asbury Park Press
Neptune, NJ

Andrew Prendimano, Designer & Art/Photo Director; Andy Mills, Photographer; Harris Siegel, ME Design & Photography; Noah K. Murray, Photographer; John Quinn, ME/Sports

Award of Excellence
Asbury Park Press
Neptune, NJ

Annette J. Vazquez, Designer; Karl Smith, News Design Editor; Andrew Prendimano, Art & Photo Director; Harris Siegel, ME/Design and Photography; John Quinn, ME/Sports; Joe Zedalis, Asst. Sports Editor; Dan Weber, Asst. Sports Editor; Celeste LaBrosse; Night Photo Editor; Kevin Shea, Photo Desk Tech

Award of Excellence
The Boston Globe
Boston, MA

Aldona Charlton, Designer; Suzanne Kreiter, Photographer; Judith Gaines, Writer

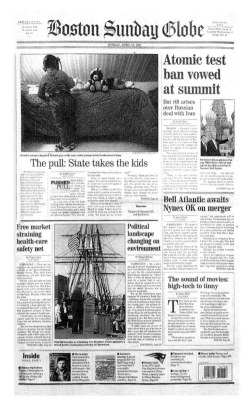

Award of Excellence
The Boston Globe
Boston, MA

Aldona Charlton, Art Director; Bill Greene, Photographer

Award of Excellence
The Charlotte Observer
Charlotte, NC

Scott Goldman, Assistant Sports Editor; Michael Persinger, Deputy Sports Editor; Monica Moses, Design Director; Sports Staff

Award of Excellence
Chicago Tribune
Chicago, IL
Staff

Award of Excellence
The Detroit News
Detroit, MI

Dale Peskin, Deputy ME; Chris Kozlowski, Design/Graphics Ed.; Chris Willis, Asst. Graphics Ed.; Shayne Bowman, Asst. Design Ed.; David Kordalski, Asst. Graphics Ed.; Tim Summers, Graphic Artist; Rick Epps, Designer; Annette Vasquez, Designer; Jim Russ, Asst. Sports Ed.; Matt Rennie, Sports Copy Ed.

Award of Excellence
The New York Times
New York, NY

Wayne Kamidoi, Designer; Joe Ward, Graphics Editor; Stephen Jesselli, Picture Editor

Silver
The New York Times
New York, NY

Joe Zeff, Designer; Pat Lyons,
Graphics Editor

Award of Excellence
The Seattle Times
Seattle, WA

Michael Kellams, Designer; Sharon Boswell, Writer; Lorraine McConaghy, Writer; Kathy
Triesch, Copy Editor; Cyndi Nash, Editor; David Miller, Art Director

Award of Excellence
The Detroit News
Detroit, MI

Dale Peskin, Deputy Managing Editor; Chris Kozlowski, Design/Graphics Director; Chris Willis, Assistant
Graphics Editor; Shayne Bowman, Assistant Design Editor; David Kordalski, Assistant Graphics Editor; Tim
Summers, Graphic Artist; Frank Lovinski, Deputy ME News

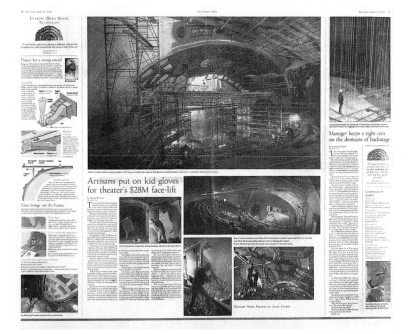

Silver
The New York Times
New York, NY

Wayne Kamidoi, Designer; Joe Ward, Graphics Editor; Stephen Jesselli, Picture Editor; Sarah Kass, Picture Editor; Sports Staff

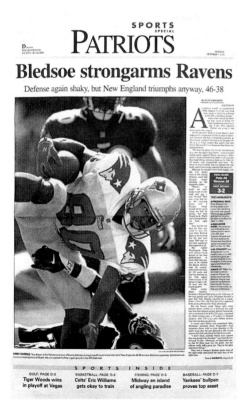

Award of Excellence
Providence Journal-Bulletin
Providence, RI
Staff

Award of Excellence
The San Diego Union-Tribune
San Diego, CA
Amy Stirnkorb, Designer/Art Director; Scott Laumann, Illustrator; Laurie Harker, Designer; Mark Nowlin, Graphics Journalist; Howard Lipin, Photographer; Leigh Fenly, Quest Editor; Scott LaFee, Staff Writer

Award of Excellence
The San Diego Union-Tribune
San Diego, CA
Staff

Silver
• Also an Award of Excellence for News Page
Chicago Tribune
Chicago, IL

Cindy Andrew, Photographer; Therese Shechter, Associate Graphics Editor; Stephen Ravenscraft, Graphic Artist; Jeanie Adams, Assistant Picture Editor; Terry Volpp, Graphics Coordinator; Bill Parker, Senior News Editor; Stacy Sweat, Graphics Editor; Staff

Award of Excellence
Asbury Park Press
Neptune, NJ

Christine A. Birch, Designer; Gary Potosky, Peter Barzilai, Night Sports Slot Eds.; David Bergeland, Michael Goldfinger, Mark R. Sullivan, Photographers; Kevin Shea, Night Photo Ed.; John Quinn; ME Sports; Andrew Prendimano, Art & Photo Director; Harris Siegel, ME Design & Photography

Award of Excellence
Reforma
Mexico City, Mexico

Juan Jesus Cortes, Illustrator; Alberto Cervantes, Photo Artist; Alejo Najera, Section Designer; Diego Trevino, Photographer; Emilio Deheza, Art Director; Eduardo Danilo, Design Consultant; Raymundo Rivapalacio, Editor; Ernesto Carrillo; Graphics Editor

Award of Excellence
The Washington Post
Washington, DC

Robert Dorrell, Graphic Journalist; Laura Stanton, Graphic Artist; Dita Smith, Graphics reporting; James Rupert, Graphics reporting

FEATURES

Regularly appearing section winners were selected after reviewing three issues. Circulation size was taken into consideration. Pages could include opinion, lifestyle/features, entertainment, food, fashion, home/real estate, travel, science/technology or any other feature page selected by the staff.

[REGULARLY APPEARING SECTIONS]

[PAGE DESIGN]

Silver
Goteborgs-Posten
Gothenburg, Sweden

Magnus Nilsson, Editor & Designer; Henrik Stromberg, Editor & Designer; Lena Stromberg, Editor & Designer

Award of Excellence
Berlingske Tidende
Copenhagen, Denmark

Per H. Larsen, Sub-Editor; Lisbeth Bredahl, Editor; Lars Vegas Nielsen, Illustrator; Carsten Gregersen, Design Editor

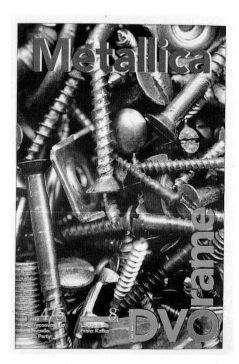

Award of Excellence
El Diario Vasco
San Sebastian, Spain

Sebastian Valencia, Graphics Editor; Jose Luis Minondo, Designer; Alberto Torregrosa, Dir/Editorial Art & Design; Jesus Aycart, Assistant Art Director

Award of Excellence
The Scotsman
Edinburgh, Scotland
Staff

Award of Excellence
Le Soleil
Quebec, Canada

Francine Julien, Designer; Michele Teller, Designer; Jacques
Samson, AME; Jean-Pascal Beaupre, AME

Award of Excellence
The Orange County Register
Santa Ana, CA

Claudia Guerrero, Daisy Teoh, Wes Bausmith, Designers; David
Medzerian, Design Team Leader; Amy Ning, Artist; Craig
Pursley, Artist; Paul E Rodriguez, Photographer; Mindy Schauer;
Photographer; Roger Bloom, Copy Editor; Travel Staff

Award of Excellence
Berlingske Tidende
Copenhagen, Denmark

Peter Frisendal, Editor; Soren Bidstrup, Photographer; Erik
Lundtang, Photographer; Niels Hjerrild, Photo Editor; Ida
Jerichow, Graphic Artist; Rie Jerichow, Art Director; Michael
Gormsen, Graphic Artist; Carsten Gregersen; Design Editor; Staff

Award of Excellence
Enfoques
Buenos Aires, Argentina

Norberto Jose Lema, Designer

Award of Excellence
Diario de Noticias
Pamplona, Spain

Javier Errea, Art Director

Award of Excellence
Folha de Sao Paulo
Sao Paulo, Brazil

Didiana Prata, Art Editor; Alcino Leite, Sunday Cultural
Supplement; Renata Buono, Page Designer

Award of Excellence
El Nuevo Herald
Miami, FL

Raul Fernandez, Designer/Illustrator

Award of Excellence
Milwaukee Journal Sentinel
Milwaukee, WI

Ruth Shattuck, Features Designer & Illustrator; Ken Miller,
Features Design Editor; Geoffrey Blaesing, Senior
Editor/Graphics & Design

Award of Excellence
NRC Handelsblad
Rotterdam, Netherlands

Jan Paul van der Wijk, Design Editor; Ugo Mulas,
Photographer

Award of Excellence
Reforma
Mexico City, Mexico

Alejo Najera, Section Designer; Enrique Portilla, Editor; Ernesto
Carrillo, Graphics Editor; Emilio Deheza, Design Consultant;
Eduardo Danilo, Design Consultant

Award of Excellence
TimesDaily
Florence, AL

Tim Buss, Design Editor; Mary Ann Kirkby, Editorial Page
Editor

Award of Excellence
The Toronto Star
Toronto, Canada

Ian Somerville, Designer; Andrew Stawicki, Photographer; Gwen Smith, Editor; Paul Watson, Writer/Reporter

Award of Excellence
The Toronto Star
Toronto, Canada

Ian Somerville, Designer; Raffi Andarian, Illustrator; Gwen Smith, Editor

Award of Excellence
The Virginian-Pilot
Norfolk, VA

Courtney D Murphy, Designer; Tom Warhover, Tony Wharton, Section Editors; Bob Voros, Artist; Hans C. Noel, Copy Editor; Eric Seidman, Art Director; Tracy Porter, Art Director

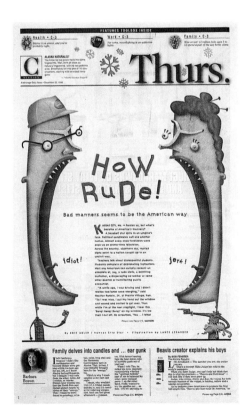

Award of Excellence
• Also an Award of Excellence for Color Illustration
The Anchorage Daily News
Anchorage, AK

Lance Lekander, Art Director, Illustrator & Designer

Award of Excellence
Chicago Tribune
Chicago, IL

Tom Heinz, Art Director

Award of Excellence
Berlingske Tidende
Copenhagen, Denmark

Bettina Soltoft, Designer/Illustrator

Silver
Berlingske Tidende
Copenhagen, Denmark
Bettina Soltoft, Designer/Illustrator

Award of Excellence
Duluth News-Tribune
Duluth, MN
Lewis H. Leung, Designer/Illustrator; Kathy Strauss, Photographer

SMAGEN AF HØJLAND

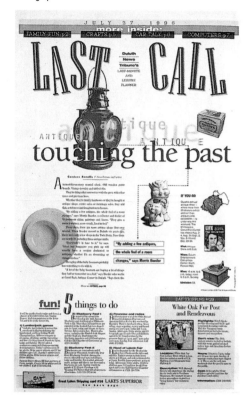

Award of Excellence
Duluth News-Tribune
Duluth, MN
Lewis H. Leung, Designer/Illustrator

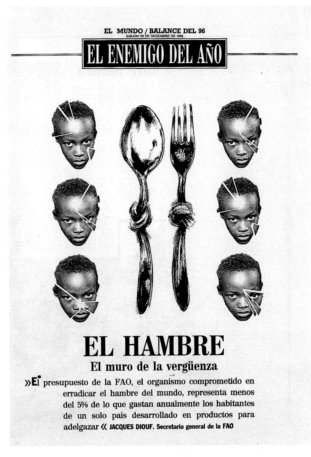

Silver
El Mundo
Madrid, Spain
Carmelo Caderot, Art
Director & Designer

Award of Excellence
El Norte
Monterrey, Mexico
Maria Teresa Tamez, Designer; Raul Braulio Martinez, Art Director; Juan Jose Ceron, Photographer; Carmen A. Escobedo, Graphics Editor; Rosa Linda Gonzalez, Editor

Award of Excellence
El Norte
Monterrey, Mexico
Carmen T Chacon, Designer; Raul Braulio Martinez, Art Director; Juan Jose Ceron, Photographer; Carmen A. Escobedo, Graphics Editor; Rosa Linda Gonzalez, Editor; Guillermo Castillo, Photo/Artist

Award of Excellence
El Norte
Monterrey, Mexico
Arturo Rangel, Illustrator; Raul Braulio Martinez, Art Director; Carlos Martinez, Co-Editor; Carmen A. Escobedo, Graphics Ed & Designer; Rosa Linda Gonzalez, Editor

Silver
NRC Handelsblad
Rotterdam, Netherlands
Karin Mathijsen Gerst, Design Editor; Geert van Kesteren, Photographer

Laaglanders schieten de hoogte in

XXL

Nederlanders zijn de snelst groeiende en inmiddels langste mensensoort in Europa. Waarom dat zo is en hoe groot we precies zullen worden, weet nog niemand. Vast staat dat een flinke lengte vaak de beste banen oplevert en nog steeds met macht, rijkdom en een lang leven wordt geassocieerd. Over het voorrecht je hoofd te stoten, je rug te forceren en in dubbelgevouwen in bad te moeten.

De meeste mensen leggen automatisch een verband tussen lengte en macht of kracht

Award of Excellence
The Globe & Mail
Toronto, Canada
Gudrun Gallo, Art Director/Designer; Michael Gregg, Executive Art Director; Joe Morse, Illustrator; Martin Levin, Books Editor

BOOKS

Shame on all of us

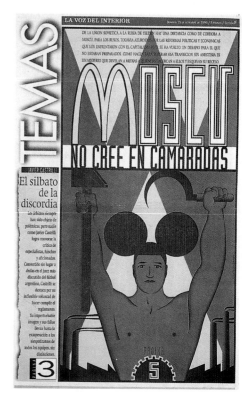

Award of Excellence
La Voz del Interior
Cordoba, Argentina
Javier Candellero, Designer & Illustrator; Miguel De Lorenzi, Art Director; Juan Carlos Gonzalez, Editor; Luis Remonda, Publisher

Award of Excellence
La Voz del Interior
Cordoba, Argentina

Javier Candellero, Designer & Illustrator; Miguel De Lorenzi, Art Director; Juan Carlos Gonzalez, Editor; Luis Remonda, Publisher

Award of Excellence
The Fox Valley Villages
Plainfield, IL

Laurie Jones, Photo Editor/Designer; Amanda Hamann, Designer; Scott Lewis, Photographer

Award of Excellence
La Voz del Interior
Cordoba, Argentina

Javier Candellero, Designer & Illustrator; Miguel De Lorenzi, Art Director; Juan Carlos Gonzalez, Editor; Luis Remonda, Publisher

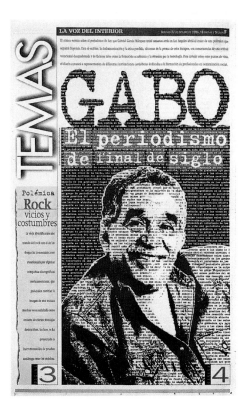

Award of Excellence
La Voz del Interior
Cordoba, Argentina

Javier Candellero, Designer & Illustrator; Miguel De Lorenzi, Art Director & Designer; Juan Carlos Gonzalez, Editor; Luis Remonda, Publisher

Award of Excellence
Morgenavisen Jyllands-Posten
Viby, Denmark

Mette Kryger, Designer

Award of Excellence
O Globo
Rio de Janeiro, Brazil
Pedro Motta, Designer; Marilia Martins, Editor

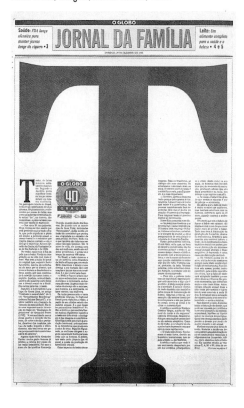

Award of Excellence
Reforma
Mexico City, Mexico
Elba Debernardi, Designer; Alberto Cervantes, Photo Artist; Celia Marin, Editor; Alberto Nava, Photo Artist; Alejandro Banuet, Graphics Editor; Emilio Deheza, Art Director; Eduardo Danilo, Design Consultant

Award of Excellence
Reforma
Mexico City, Mexico
Alejandro Banuet, Designer; Celia Marin, Editor; Emilio Deheza, Art Director; Eduardo Danilo, Design Consultant

Award of Excellence
Reforma
Mexico City, Mexico
Xochitl Gonzalez, Section Designer; Alberto Nava, Photo Artist; Dinorah Basanez, Editor; Alejandro Banuet, Graphics Editor; Emilio Deheza, Art Director; Eduardo Danilo, Design Consultant

Award of Excellence
Reforma
Mexico City, Mexico
Elba Debernardi, Designer; Monica Solorzano, Photo Artist; Jose Diego Gomez, Photographer; Celia Marin, Editor; Alejandro Banuet, Graphics Editor; Emilio Deheza, Art Director; Eduardo Danilo, Design Consultant

Award of Excellence
The Scotsman
Edinburgh, Scotland
Staff

Award of Excellence
The Star-Ledger
Newark, NJ

Elise Levine, Designer; Chris Buckley, Features Art Director; Jason Jett, Section Editor; David G. Klein, Illustrator; George Frederick, AME/Design Director

Award of Excellence
The Star-Ledger
Newark, NJ

Bob Bogert, Designer; David McLimans, Illustrator; Steven Needham, Photographer; Chris Buckley, Art Director/Features; Mark Di Ionno, Section Editor; George Frederick, AME/Design; Susan Olds, AME/Features

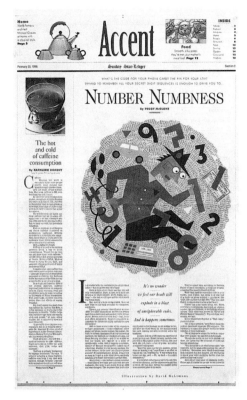

Award of Excellence
The Virginian-Pilot
Norfolk, VA

Sam Hundley, Illustrator/Designer; Eric Sundquist, Editor; Lorraine Eaton, Editor

Award of Excellence
The Anchorage Daily News
Anchorage, AK

Lance Lekander, Designer

Award of Excellence
The Anchorage Daily News
Anchorage, AK

Lance Lekander, Designer; Shawn Mortensen, Photographer

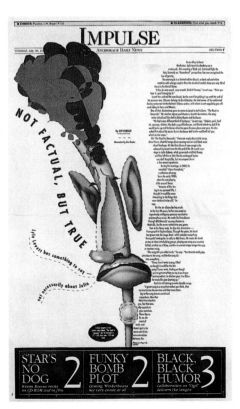

Award of Excellence
The Anchorage Daily News
Anchorage, AK

Dee Boyles, Illustrator & Designer

Silver
The Anchorage Daily News
Anchorage, AK
Dee Boyles, Designer

Award of Excellence
The Anchorage Daily News
Anchorage, AK
Lance Lekander, Art Director & Designer

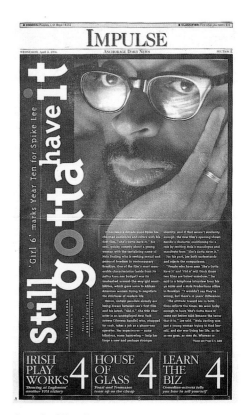

Award of Excellence
The Anchorage Daily News
Anchorage, AK
Lance Lekander, Designer; Robert Cauthier, Photographer

Award of Excellence
The Anchorage Daily News
Anchorage, AK
Dee Boyles, Designer; Michael Halsband, Photographer

Award of Excellence
The Anchorage Daily News
Anchorage, AK
Lance Lekander, Designer; Dana Lixenberg, Photographer

Award of Excellence
The Anchorage Daily News
Anchorage, AK
Dee Boyles, Designer; Juergen Teller, Photographer

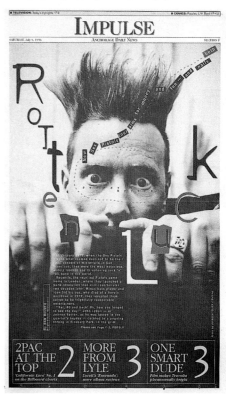

Award of Excellence
El Norte
Monterrey, Mexico
Nohemi Bernal, Designer; Raúl Braulio Martínez, Art Director; Carmen A. Escobedo, Graphics Editor; Edgardo Reséndiz, Editor

Award of Excellence
Austin American-Statesman
Austin, TX
Mike Sutter, Designer; G.W. Babb, Design Director

Award of Excellence
El Periodico de Catalunya
Barcelona, Spain
Olga Puig, Designer; Jaume Mor, Picture Editor; Javier Jubierre, Photo Editor; Miguel Angel Maestro, News Editor

Award of Excellence
Le Devoir
Montreal, Canada

Lise Bissonnette, Publisher; Bernard Descoteaux, Editor-in-Chief; Claude Bearuegard, News Editor; Roland-Yves Carignan, Art Director & Designer; Normand Theriault, Section Editor; Michel Belair, Copy Editor; Gilbert David, Copy Writer

Award of Excellence
Le Devoir
Montreal, Canada

Lise Bissonnette, Publisher; Bernard Descoteaux, Editor-in-Chief; Claude Bearuegard, News Editor; Roland-Yves Carignan, Art Director & Designer; Normand Theriault, Section Editor; Michel Belair, Copy Editor; Mario Cloutier, Copy Writer

Award of Excellence
The New York Times
New York, NY

Linda Brewer, Art Director; J. Otto Siebold, Illustrator

Award of Excellence
La Presse
Montreal, Canada

Julien Chung, AME Photo & Graphics; Alain de Repentigny, AME Entertainment; Helene de Guise, Designer; Bernard Brault, Christian Guay, Photographers

Award of Excellence
The Montreal Gazette
Montreal, Canada

Gayle Grin, Design Editor; Arthur Kaptainis, Writer; Lucinda Chodan, Entertainment Editor

Award of Excellence
The Toronto Star
Toronto, Canada

Neil Cochrane, Designer; Kathleen Kenna, Editor

Award of Excellence
• Also an Award of Excellence for Entertainment Section
The Virginian-Pilot
Norfolk, VA
Sam Hundley, Designer; Roberta Vowell, Editor

Silver
El Norte
Monterrey, Mexico

Graciela Sanchez, Designer; Raul Braulio Martinez, Art Director; Andres Reyes, Photographer; Carmen A. Escobedo, Graphics Editor; Altagracia Fuentes, Editor; Angela Cervantes, Photo Artist

Award of Excellence
The Boston Globe
Boston, MA
Jane Martin, Art Director & Designer

Award of Excellence
El Norte
Monterrey, Mexico

Graciela Sanchez, Designer; Raúl Braulio Martinez, Art Director; Carmen A. Escobedo, Graphics Editor; Altagracia Fuentes, Editor; Juan Jose Ceron, Photographer

Award of Excellence
El Norte
Monterrey, Mexico

Graciela Sanchez, Designer; Juan Jose Ceron, Photographer; Yamil Lopez, Photographer; Raul Braulio Martinez, Art Director; Carmen A. Escobedo, Graphics Ed.; Altagracia Fuentes, Ed.

Award of Excellence
El Norte
Monterrey, Mexico

Graciela Sanchez, Designer; Juan Jose Ceron, Photographer; Rosa Ma Castellanos, Photo Artist; Raul Braulio Martinez, Art Director; Carmen A. Escobedo, Graphics Ed.; Altagracia Fuentes, Ed.

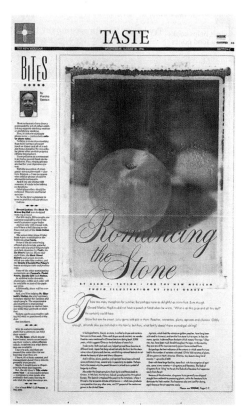

Award of Excellence
El Norte
Monterrey, Mexico

Graciela Sanchez, Designer; Raúl Braulio Martinez, Art Director; Juan Jose Ceron, Photographer; Carmen A. Escobedo, Graphics Editor; Alejandra Garcia, Photo Artist; Altagracia Fuentes, Editor

Award of Excellence
The Hartford Courant
Hartford, CT

Christopher Moore, Graphic Designer; Christian Potter Drury, Art Director; Cecilia Prestamo, Features Photo Editor; Richard Messina, Photographer

Award of Excellence
The New Mexican
Santa Fe, NM

Deborah Villa, Designer; Julie Graber, Photo Illustration

Award of Excellence
San Antonio Express-News
San Antonio, TX
John Camejo, Chief Artist/Features

Award of Excellence
San Francisco Examiner
San Francisco, CA
Richard Paoli, Director/Photography; Jo Mancuso, Epicure Editor; Don McCartney, Designer; Kelly Frankeny, AME Design; Elizabeth Mangelsdorf, Photographer

Award of Excellence
• Also an Award of Excellence for Features Portfolio
San Francisco Examiner
San Francisco, CA
Richard Paoli, Director/Photography; Jo Mancuso, Epicure Editor; Don McCartney, Designer; Kelly Frankeny, AME Design; Paul Chinn, Photographer

Award of Excellence
El Norte
Monterrey, Mexico
Lourdes de la Rosa, Designer; Raúl Braulio Martinez, Art Director; Carmen A. Escobedo, Graphics Editor; Arturo Lopez, Photographer; Rocio Diaz, Editor; Juan Jose Ceron, Photographer

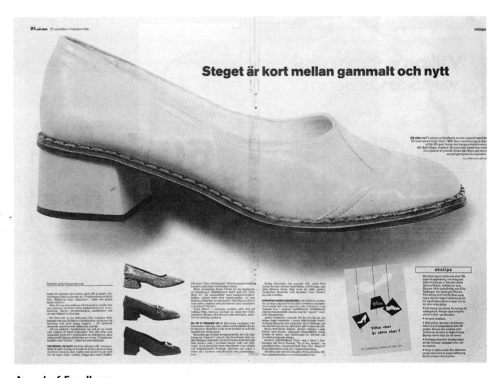

Award of Excellence
Dagens Nyheter
Stockholm, Sweden
Lotten Ekman, Layout; Maria Wahlstrom, Photographer

Award of Excellence
The Montreal Gazette
Montreal, Canada

Gayle Grin, Feature Design Editor & Designer; Iona Monahan, Fashion Editor; Cecelia McGuire, Living Editor; Helene Majera, Illustrator

Award of Excellence
O Globo
Rio de Janeiro, Brazil

Leonardo Drummond, Designer; Mara Caballero, Editor; Patricia Veiga, Reporter; Vicente de Paulo, Photographer

Award of Excellence
Reforma
Mexico City, Mexico

Tsuki Shiraishi, Section Designer/Designer; Moramay Juarez, Photo Artist; Valeria Ascencio, Photographer; Eduardo Danilo, Design Consultant; Alejandro Banuet, Graphics Editor; Emilio Deheza, Art Director

Award of Excellence
Reforma
Mexico City, Mexico

Tsuki Shiraishi, Section Designer; Alejandro Banuet, Designer; Moramay Juarez, Photo Artist; Valeria Ascencio, Photographer; Celia Marin, Editor; Alejandro Banuet, Graphics Editor; Emilio Deheza, Art Director; Eduardo Danilo; Design Consultant

Award of Excellence
The Anchorage Daily News
Anchorage, AK

Pamela Dunlap-Shohl, Designer; Mindy Dwyer, Illustrator

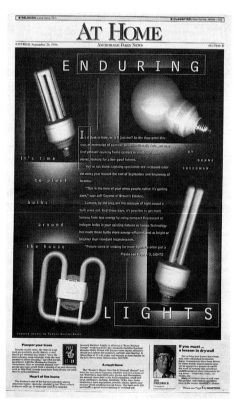

Award of Excellence
The Anchorage Daily News
Anchorage, AK

Pamela Dunlap-Shohl, Designer & Illustrator

Award of Excellence
The Boston Globe
Boston, MA

Keith A. Webb, Art Director & Designer

Silver
The Anchorage Daily News
Anchorage, AK

Pamela Dunlap-Shohl, Art Director, Designer & Illustrator

Award of Excellence
The Flint Journal
Flint, MI

Rickard Watkins, Graphic Artist; Michael Robb, Graphics Editor; Jennifer Walkling, At Home Editor; Cookie Wascha, Tempo Editor; John Dickson, AME

Silver
Dagens Nyheter
Stockholm, Sweden

Stina Wirsén, Illustrator; Karrin Jacobsson, Art Director

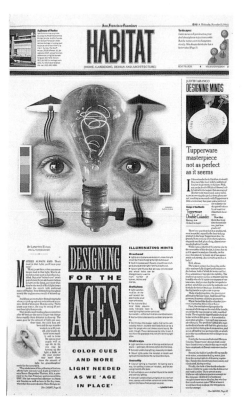

Award of Excellence
San Francisco Examiner
San Francisco, CA

Richard Paoli, Director/Photography; Jo Mancuso, Habitat Editor; Pat Sedlar, Designer/Illustrator; Kelly Frankeny, AME Design

Award of Excellence
The Star-Ledger
Newark, NJ

Richard Bigelow, Designer; Pablo Colon, Designer; Mark Di Ionno, Section Designer; Chris Buckley, Art Director; George Frederick, AME Design

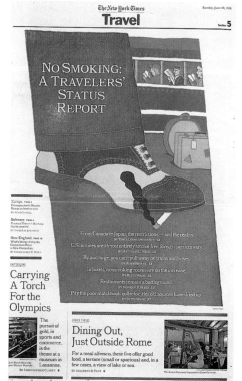

Award of Excellence
The New York Times
New York, NY

Nicki Kalish, Art Director; Seymour Chwast, Illustrator; Carol Dietz, Designer

Award of Excellence
The Oregonian
Portland, OR

Beth Weissman, Designer; Nancy Casey, Features Art Director;
Lydia Hess, Illustrator

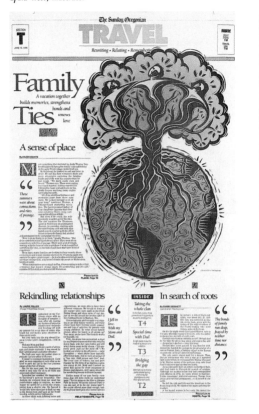

Silver
Reforma
Mexico City, Mexico

Fernando Calderon Escartin, Section Designer; Maria del Socorro Ceballos, Photographer; Lourdes Lopez, Editor; Alejandro Banuet, Graphics Editor; Emilio Dehesa, Art Director; Eduardo Danilo, Design Consultant

Award of Excellence
San Francisco Examiner
San Francisco, CA

Richard Paoli, Director/Photography; John Flinn, Travel Editor;
Don McCartney, Designer; Kelly Frankeny, AME Design; Peter
Spino, Illustrator

Silver
Berlingske Tidende
Copenhagen, Denmark
Ida Jerichow, Graphic Artist

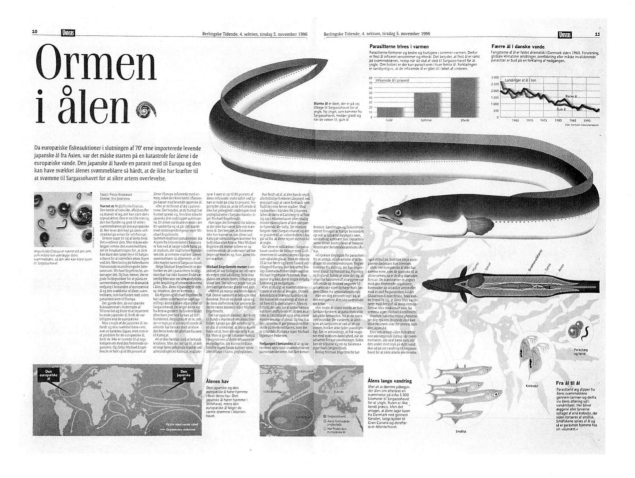

Ormen
i ålen

Da europæiske fiskeauktioner i slutningen af 70'erne importerede levende japanske ål fra Asien, var det måske starten på en katastrofe for ålene i de europæiske vande. Den japanske ål havde en parasit med til Europa og den kan have svækket ålenes svømmeblære så hårdt, at de ikke har kræfter til at svømme til Sargassohavet for at sikre artens overlevelse.

Award of Excellence
Diario de Noticias
Pamplona, Spain
Silvia De Luis, Designer

14 • En portada

Tras
las huellas del santo:
Malaca

LA CIUDAD PORTUARIA DE MALASIA CONSERVA ALGUNOS VESTIGIOS Y LE VENERA, 451 AÑOS DESPUÉS, COMO EL APÓSTOL DEL ESTE

En portada • 15

TRAVEL

Along the California coast in a square-topsail schooner

SAILING
Tall

Award of Excellence
San Francisco Examiner
San Francisco, CA

Richard Paoli, Director/Photography; John Flinn, Travel Editor;
Don McCartney, Designer; Kelly Frankeny, AME Design

Award of Excellence
Chicago Tribune
Chicago, IL
Kristin Fitzpatrick, Art Director/Illustrator; Steven Duenes, Illustrator

Silver
The Boston Globe
Boston, MA
Cindy Daniels, Art Director & Designer; Henrik Drescher, Illustrator; Nils Bruzelius, Editor; Kathy Everly, Editor; Alison Bass, Writer

Award of Excellence
The Boston Globe
Boston, MA
Cindy Daniels, Art Director & Designer

Silver
NRC Handelsblad
Rotterdam, Netherlands

Marinka Reuten, Design Editor; Rik
van Schagen, Graphics Editor

Award of Excellence
The Boston Globe
Boston, MA

Cindy Daniels, Art Director & Designer; Nils Bruzelius, Editor;
Kathy Everly, Editor; David L. Chandler, Writer

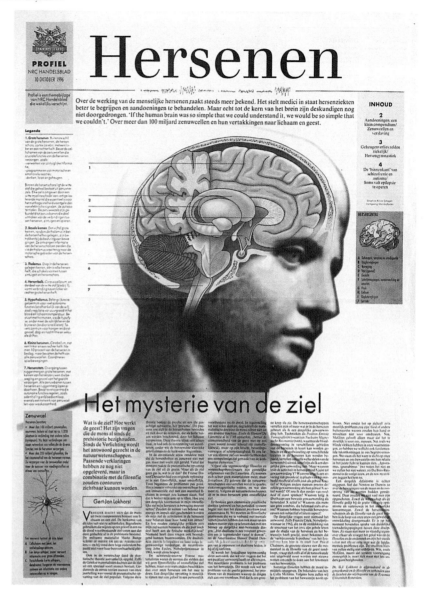

Award of Excellence
Detroit Free Press
Detroit, MI

Elio Leturia, Designer; J. Kyle Keener, Photo Illustration; Chris Magerl, Picture Editor

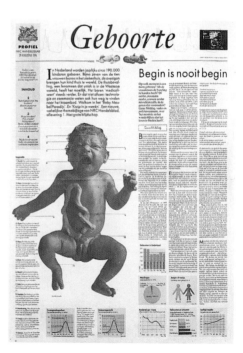

Award of Excellence
NRC Handelsblad
Rotterdam, Netherlands

Stephan Saaltink, Design Editor; Maarten Boddaert, Graphics
Editor; Hilly Versprille, Photographer

Award of Excellence
The San Diego Union-Tribune
San Diego, CA

Amy Stirnkorb, Art Director & Designer; Scott Laumann, Illustrator; Howard Lipin, Photographer

Award of Excellence
The San Diego Union-Tribune
San Diego, CA

Channon Seifert, Designer; Phillip Dvorak, Illustrator

Award of Excellence
NRC Handelsblad
Rotterdam, Netherlands

Henry Cannon, Design Editor; Rik van Schagen, Graphics Editor; Jeanette van Bommel, Graphics Editor

Award of Excellence
The San Diego Union-Tribune
San Diego, CA

Amy Stirnkorb, Designer; Scott Laumann, Illustrator; Mark Nowlin, Graphics Journalist

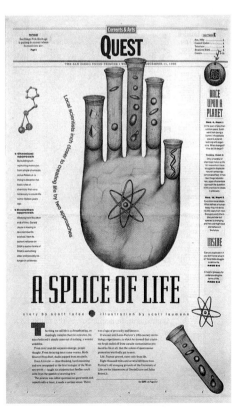

Award of Excellence
The San Diego Union-Tribune
San Diego, CA

Laurie Harker, Designer; Amy Stirnkorb, Designer; Scott Laumann, Illustrator

Award of Excellence
San Jose Mercury News
San Jose, CA

Martin Gee, Designer

Silver
• Also an Award of Excellence
for Color Illustration
Dagens Nyheter
Stockholm, Sweden

Lotten Ekman, Layout; Stina
Wirsen, Illustrator

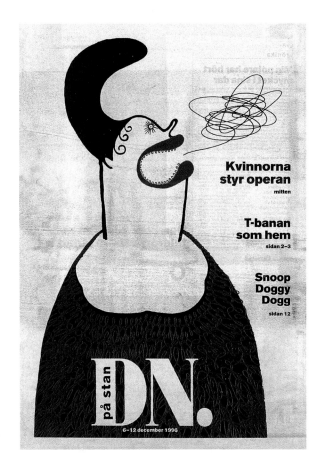

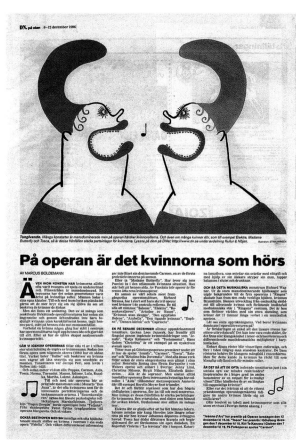

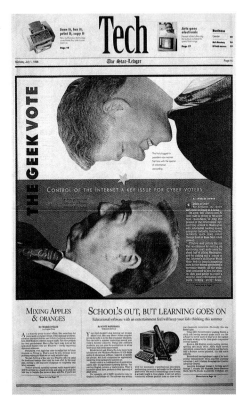

Award of Excellence
La Gaceta
San Miguel de Tucuman, Argentina

Sergio Fernandez, Art Director; Mario Garcia, Design
Consultant; Ruben Falci, Designer

Award of Excellence
• Also an Award of Excellence for Color Illustration
The Anchorage Daily News
Anchorage, AK

Lance Lekander, Art Director & Designer & Illustrator

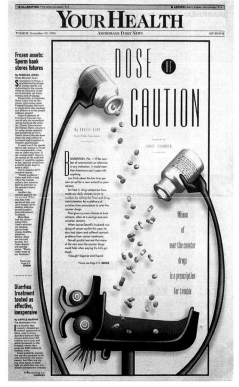

Award of Excellence
The Anchorage Daily News
Anchorage, AK
Lance Lekander, Art Director, Designer & Illustrator

Silver
Diario de Noticias
Pamplona, Spain
Jose Javier Aos, Designer

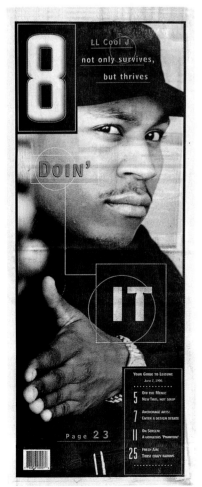

Award of Excellence
The Anchorage Daily News
Anchorage, AK
Lance Lekander, Art Director & Designer

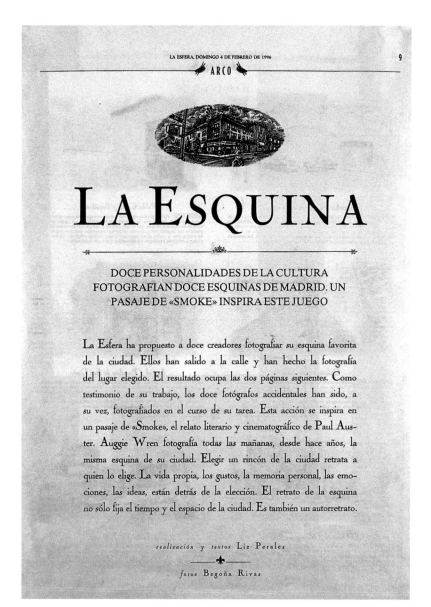

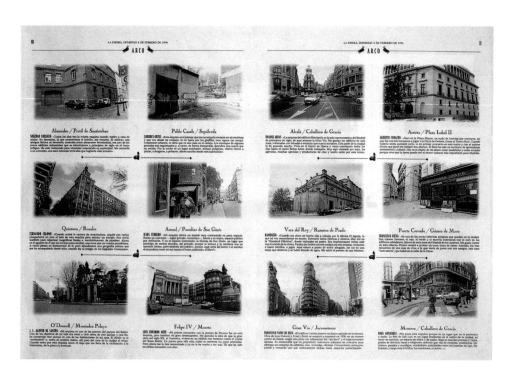

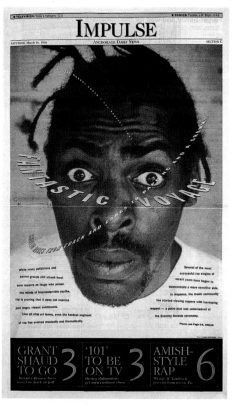

Award of Excellence
• Also an Award of Excellence for Features Portfolio
Berlingske Tidende
Copenhagen, Denmark
Gregers Jensen, Designer

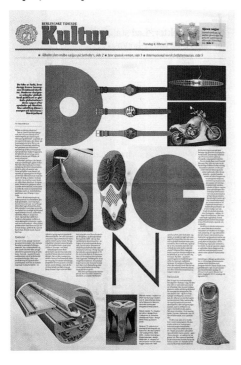

Silver
El Pais
Madrid, Spain
Jesus Martinez, Designer; Luis Galan, Designer

Award of Excellence
Berlingske Tidende
Copenhagen, Denmark
Gregers Jensen, Designer

Award of Excellence
Dagens Nyheter
Stockholm, Sweden
Anders Frelin, Designer; John Bark, Design Director; Tommy Svenson, Photographer

Award of Excellence
Dagens Nyheter
Stockholm, Sweden
Kerstin Wigstrand, Design Director; John Bark, Design Director; Fredrik Funck, Photographer

Award of Excellence
Dagens Nyheter
Stockholm, Sweden
Hans Kronbrink, Designer; John Bark, Design Director

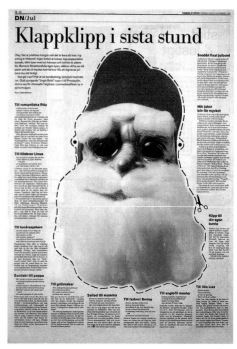

Award of Excellence
The Dallas Morning News
Dallas, TX
Lesley Becker, Designer

Award of Excellence
Duluth News-Tribune
Duluth, MN
Lewis H. Leung, Designer/Illustrator; Dave Ballard, Photographer

Award of Excellence
Dagens Nyheter
Stockholm, Sweden
Hakan Burell, Designer; John Bark, Design Director

Award of Excellence
El Mundo
Madrid, Spain

Carmelo Caderot, Art Director & Designer; Ulises Culebro, Illustrator

Award of Excellence
El Mundo
Madrid, Spain

Carmelo Caderot, Art Director & Designer; Raul Arias, Illustrator

Award of Excellence
El Mundo
Madrid, Spain

Carmelo Caderot, Art Director & Designer; Tono Benavides, Illustrator

Award of Excellence
El Norte
Monterrey, Mexico

Rebeca Ayala, Designer & Photo Artist; Angela Cervantes, Illustrator; Raul Braulio Martinez, Art Director; Andres Reyes, Photographer; Marcela Amaya, Graphics Editor; Katya Garza, Editor; Cristina Cuellar; Editor

Award of Excellence
El Norte
Monterrey, Mexico

Rebecca Ayala, Designer; Angela Cervantes, Illustrator, Photo Artist; Rebeca Ayala, Photo Artist; Raul Braulio Martinez, Art Director; Andres Reyes, Photographer; Marcela Amaya, Graphics Editor; Katya Garza, Editor; Cristina Cuellar, Editor; Adriana Ortiz, Illustrator; Miguel Angel Chavez, Photographer

Award of Excellence
El Pais
Madrid, Spain
Luis Galan, Designer; Jesus Martinez, Designer

Award of Excellence
El Nuevo Dia
San Juan, PR
Jose L. Diaz de Villegas, Jr, Art Director, Designer & Illustrator

Award of Excellence
The Flint Journal
Flint, MI
Jeff Johnston, Page Designer; Stuart Bauer, Todd Wharton, Photographers; Tina Beirne, Photo Ed.; Michael Robb, Graphics Ed.; John Dickson, AME

Award of Excellence
La Gaceta
San Miguel de Tucuman, Argentina
Sergio Fernandez, Art Director; Mario Garcia, Design Consultant; Sebastian Rosso, Designer

Award of Excellence
La Gaceta
San Miguel de Tucuman, Argentina
Sergio Fernandez, Art Director; Mario Garcia, Design Consultant; Sebastian Rosso, Designer; Guillermo Monti, Editor

Award of Excellence
La Gaceta
San Miguel de Tucuman, Argentina
Sergio Fernandez, Art Director; Mario Garcia, Design Consultant; Bellen Bestani, Designer

Award of Excellence
La Presse
Montreal, Canada
Julien Chung, AME Graphics/Photography; Guy Pinard, Editor; Steve Adams, Illustrator & Designer

Award of Excellence
La Gaceta
San Miguel de Tucuman, Argentina
Sergio Fernandez, Art Director; Mario Garcia, Design Consultant; Sebastian Rosso, Designer

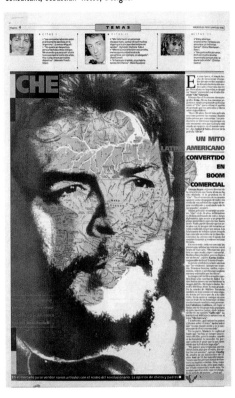

Award of Excellence
Listin Diario
Santo Domingo, Dominican Republic
Javier Errea, Design Consultant; Ricardo Bermejo, Design Consultant; Luis Garbayo, Design Consultant; Elena Moreno, Design Consultant; Humberto Martinez, Artist

Award of Excellence
The New York Times
New York, NY
John Cayea, Art Director

Award of Excellence
Reforma
Mexico City, Mexico
Mayte Amezcua, Section Designer; Jorge Penaloza, Illustrator & Designer; Beatriz de Leon Lugo, Editor; Eduardo Danilo, Design Consultant; Alejandro Banuet, Graphics Editor; Emilio Deheza, Art Director

Award of Excellence
Morgenavisen Jyllands-Posten
Viby, Denmark
Hans Bjarne Hansen, Journalist; Rina Kjeldgaard, Graphic Artist

Award of Excellence
Reforma
Mexico City, Mexico

Mayte Amezcua, Section Designer; Jorge Penaloza, Illustrator; Beatriz de Leon Lugo, Editor; Eduardo Danilo, Design Consultant; Alejandro Banuet, Graphics Editor; Emilio Deheza, Art Director

Award of Excellence
Reforma
Mexico City, Mexico

Mayte Amezcua, Section Designer; Cristina Medrano, Illustrator; Beatriz de Leon Lugo, Editor; Eduardo Danilo, Design Consultant; Alejandro Banuet, Graphics Editor; Emilio Deheza, Art Director

Award of Excellence
Chicago Tribune
Chicago, IL

David Syrek, Associate Design Editor; David Cowles, Illlustrator; Robin Johnston, Art Director

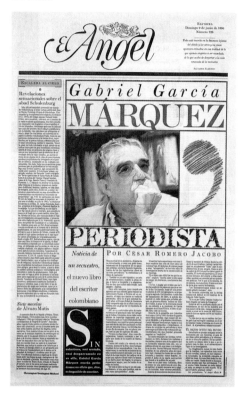

Award of Excellence
The Akron Beacon Journal
Akron, OH

Dennis Balogh, Illustrator & Designer

Award of Excellence
El Norte
Monterrey, Mexico

Nora Diaz, Designer; Raúl Braulio Martinez, Art Director; Romel Luna, Photographer; Marcela Amaya, Graphics Editor; Rossana Garza, Editor

Silver
El Norte
Monterrey, Mexico

Carmen T. Chacon, Designer & Photo Artist; Raul Braulio Martinez, Art Director; Andres Reyes, Photographer; Angeles Nasar, Graphics Editor; Katya Garza, Editor; Cristina Cuellar, Editor

Award of Excellence
El Norte
Monterrey, Mexico

Alejandra Delgado, Designer & Photo Artist; Raúl Braulio Martinez, Art Director; Guillermo Castillo, Illustrator; Marcela Amaya, Graphics Editor; Eduardo Crisostomo, Editor

Award of Excellence
Goteborgs-Posten
Gothenburg, Sweden
Rune Stenberg, Designer

Award of Excellence
El Norte
Monterrey, Mexico
Angeles Nassar, Designer & Graphics Editor; Raúl Braulio Martinez, Art Director; Cristina Cuellar, Editor

Award of Excellence
The Stuart News
Stuart, FL
Jim Sergent, Chief Designer

MAGAZINES

Magazines had to be distrib-
uted with a newspaper to qual-
ify for this category.
Magazines could enter the
Special Section category if
the sections appeared fewer
than four times a year. Covers
were judged in two divisions:
Black & white and/or one color
and two or more colors. Three
complete issues of the magazine had to be entered for
overall design.

[OVERALL DESIGN]

[SPECIAL SECTIONS]

[COVER DESIGN]

[PAGE DESIGN]

Dagens Nyheters Månadsmgasin was awarded a Gold Medal for its thoughtful and creative use of imagery through composition content and editing – successfully contrasting with bold and simple typography.

Gold
Dagens Nyheter
Stockholm, Sweden
Pompe Hedengren, Art Director; Peter Alenas, Art Director; Hakan Lindgren, Picture Editor

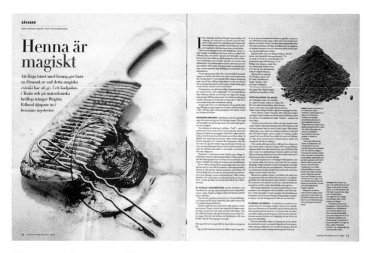

Dagens Nyheters Mánadsmgasin se ganó una Medalla de Oro por su uso bien pensado y creativo de imágenes mediante composición, contenido y compaginación – con éxito puestos en contraste mediante una tipografía audaz y sencilla.

Praga

por detrás da Cortina de Veludo

Gold
Diario de Noticias
Lisboa, Portugal
Mario Resendes, Editor-in-Chief;
Pedro Rolo Duarte, Editor;
Jose Maria Ribeirinho, Art
Director; Luis Silva Dias,
Design Editor; Gabriel Morón,
Designer

Diario de Noticias was awarded a Gold Medal for its fresh, sharp, sophisticated, dynamic, clean, surprising, thoroughly graphic and bold visual look.

Diario de Noticias se ganó una Medalla de Oro por su aspecto visual audaz, completamente gráfico y de enfoque fresco, agudo, sofisticado, dinámico, limpio y sorprendente.

Corpo
e alma

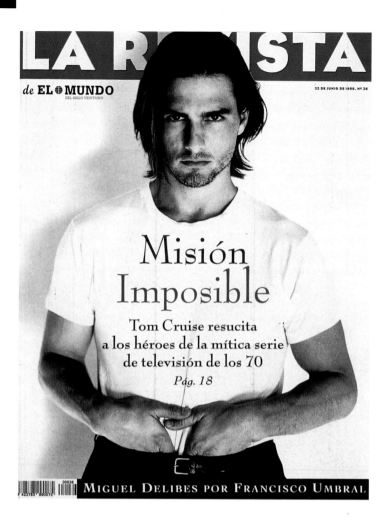

Silver
La Revista
Madrid, Spain

Rodrigo Sanchez,
Art Director;
Carmelo Caderot,
Design Director

Award of Excellence
La Vanguardia
Barcelona, Spain

Carlos Pérez de Rozas Arribas, Art Director; Rosa Mundet
Poch, Chief of Design & iInfographics; Emilio Alvarez, Designer;
Antonio Soto, Designer; Ma Jose Oriol, Designer; Monica
Caparros, Designer

Award of Excellence
El Pais de las Tentaciones
Madrid, Spain

Fernando Gutierrez, Designer; Nuria Muina, Art Editor;
Wladimir Marnich, Art Editor; Guillermo Trigo, Art Dept;
Santiago Carbajo, Art Dept; Cesar Paredes, Art Dept

Award of Excellence
El Pais de las Tentaciones
Madrid, Spain

Fernando Gutierrez, Designer; Nuria Muina, Art Editor;
Wladimir Marnich, Art Editor; Guillermo Trigo, Art Dept;
Santiago Carbajo, Art Dept; Cesar Paredes, Art Dept

Silver
El Pais Semanal
Madrid, Spain

Fernando Gutierrez, Art Director; Ignacio Rubio, Designer; Ignacio Tamargo, Designer; Ricardo Martin, Picture Editor

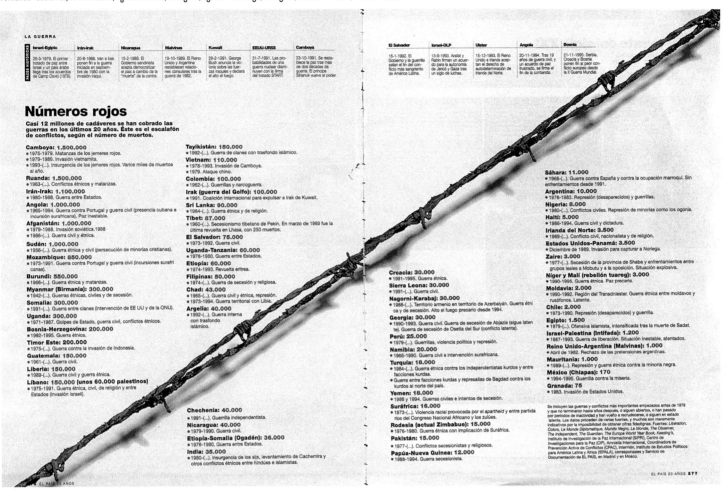

Award of Excellence
El Pais Semanal
Madrid, Spain

David Garcia, Art Director; Eugenio Gonzalez, Design Director; Maria Paz Domingo, Designer; Gustavo Sanchez, Designer; Alex Martinez, Chief Editor

Award of Excellence
The Boston Globe
Boston, MA

Cindy Daniels, Art Director; Michael J. Larkin, AME; Robert F. Cutting, Special Sections Editor; Gail Ravgiala, Content Editor

Silver
El Pais Semanal
Madrid, Spain

David Garcia, Art Director; Eugenio Gonzalez, Design Director; Maria Paz Domingo, Designer; Gustavo Sanchez, Designer; Alex Martinez, Editor

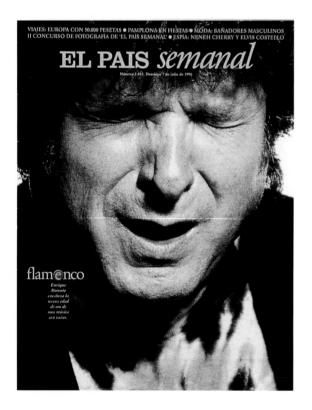

Silver
El Pais Semanal
Madrid, Spain

David Garcia, Art Director; Eugenio Gonzalez, Design Director; Maria Paz Domingo, Designer; Gustavo Sanchez, Designer; Alex Martinez, Editor

Silver
La Revista
Madrid, Spain
Rodrigo Sanchez, Art Director; Carmelo Caderot, Design Director

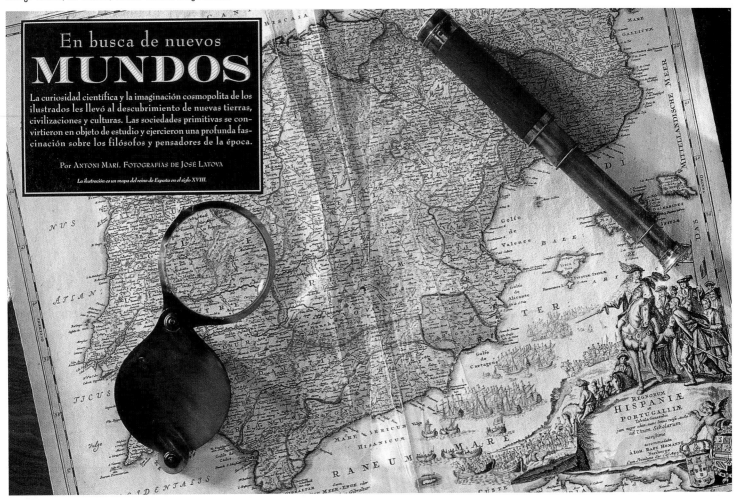

Award of Excellence
La Revista
Madrid, Spain
Rodrigo Sanchez, Art Director; Miguel Buckenmeyer, Designer;
Maria Gonzalez, Designer; Amparo Redondo, Designer; Carmelo
Caderot, Design Director; Chema Conesa, Photo Editor

Award of Excellence
El Pais Semanal
Madrid, Spain
David Garcia, Art Director; Eugenio Gonzalez, Design Director;
Maria Paz Domingo, Designer; Gustavo Sanchez, Designer; Alex
Martinez, Chief Editor

Award of Excellence
The New York Times Magazine
New York, NY
Janet Froelich, Art Director; Catherine Gilmore-Barnes, Art
Director; Kathy Ryan, Photo Editor; John Walker, Designer

Award of Excellence
La Vanguardia
Barcelona, Spain

Carlos Pérez de Rozas Arribas, Art Director; Rosa Mundet
Poch, Chief of Design and Infographics; Emilio Alvarez,
Designer; Antonio Soto, Designer; Ma Jose Oriol, Designer;
Monica Caparros, Designer; Jordi Labanda, Illustrator

Award of Excellence
The New York Times Magazine
New York, NY

Janet Froelich, Art Director; Joel Cuyler, Art Director; Kathy
Ryan, Photo Editor; John Walker, Designer

Award of Excellence
The New York Times Magazine
New York, NY

Janet Froelich, Art Director; Lisa Naftolin, Art Director; Kathy
Ryan, Photo Editor; Joel Cuyler, Designer; Jody Quon, Assistant
Photo Editor; Susan Dazzo, Designer

Award of Excellence
El Dominical/
El Periodico de Catalunya
Barcelona, Spain
Ferran Sendra, Designer; Nuria Miguel, Designer; Kim Salomon, Designer; Gerardo Della Santa, Designer; Ricardo Feriche, Creative Director; Alejandro Yofre, Photo Editor; Hector Chimirri, News Editor; Rafael Nadal; Vice-Editor

Award of Excellence
The New York Times Magazine
New York, NY
Janet Froelich, Art Director; Cathy Gilmore-Barnes, Designer

Award of Excellence
The Philadelphia Inquirer Magazine
Philadelphia, PA
Christine Dunleavy, Art Director; Susan Syrnick, Assistant Art Director & Designer; Nick Kelsh, Photographer

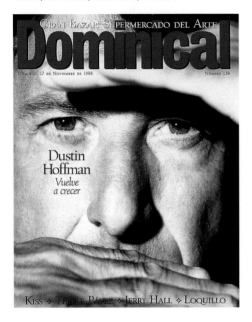

Award of Excellence
The Seattle Times
Seattle, WA
Rhonda Prast, Pacific Art Director

Award of Excellence
Dagens Nyheter
Stockholm, Sweden
Lotten Ekman, Layout; Sam Stadener, Photo

Award of Excellence
El Mundo Metropoli
Madrid, Spain
Rodrigo Sanchez, Art Director & Designer; Carmelo Caderot, Design Director

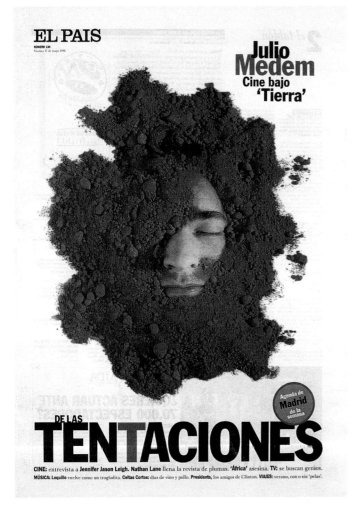

Silver
El Pais de las Tentaciones
Madrid, Spain

Fernando Gutierrez, Designer; Nuria Muina, Art Editor;
Wladimir Marnich, Art Editor; Guillermo Trigo, Art Dept;
Santiago Carbajo, Art Dept; Cesar Paredes, Art Dept

Silver
El Mundo Metropoli
Madrid, Spain

Rodrigo Sanchez, Art Director & Designer; Carmelo Caderot, Design Director

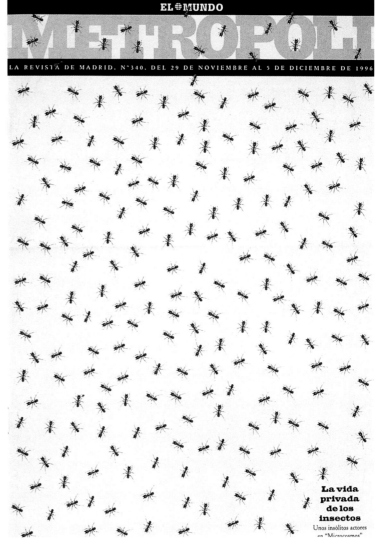

Silver
• Also an Award of Excellence for Photo Illustration
El Pais de las Tentaciones
Madrid, Spain

Fernando Gutierrez, Designer; Nuria Muina, Art Editor;
Wladimir Marnich, Art Editor; Guillermo Trigo, Art Dept;
Santiago Carbajo, Art Dept; Cesar Paredes, Art Dept; Pedro
Laguna, Photographer

Silver
The New York Times Magazine
New York, NY
Janet Froelich, Art Director; Joel Cuyler, Designer; Rimma Gerlovin, Valeriy Gerlovin, Photographers; Kathy Ryan, Photo Editor

Award of Excellence
El Mundo Metropoli
Madrid, Spain
Rodrigo Sanchez, Art Director and Designer; Carmelo Caderot, Design Director

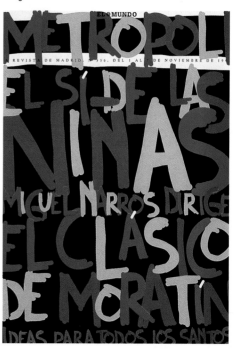

Award of Excellence
El Nuevo Dia
San Juan, PR
Jose L. Diaz de Villegas, Jr, Art Director, Designer & Illustrator

Award of Excellence
El Pais de las Tentaciones
Madrid, Spain
Fernando Gutierrez, Designer; Nuria Muina, Art Director; Guillermo Trigo, Art Dept; Santiago Carbajo, Art Dept; Cesar Paredes, Art Dept

Award of Excellence
El Pais de las Tentaciones
Madrid, Spain
Fernando Gutierrez, Designer; Nuria Muina, Art Director; Wladimir Marnich, Art Director; Guillermo Trigo, Art Dept; Santiago Carbajo, Art Dept; Cesar Paredes, Art Dept

Award of Excellence
El Pais de las Tentaciones
Madrid, Spain
Fernando Gutierrez, Designer; Nuria Muina, Art Editor; Wladimir Marnich, Art Editor; Guillermo Trigo, Art Dept; Santiago Carbajo, Art Dept; Cesar Paredes, Art Dept

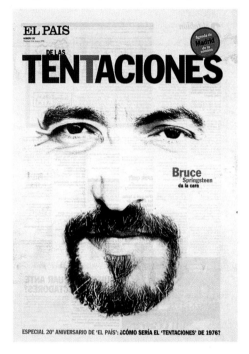

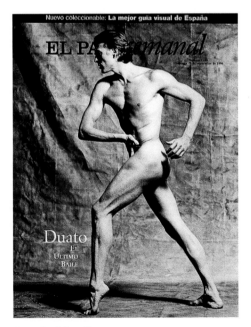

Award of Excellence
El Pais Semanal
Madrid, Spain
David Garcia, Art Director; Eugenio Gonzalez, Design Director; Maria Paz Domingo, Designer; Gustavo Sanchez, Designer; Jordi Socias, Photographer; Alex Martinez, Chief Editor

Award of Excellence
El Pais Semanal
Madrid, Spain
David Garcia, Art Director; Eugenio Gonzalez, Design Director; Maria Paz Domingo, Designer; Gustavo Sanchez, Designer; Joan Tomas, Photographer; Alex Martinez, Chief Editor

Award of Excellence
El Pais Semanal
Madrid, Spain
David Garcia, Art Director; Eugenio Gonzalez, Design Director; Maria Paz Domingo, Designer; Gustavo Sanchez, Designer; Juan Sesen, Photographer; Alex Martinez, Editor

Award of Excellence
El Pais Semanal
Madrid, Spain

David Garcia, Art Director; Eugenio Gonzalez, Design Director; Maria Paz Domingo, Designer; Gustavo Sanchez, Designer; Alex Martinez, Editor; Heriberto Muela, Illustrator

Award of Excellence
El Dominical/
El Periodico de Catalunya
Barcelona, Spain

Ferran Sendra, Designer; Nuria Miguel, Designer; Kim Salomon, Designer; Gerardo Della Santa, Designer; Ricardo Feriche, Creative Director; Alejandro Yofre, Photo Editor; Hector Chimirri, News Editor; Rafael Nadal, Vice-Editor; Jorge Represa, Photographer

Award of Excellence
El Dominical/
El Periodico de Catalunya
Barcelona, Spain

Ferran Sendra, Designer; Nuria Miguel, Designer; Kim Salomon, Designer; Gerardo Della Santa, Designer; Ricardo Feriche, Creative Director; Alejandro Yofre, Photo Editor; Hector Chimirri, News Editor; Rafael Nadal, Vice-Editor; Jorge Represa, Photographer

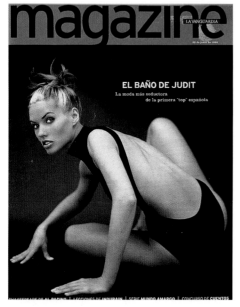

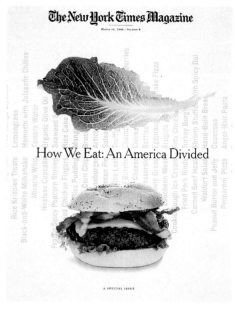

Award of Excellence
La Vanguardia
Barcelona, Spain

Carlos Pérez de Rozas Arribas, Art Director; Rosa Mundet Poch, Chief of Design and Infographics; Emilio Alvarez, Section Designer; Antonio Soto, Designer; Ma José Oriol, Designer; Monica Caparrós, Designer

Award of Excellence
The New York Times Magazine
New York, NY

Janet Froelich, Art Director & Designer; Chip Kidd, Designer

Award of Excellence
The New York Times Magazine
New York, NY

Janet Froelich, Art Director; Lisa Naftolin, Designer; Kenji Toma, Photographer; Kathy Ryan, Photo Editor

Award of Excellence
El Periodico de Catalunya/El Dominical
Barcelona, Spain

Ferran Sendra, Designer; Nuria Miguel, Designer; Kim Salomon, Designer; Gerardo Della Santa, Designer; Ricardo Feriche, Creative Director; Alejandro Yofre, Photo Editor; Hector Chimirri, News Editor; Rafael Nadal; Vice-Editor; Jorge Represa, Photographer

Award of Excellence
• Also an Award of Excellence for Color Illustration
The New York Times Magazine
New York, NY

Janet Froelich, Art Director; Joel Cuyler, Designer; C.F. Payne, Illustrator

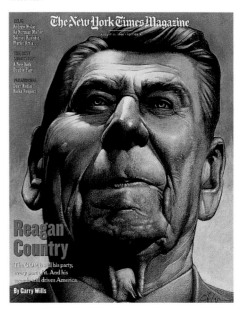

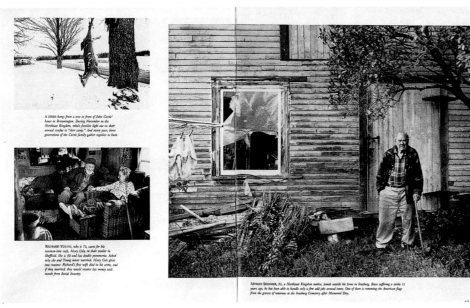

Award of Excellence
The Boston Globe
Boston, MA

Catherine Aldrich, Art Director & Designer; Bill Greene, Photographer

Award of Excellence
El Pais de las Tentaciones
Madrid, Spain

Fernando Gutierrez, Designer; Nuria Muina, Art Editor; Wladimir Marnich, Art Editor; Guillermo Trigo, Art Dept; Santiago Carbajo, Art Dept; Cesar Paredes, Art Dept

El Pais Semanal was awarded a Gold Medal for the bold and daring use of photography, color and photo editing, as well as using restraint in the design to let the pictures tell the story.

Gold
El Pais Semanal
Madrid, Spain

David Garcia, Art Director; Eugenio Gonzalez, Design Director; Maria Paz Domingo, Designer; Gustavo Sanchez, Designer; Francis Giacobetti, Photographer; Alex Martinez, Chief Editor

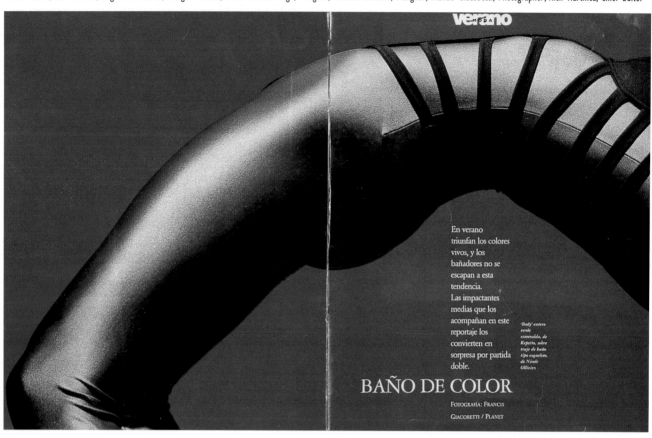

En verano triunfan los colores vivos, y los bañadores no se escapan a esta tendencia. Las impactantes medias que los acompañan en este reportaje los convierten en sorpresa por partida doble.

'Body' entero verde esmeralda, de Repetto, sobre traje de baño tipo esqueleto, de Nicole Ollivier.

BAÑO DE COLOR

FOTOGRAFÍA: FRANCIS GIACOBETTI / PLANET

Medias de Repetto que acompañan a un bañador blanco con rayas, de Sun Valley.

El blanco y el negro, dos ases seguros que combinan con todo

A la derecha, unas coloristas medias de rayas, de Nally Bit, animan un bañador negro con estrellas naranjas de la firma Spalding para Interport.

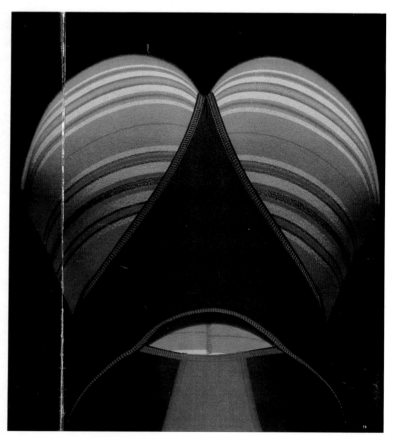

El País Semanal se ganó una Medalla de Oro por su uso atrevido de la fotografía, el color y la edición de fotos, así como por su moderación en el diseño, para dejar que las imágenes relaten el evento.

Silver
The New York Times Magazine
New York, NY

Janet Froelich, Art Director; Matthew Rolston, Photographer; Elizabeth Stewart, Stylist

3. If courage fails, go for the nails. These were lacquered in Snow by Urban Decay. Gold body makeup, right, from Naimie's Beauty Supply. M.A.C. lipstick in Cyber and Laura Mercier Classique Eye Colour in Lavender Field. Yves Saint Laurent's plum mascara No. 4.

The Cuts
That Go Deeper

As costs drop and guilt recedes, more women – and men – are having cosmetic surgery. But in the process something other than flesh is being altered. By Charles Siebert

"NOW, WHAT IS IT YOU'D like done?" Tracy Martin asked as I took a seat beside her and stared into a wall-size mirror. Martin, a tall, slender blonde in her early 30's, is a computer-imaging technician and health educator at the Institute for Aesthetic and Reconstructive Surgery in Nashville, the country's first all-purpose plastic surgery center and one of the most advanced facilities of its kind in the world. Founded seven years ago at Nashville's Baptist Hospital, the institute features a staff of 22 plastic surgeons, its own state-of-the-art surgical unit and private recovery suites, a wide variety of pre- and post-operative cosmetic salon services, a fitness center, a skin-assessment center and a separate resource center with a library, a video room and a year-round program of free seminars to educate both patients and doctors about the latest developments in plastic surgery. Each year at the institute, thousands of people visit the computer-imaging center; there, the designs they have on themselves are modified by, and electronically

melded with, the designs now made possible by modern plastic surgery.

As Martin fixed my image on her computer – it has a big TV-size screen with a camera mounted on top — I sat reviewing the institute's extensive makeover menu. Starting from the top, it includes:

Hair replacement surgery. Through a variety of techniques, among them "scalp reduction, tissue expansion, strip grafts, scalp flaps or clusters of punch grafts (plugs, miniplugs and microplugs)."

Brow lift. To minimize creases in the forehead and hooding over the eyes.

Blepharoplasty. To cut away excess skin and fat around the eyes, eliminating drooping upper eyelids and puffy bags below.

Otoplasty. To reshape ears.

Rhinoplasty. To reduce, increase or reshape the nose.

Collagen and fat injections. To enhance the lips or plump up sunken facial skin.

Liposuction. To remove fat deposits.

Chemical peel. To eliminate wrinkled, blemished, unevenly pigmented or sun-damaged skin.

Dermabrasion. To remove scarring from acne using a high-speed rotary wheel or laser surgery.

Rhytidectomy (face lift). To tighten sagging skin and the underlying facial muscles over which the skin is then redraped.

Facial implants. To change the basic

Charles Siebert is a contributing writer to the Magazine. His article "The DNA We've Been Dealt" appeared in September.

Photographs by Rimma Gerlovina and Valeriy Gerlovin

Silver
The New York Times Magazine
New York, NY

Janet Froelich, Art Director; Nancy Harris, Designer; Valeriy Gerlovin, Photographer; Rimma Gerlovina, Photographer; Kathy Ryan, Photo Editor

Silver
The New York Times Magazine
New York, NY

Janet Froelich, Art Director; Susan Dazzo, Designer; Lisa Naftolin, Designer; Daniel Adel, Illustrator

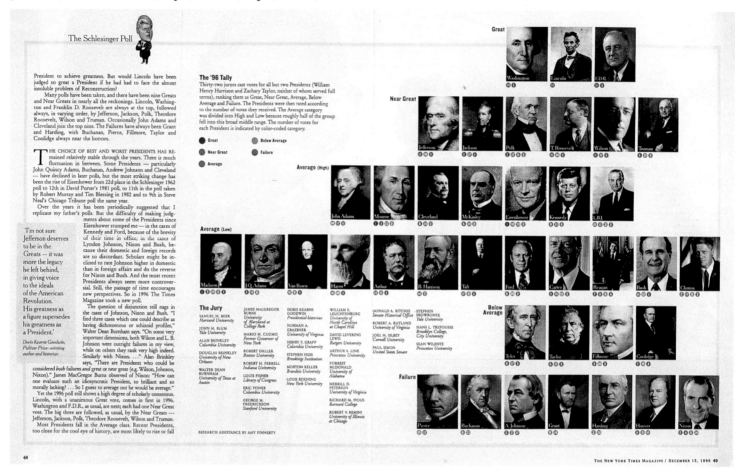

Award of Excellence
El Pais de las Tentaciones
Madrid, Spain

Fernando Gutierrez, Designer; Nuria Muina, Art Editor; Wladimir Marnich, Art Editor; Guillermo Trigo, Art Department; Cesar Paredes, Art Department

Award of Excellence
El Pais de las Tentaciones
Madrid, Spain

Fernando Gutierrez, Designer; Nuria Muina, Art Editor; Wladimir Marnich, Art Editor; Guillermo Trigo, Art Dept; Santiago Carbajo, Art Dept; Cesar Paredes, Art Dept

Award of Excellence
El Pais de las Tentaciones
Madrid, Spain

Fernando Gutierrez, Design; Nuria Muina, Art Editor; Wladimir Marnich, Art Editor; Guillermo Trigo, Art Department; Santiago Carbajo, Art Department; Cesar Paredes, Art Department

Award of Excellence
El Pais de las Tentaciones
Madrid, Spain

Fernando Gutierrez, Design; Nuria Muina, Art Editor; Wladimir Marnich, Art Editor; Guillermo Trigo, Art Department; Santiago Carbajo, Art Department; Cesar Paredes, Art Department

Award of Excellence
El Pais de las Tentaciones
Madrid, Spain

Fernando Gutierrez, Design; Nuria Muina, Art Editor; Wladimir Marnich, Art Editor; Guillermo Trigo, Art Department; Santiago Carbajo, Art Department; Cesar Paredes, Art Department

Award of Excellence
El Pais Semanal
Madrid, Spain

David Garcia, Art Director; Eugenio Gonzalez, Design Director; Maria Paz Domingo, Designer; Gustavo Sanchez, Designer; Isabel Munoz, Photographer; Alex Martinez, Chief Editor

Award of Excellence
El Pais Semanal
Madrid, Spain

David Garcia, Art Director; Eugenio Gonzalez, Design Director;
Maria Paz Domingo, Designer; Gustavo Sanchez, Designer; Juan
Sesen, Photographer; Alex Martinez, Chief Editor

Award of Excellence
The New York Times Magazine
New York, NY

Janet Froelich, Art Director; Nancy Harris, Designer; Serge
Lutens, Photographer; Franciscus Ankone, Stylist

Award of Excellence
El Pais Semanal
Madrid, Spain

David Garcia, Art Director; Eugenio Gonzalez, Design Director;
Maria Paz Domingo, Designer; Gustavo Sanchez, Designer; Juan
Sesen, Photographer; Alex Martinez, Chief Editor

Award of Excellence
El Periodico de Catalunya/El Dominical
Barcelona, Spain

Ferran Sendra, Designer; Nuria Miguel, Designer; Kim Salomon, Designer; Gerardo Della Santa, Designer; Ricardo Feriche, Creative Director; Alejandro Yofre, Photo Editor; Hector Chimirri, News Editor; Rafael Nadal, Vice-Editor

Award of Excellence
El Periodico de Catalunya/El Dominical
Barcelona, Spain

Ferran Sendra, Designer; Nuria Miguel, Designer; Kim Salomon, Designer; Gerardo Della Santa, Designer; Ricardo Feriche, Creative Director; Alejandro Yofre, Photo Editor; Hector Chimirri, News Editor; Rafael Nadal, Vice-Editor

Award of Excellence
La Vanguardia
Barcelona, Spain

Carlos Perez de Rozas Arribas, Art Director; Rosa Mundet Poch, Chief of Design and Infographicss; Emilio Alvarez, Chief of Design Section; Antonio Soto, Designer; Ma Jose Oriol, Designer; Monica Caparros, Designer

Award of Excellence
El Periodico de Catalunya/El Dominical
Barcelona, Spain

Ferran Sendra, Designer; Nuria Miguel, Designer; Kim Salomon, Designer; Gerardo Della Santa, Designer; Ricardo Feriche, Creative Director; Alejandro Yofre, Photo Editor; Hector Chimirri, News Editor; Rafael Nadal, Vice-Editor; Jorge Represa, Photographer

Award of Excellence
The New York Times Magazine
New York, NY

Janet Froelich, Art Director; Joel Cuyler, Designer; Kathy Ryan, Photo Editor; Lisa Naftolin, Designer; Michael O'Neil, Photographer

Award of Excellence
The New York Times Magazine
New York, NY

Janet Froelich, Art Director; Nancy Harris, Designer; Walter Iooss, Photographer; Elizabeth Stewart, Stylist

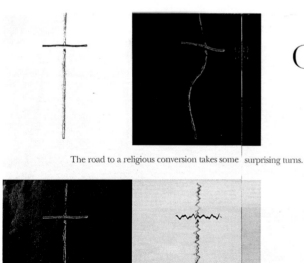

The road to a religious conversion takes some surprising turns.

Award of Excellence
San Jose Mercury News
San Jose, CA

Tracy Cox, Designer

Award of Excellence
San Jose Mercury News
San Jose, CA

Tracy Cox, Art Director & Designer; Sue Morrow, Photo Editor; Nuri Ducassi, Illustrator

SPECIAL SECTIONS

Single-subject series winners
were based on submissions from
three or more consecutive publication dates of preplanned
coverage. Special sections
could include news, sports,
business and all "soft news"
or features special projects.
Inside pages were divided into
two groups: Those with ads or
those with no ads.

[SINGLE-SUBJECT SERIES]

[COVER PAGE]

[INSIDE PAGES]

Award of Excellence
Asbury Park Press
Neptune, NJ

Christine A. Birch, Designer; Gary Potosky, Peter Barzilai, Night Sports Slot Editors; David Bergeland, Michael Goldfinger, Mark R. Sullivan, Photographers; Kevin Shea, Night Photo Editor; John Quinn; ME Sports; Andrew Prendimano, Art & Photo Director; Harris Siegel, ME Design & Photography

Award of Excellence
Chicago Tribune
Chicago, IL

Steve Layton, Artist; Lara Weber, Graphics Coordinator; Robin Johnston, Art Director; Stacy Sweat, Graphics Editor; Therese Shechter, Associate Graphics Editor

Award of Excellence
Chicago Tribune
Chicago, IL

Julie Frady, Art Director; Kristin Fitzpatrick, Art Director; Randy Curwen, Editor; Robert Cross, Writer; Joe LeMonnier, Map Illustrator

Award of Excellence
El Correo
Bilbao, Spain

Tomas Ondarra, Art & Infographic Director; Javier Zarracina, Artist; Fernando G. Baptista, Artist; Aitor Eguinoa, Artist; Alberto Torregrosa, Dir/Editorial Art & Design; Jesus Aycart, Assistant Art Director

Award of Excellence
The Spokesman-Review
Spokane, WA

Lisa A. Cowan, Page Designer; John Sale, Photo Editor; Sandra Bancroft-Billings, Photographer; Warren Huskey, Assistant Graphics Editor

Award of Excellence
The Seattle Times
Seattle, WA

Marian Wachter, Liz McClure, Christine Cox, Sheryl Cabana, Designers; Betty Udeson, Fred Nelson, Photographers; Terry Tazioli, Editor; David Miller, Art Director

Award of Excellence
The Seattle Times
Seattle, WA

David Miller, Art Director; Liz McClure, Designer; Michael Kellams, Designer; Karen Kerchelich, Graphics Reporting and Editing; James McFarlane, Graphic Artist; Jeff Neumann, Graphic Artist; Jimi Lott, Photographer; Fred Nelson; Photographer

Award of Excellence
The Boston Globe
Boston, MA

Aldona Charlton, Art Director & Designer; Sue Dawson, Art Director & Designer; Charles Sennott, Writer

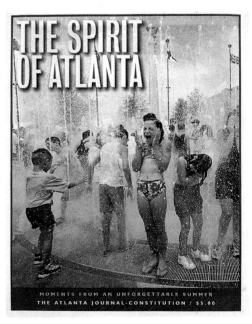

Award of Excellence
The Atlanta Journal & Constitution
Atlanta, GA

Tony Deferia, AME News Art & Photography; Kim Buckner, Designer; Hyde Post, ME; Richard Halicks, Project Editor; John Glenn, Photographer; John Tornoe, Designer

Award of Excellence
• Also an Award of Excellence for Special Section Cover Page

Columbus Dispatch
Columbus, OH

Scott Minister, Art Director & Designer; Tricia Barry, Sherri Rinderle, Designers; Nancy McCloud Wygle, Infographics Editor; Doug Miller, Production Artist; Eric Albrecht, Photographer; Becky Kover, Section Coordinator; Mary Lynn Plageman, AME

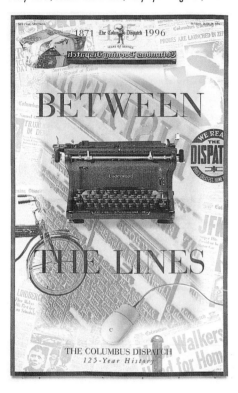

Award of Excellence
Chicago Tribune
Chicago, IL

Stacy Sweat, Graphics Editor; Therese Shechter, Nancy I.Z. Reese, Asst. Graphics Editors; John Crewdson, Senior Writer; Steve Layton, Steven Duenes, Scott Holingue, David Jahntz; Stephen Ravenscraft, Graphic Artists; Kevin Irby, Illustrator

Award of Excellence
The Oregonian
Portland, OR

Steve Cowden, Graphic Artist; Michelle D Wise, Designer; Paul Kitagaki Jr, Photographer; Steven Nehl, Photographer; Pete Lesage, Copy Editor; Serge McCabe, Photo Director; Jacqui Banaszynski, Project Editor

Award of Excellence
• Also an Award of Excellence for Photo Series or Story

Press-Telegram
Long Beach, CA

Paul Hu, Photographer; Leo Hetzel, Photographer; Juanito Holandez, Photographer; Kenny Kwok, Photographer; Suzette Van Bylevelt, Photographer; Staff

Award of Excellence
The San Diego Union-Tribune
San Diego, CA

Channon Seifert, Designer; Michael Franklin, Photo Editor; Karen Clark, Editor; Howard Lipin, Nelvin Cepeda, Gerald McClard, Charlie Neuman, Laura Embry; Nancee E. Lewis, Roni Galgano, Photographers

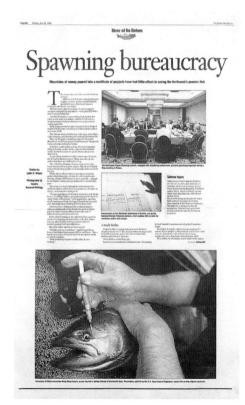

Award of Excellence
The Spokesman-Review
Spokane, WA

Lisa A. Cowan, Designer; John Sale, Photo Editor; Sandra Bancroft-Billings, Photographer; Warren Huskey, Assistant Graphics Editor

Award of Excellence
The Boston Globe
Boston, MA

Keith A. Webb, Art Director & Designer; Robin Romano, Coordinator

Silver
The San Diego Union-Tribune
San Diego, CA

Channon Seifert, Designer; Chris Ross, Designer; Bill Gaspard, Designer; Mike Canepa, Designer; Stacy Seifert, Designer; Greg Epkes, Illustrator; Bill Osborne, News Editor

Award of Excellence
The Los Angeles Times
Los Angeles, CA

David Montesino, Art Director; Leah Reiter, Sports Editor; Rebecca Perry, Artist; Mark Hafer, Artist; Jayne Kamin-Oncea, Photographer; Ricardo DeAratanha, Photographer; Brian Vander Brug, Photographer; Mark Savage; Photographer

Award of Excellence
The San Diego Union-Tribune
San Diego, CA

Channon Seifert, Designer; Chris Ross, Designer; Bill Gaspard, Designer; Mike Canepa, Designer; Stacy Seifert, Designer; Greg Epkes, Illustrator; Bill Osborne, News Editor

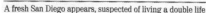

Award of Excellence
The Boston Globe
Boston, MA

Keith A. Webb, Art Director & Designer

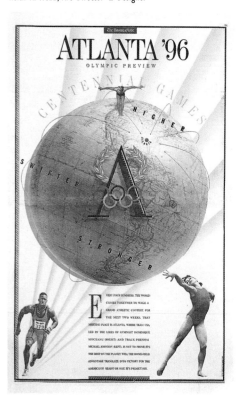

Award of Excellence
The New York Times
New York, NY

Steven Heller, Art Director & Designer; Charles McGrath, Editor; Mark Summers, Illustrator

Award of Excellence
The Seattle Times
Seattle, WA

Jeff Neumann, Illustrator/Designer; Benjamin Benschneider, Photographer; Mark Watanabe, Editor; David Miller, Art Director

Award of Excellence
The Scotsman
Edinburgh, Scotland

Ally Palmer, Art Director; Terry Watson, Design Editor

Award of Excellence
Colorado Springs Gazette Telegraph
Colorado Springs, CO
Trich Redman, Art Director & Designer; Mary Kelley,
Photographer

Silver
The Boston Globe
Boston, MA
Aldona Charlton, Art Director & Designer; Sue Dawson, Art Director & Designer; Charles Sennott, Writer

Award of Excellence
The Detroit News
Detroit, MI
Dale Peskin, Deputy ME; Chris Kozlowski, Design/Graphics
Director; Brad Stertz, Automotive Editor; Tom Hardin, Photo
Editor; James Higgins, Deputy Business Editor

Award of Excellence
Lexington Herald-Leader
Lexington, KY

Steve Dorsey, Presentation Director/Designer; Michelle Patterson-Thomas, Photographer; Karen Samples, Reporter; Harry Merritt, Project Editor; Amy Butters, Copy Editor; Ron Garrison, Photo Director; Russell Lee, Photographer (National Archive)

Award of Excellence
La Presse
Montreal, Canada

Julien Chung, AME Graphics/Photography; Philippe Dubuisson, AME/Business & Politics; Steve Adams, Illustrator & Designer; Rudy Le Cours, Business Editor

Award of Excellence
Pittsburgh Post-Gazette
Pittsburgh, PA

Ted Crow, Illustrator & Designer; Christopher Pett-Ridge, AME Graphics; Tracy Collins, Associate Editor/Graphics; Bill Pliske, Deputy Editor/Graphics; Anita Dufalla, Art Director

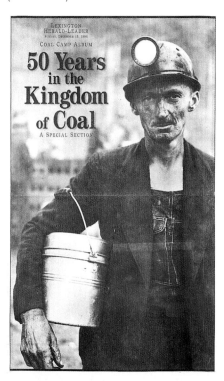

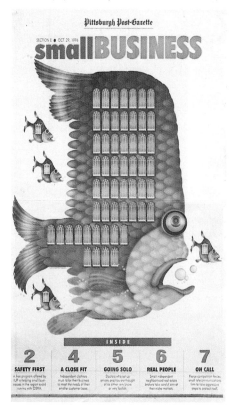

Award of Excellence
Wall Street Journal Reports
New York, NY

Greg Leeds, Design Director & Designer; Dan Yaccarino, Illustrator

Award of Excellence
Asbury Park Press
Neptune, NJ

Stephen Cavendish, News Designer; Janet Michaud, Night Layout Editor; Harris Siegel, ME Design & Photo; Celeste LaBrosse, Night Photo Editor

Award of Excellence
The Wichita Eagle
Wichita, KS
Derek Simmons, Designer; Jeff Tuttle, Photographer

Award of Excellence
Chicago Tribune
Chicago, IL
Joan Cairney, Art Director; Antonio Perez, Photographer; Jose More, Photographer; Torry Bruno, Picture Editor; Jeanie Adams, Assistant Picture Editor

Award of Excellence
Asbury Park Press
Neptune, NJ
Andrew Prendimano, Art and Photo Director; David Bergeland, Photographer; Harris Siegel, ME Design & Photo/Designer; Joe Zedalis, Assistant Sports Editor

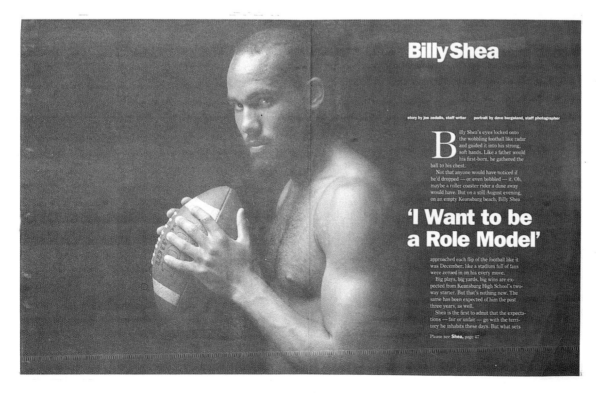

Award of Excellence
• Also an Award of Excellence for Color Informational Graphics
The Washington Post
Washington, DC

Laura Stanton, Graphic Artist

Award of Excellence
Chicago Tribune
Chicago, IL

Steve Layton, Graphic Artist

Award of Excellence
The Philadelphia Inquirer
Philadelphia, PA

David Milne, AME Design; Bill Marsh, Design
Director; Lisa Zollinger, Page Designer; Nan
Winterstellar, Deputy Photo Director

DESIGN PORTFOLIO

Portfolios had to include six pages by one designer in any one of four areas: News, feature, magazine or a combination of any of these. Entries were divided into three circulation groups: Circulation 175,000 and above, circulation 50,000 though 174,999 and circulation 49,999 and below.

[NEWS]

[FEATURE]

[MAGAZINE]

[COMBINATION]

Award of Excellence
The Boston Globe
Boston, MA
Janet L. Michaud, Designer

Award of Excellence
The Home News & Tribune
East Brunswick, NJ
Harris Siegel, ME/Design & Photo/Designer

Award of Excellence
The Detroit News
Detroit, MI
David Kordalski, Assistant Graphics Editor

Award of Excellence
The Miami Herald
Miami, FL
Ana Lense Larrauri, Graphic Artist

Award of Excellence
The New York Times
New York, NY
Wayne Kamidoi, Designer

Award of Excellence
The New York Times
New York, NY
Tim Oliver, Presentation Editor

Award of Excellence
The Stuart News
Stuart, FL
Jim Sergent, Chief Designer

Award of Excellence
The Virginian-Pilot
Norfolk, VA
Latane Jones, Designer

Award of Excellence
Star Tribune
Minneapolis, MN
Denise M. Reagan, Designer

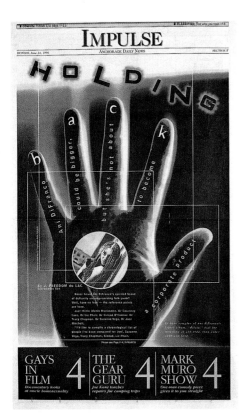

Award of Excellence
The Anchorage Daily News
Anchorage, AK
Dee Boyles, Designer

Award of Excellence
The Boston Globe
Boston, MA
Keith A. Webb, Art Director & Designer

Award of Excellence
The Boston Globe
Boston, MA
Natalie Diffloth, Art Director & Designer

Silver
• Also an Award of Excellence for Inside Page
The Boston Globe
Boston, MA
Cindy Daniels, Art Director & Designer; David L. Chandler, Writer; Sean McNaughton, Informational Graphic Designer; Nils Bruzelius, Editor; Kathy Everly, Editor

Award of Excellence
Columbus Dispatch
Columbus, OH
Scott Minister, Art Director & Designer

Award of Excellence
The Boston Globe
Boston, MA
Natalie Diffloth, Art Director & Designer

Silver
El Mundo
Madrid, Spain
Carmelo Caderot, Art Director & Designer

Los Documentos Del 3.M

SÁBADO 17 DE FEBRERO DE 1996

RADIOGRAMAS ELECTORALES

Los Documentos Del 3.M

MIÉRCOLES 7 DE FEBRERO DE 1996

RADIOGRAMAS ELECTORALES

BORJA HERMOSO

⑨ *Cultura*

La atracción del escaparatismo

Un innegable avance en el tejido de infraestructuras y equipamientos, cierta pobreza de textos legislativos y no pocas dosis de escaparatismo y ampulosidad financiera en operaciones como la compra de la Colección Thyssen o la interminable reapertura del Teatro Real, han sido quizá los tres vértices de la gestión socialista de la Cultura desde la llegada del PSOE al poder en 1982.

En 13 años, cuatro inquilinos han pasado por el Ministerio situado en la madrileña Plaza del Rey, y esas cuatro gestiones han sido, desde luego, bien distintas tanto en su personalidad como en su quehacer.

Javier Solana (1982-1988) fue designado por Felipe González como el primer encargado de reducir en realidades aquella progresiva accesibilidad a la cultura prometida por el programa del PSOE. El actual secretario general de la OTAN fue sólo el ministro de Cultura más longevo de la era socialista, si es que esa era

toca a su fin como apuntan los sondeos. Y fue, sobre todo, el más esforzado de todos al menos en lo relativo a la preparación y promulgación de leyes: suyas son la Ley del Patrimonio Histórico Español de 1985 y la de la Propiedad Intelectual de 1987, además de

una decena de decretos fundamentalmente referentes a las ayudas al cine español.

A un político-político le sustituyó un escritor-cineasta metido a político cuya gestión acabaría volviéndose contra él. Jorge Semprún llegó a la Plaza del Rey en julio del

88 con el valioso aval de ser uno de los intelectuales españoles de mayor prestigio en el extranjero. Semprún no logró aupar su gestión ministerial a la altura de su sabiduría literaria y cinematográfica. Siempre aseguró, siendo ministro, que le había costado

mucho decir «sí» a Felipe González. El tiempo le daría su razón.

Prometió una Ley de Mecenazgo y Fundaciones que nunca pudo firmar (lo haría Carmen Alborch); emprendió una personal cruzada contra las subvenciones automáticas al cine, que le hizo acreedor del varapalo de gran parte del sector y, sobre todo, pasó a la posteridad con el martirio de ser el ministro de Cultura bajo cuyo mandato se cesó a tres altos cargos públicos por el simple hecho de haber manifestado su opiniones: Jaime Brihuega y Juan Manuel Velasco, directores generales de Bellas Artes y del Libro respectivamente, fueron fulminantemente cesados en febrero del 91 tras haber firmado un manifiesto contra la participación española en la guerra del Golfo.

Al día siguiente, el director del Prado, Alfonso Pérez Sánchez, también firmante del manifiesto, presentó su dimisión, aceptada por Felipe González. Jorge Semprún justificó los ceses alegando que los cargos públicos no podían estar en «una sintonía diferente a la del gobierno».

(Pasa a la página siguiente)

VICENTE MATEU

① *Sanidad*

La historia interminable

Catorce años después, la Sanidad sigue siendo una asignatura pendiente de la modernización de España. Han sido casi tres lustros de continuos bandazos de una política sanitaria socialista que hoy día la encuentra, ideológicamente, en las antípodas de sus comienzos. La libre elección de especialista con que la actual ministra, Ángeles Amador, ha querido contribuir a la campaña electoral en ciernes hubiera sido anatemizada, sin duda alguna, por casi la práctica totalidad de sus antecesores en el cargo.

Como también habrían condenado un «catálogo de prestaciones» cuyo objetivo último no es otro que recortar gastos a costa de suprimir tratamientos, o un «medicamentazo que, con el mismo argumento, ha expulsado cientos de fármacos de la Seguridad Social.

Catorce años después, la Sanidad sigue también enquistada casi en los mismos problemas de entonces y, a golpe de déficit, se

ha convertido en un problema financiero de primer orden, incluido como capítulo estrella en los planes de convergencia de la Unión Europea.

La ingente partida presupuestaria de la Sanidad –casi cuatro billones en estos momentos–, no ha dado de sí lo suficiente para

construir los hospitales del siglo XXI, a pesar de los indudables esfuerzos de los gestores socialistas.

Antes bien, nuestros grandes centros sanitarios, con 25 años en sus espaldas, apenas sí han conseguido mantenerse en pie y limitarse a ir tirando con la historia

interminable de las listas de espera. La reforma de la Atención Primaria, por su parte, no ha resuelto tampoco los problemas de masificación y las urgencias aún todavía la puerta falsa que los pacientes utilizan para poder llegar hasta los quirófanos.

El conflicto con los trabajadores

de la Sanidad, desde los médicos a los celadores, sigue siendo, como hace más de una década, una de las patologías crónicas del sistema, a la espera de que alguien se atreva a adaptar a los nuevos tiempos su régimen laboral. Ahí está para recordarlo la huelga de médicos de hospitales que puso al Insalud al borde del caos la pasada primavera.

Catorce años después, que del PSOE como desde el PP las soluciones que se ofrecen para salir de la crisis de la Sanidad tienen una similitud más que evidente. La panacea electoral de marzo del 96 apunta a una Sanidad que de publica ya sólo tendría la financiación. Quién cure al enfermo es ya lo de menos para ambos partidos, por mucho que desde las filas socialistas se intente colgar a los populares el sambenito de la «privatización».

Unos y otros ofrecen a los ciudadanos libertad para elegir su médico, pero de momento es sólo una libertad para elegir dónde esperar.

(Pasa a la página siguiente)

Award of Excellence
Goteborgs-Posten
Gothenburg, Sweden
Karin Nilsson, Designer

Manos blancas por la paz

El «*éxtasis*» de los fines de semana

La próxima pastilla puede ser la última

Award of Excellence
El Mundo
Madrid, Spain
Carmelo Caderot, Art Director

Silver
El Mundo
Madrid, Spain
Miguel Arzoz, Designer

Award of Excellence
El Mundo
Madrid, Spain
Manuel de Miguez, Designer

Award of Excellence
La Gaceta
San Miguel de Tucuman, Argentina
Sebastian Rosso, Designer

Award of Excellence
Le Devoir
Montreal, Canada
Roland-Yves Carignan, Art Director & Page Designer

Silver
El Mundo
Madrid, Spain
Carmelo Caderot, Art Director

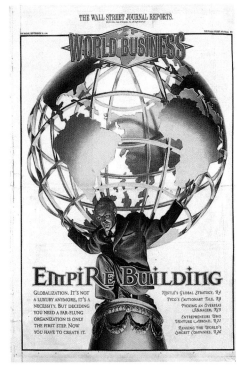

Award of Excellence
The Wall Street Journal Reports
New York, NY
Greg Leeds, Designer & Design Director

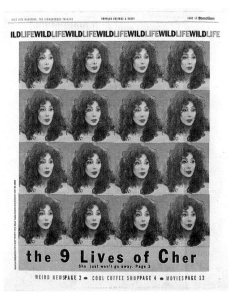

Award of Excellence
The Albuquerque Tribune
Albuquerque, NM
Leanne Potts, Designer

Award of Excellence
The Boston Globe
Boston, MA
Catherine Aldrich, Art Director & Designer

Silver
L.A. Weekly
Los Angeles, CA
Bill Smith, Art Director & Designer

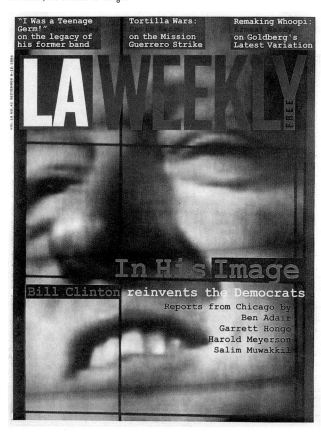

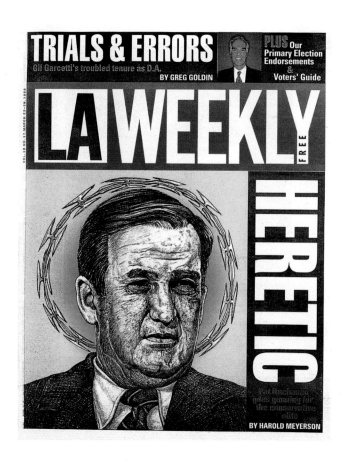

Silver
L.A. Weekly
Los Angeles, CA
Bill Smith, Art Director

Silver
El Mundo Metropoli
Madrid, Spain
Rodrigo Sanchez, Art Director & Designer

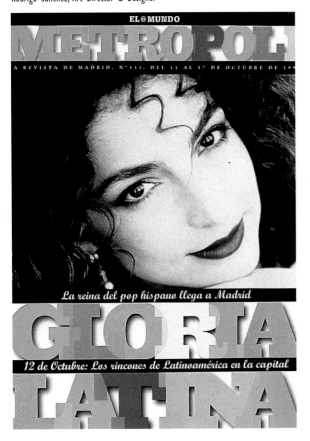

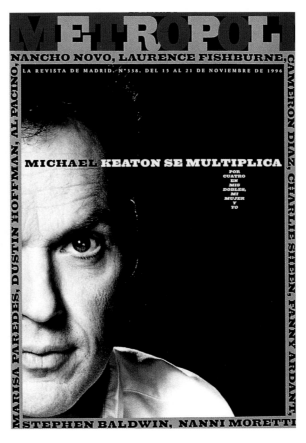

Award of Excellence
The San Diego Union-Tribune
San Diego, CA
Channon Seifert, Designer

Award of Excellence
La Revista
Madrid, Spain
Rodrigo Sanchez, Art Director

Award of Excellence
La Revista
Madrid, Spain
Rodrigo Sanchez, Art Director

A Gold Medal was awarded to El Mundo for the way its Metropoli nameplate could be changed, which breaks the rules, yet maintains its identity through a consistent use of high-level design.

Gold
• Also an Award of Excellence for Magazine Cover
El Mundo Metropoli
Madrid, Spain
Rodrigo Sanchez, Art Director & Designer; Carmelo Caderot, Design Director; Luis Iglesias, Photographer

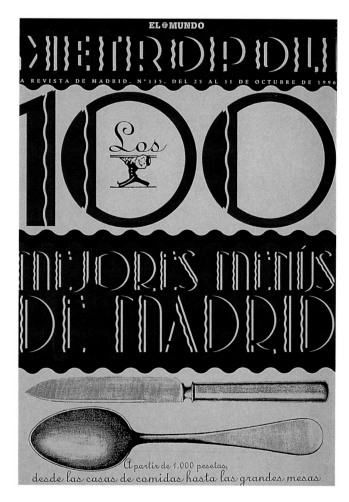

El Mundo se ganó una Medalla de Oro por la forma en que el letrero de su nombre se podía cambiar, lo cual rompe las reglas, a la vez de mantener su identidad a través de un uso consistente de diseño de alto nivel.

Silver
El Mundo
Metropoli
Madrid, Spain
Rodrigo Sanchez,
Art Director &
Designer

Silver
La Revista
Madrid, Spain
Rodrigo Sanchez,
Art Director

Silver
The Washington Post Magazine
Washington, DC
Kelly Doe, Art Director & Designer

Silver
La Revista
Madrid, Spain
Rodrillo Sanchez,
Art Director

Silver
Le Soleil
Quebec, Canada
Andre Bernard,
Graphic Designer

Award of Excellence
Goteborgs-Posten
Gothenburg, Sweden
Mats Widebrant, Designer

Award of Excellence
Eastsideweek
Seattle, WA
Barbara Dow, Art Director & Designer

Award of Excellence
The Albuquerque Tribune
Albuquerque, NM

Joan Carlin, Designer

Award of Excellence
Ball State Daily News
Muncie, IN

Bill Webster, Editor/Art Director

Award of Excellence
Providence Journal-Bulletin
Providence, RI

Lynn Rognsvoog, Picture Editor & Designer

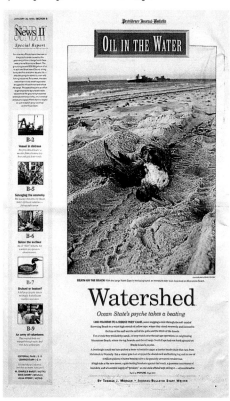

Award of Excellence
The Baltimore Sun
Baltimore, MD

Peter Yuill, Features Design

Award of Excellence
The Greenville News
Greenville, SC

Scott Stoddard, Art Director

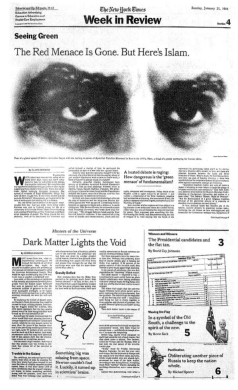

Award of Excellence
The New York Times
New York, NY

Greg Ryan, Art Director & Designer

ILLUSTRATION

Work must have been staff-generated or first-use. Entries
were divided into two groups:
Black & white and/or one
color, two or more colors. Six
pieces of work must have been
submitted for each portfolio.
Portfolio entries were divided
into two groups: Portfolio by
one artist, portfolio by more
than one artist.

[BLACK & WHITE AND/OR ONE COLOR]

[TWO OR MORE COLORS]

[PORTFOLIO BY ONE ARTIST]

[PORTFOLIO BY MORE THAN ONE ARTIST]

El Mundo Del Siglo XXI received two Gold Medals (also next page) for superb technique and subtle, yet powerful, use of symbolism.

El Mundo del Siglo XXI recibió dos Medallas de Oro (también en la próxima página) por su técnica exquisita y uso sutil, aunque poderoso, de simbolismo.

Gold
• Also a Silver for Illustration Portfolio
El Mundo Del Siglo XXI
Madrid, Spain
Ricardo Martinez, Illustration Director

Gold
El Mundo Del Siglo XXI
Madrid, Spain
Ricardo Martinez, Illustration Director

Award of Excellence
The Anchorage Daily News
Anchorage, AK

Dee Boyles, Designer/Illustrator

Award of Excellence
The Boston Globe
Boston, MA

Natalie Diffloth, Art Director &
Designer; Christopher Bing, Illustrator

Award of Excellence
Chicago Tribune
Chicago, IL

Henrik Drescher, Illustrator; Tom Heinz, Art Director

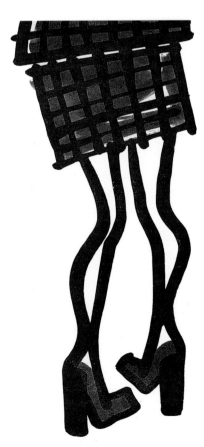

Award of Excellence
Dagens Nyheter
Stockholm, Sweden

Stina Wirsen, Illustrator; Peter Alenas, Layout

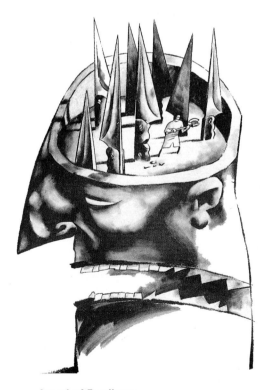

Award of Excellence
El Mundo
Madrid, Spain

Tono Benavides, Illustrator

Award of Excellence
Dagens Nyheter
Stockholm, Sweden

Stina Wirsen, Illustrator

Award of Excellence
El Pais
Madrid, Spain
Agustin Sciammarella, Illustrator

Award of Excellence
El Nuevo Herald
Miami, FL
Raul Fernandez, Designer/Illustrator

Award of Excellence
El Mundo
Madrid, Spain
Ulises Culebro, Illustrator

Award of Excellence
Reforma
Mexico City, Mexico
Ricardo del Castillo, Section Designer/Designer; Alejandro Banuet, Graphics Editor; Fabricio Vanden Broeck, Illustrator; Eduardo Danilo, Design Consultant; Emilio Deheza, Art Director; Roberto Zamarripa, Editor

Award of Excellence
The Globe & Mail
Toronto, Canada
Douglas Fraser, Illustrator; Eric Nelson, Art Director & Designer; Sarah Murdoch, Focus Editor

Award of Excellence
Maine Sunday Telegram
Portland, ME
Pete Gorski, News Artist

Award of Excellence
The Miami Herald
Miami, FL
Patterson Clark, Artist/Designer

Award of Excellence
San Jose Mercury News
San Jose, CA
David Frazier, Page Designer and Illustrator; Nuri Ducassi, Design Director

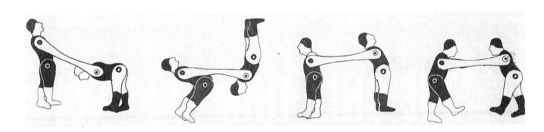

Award of Excellence
The New York Times
New York, NY
Istvan Banyai, Illustrator; Nicholas Blechman, Art Director

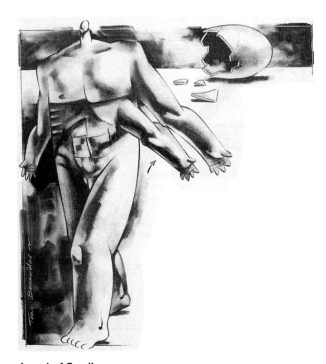

Award of Excellence
El Mundo Del Siglo XXI
Madrid, Spain
Toño Benavides, Illustrator

Award of Excellence
El Mundo
Madrid, Spain
Ricardo Martínez, Illustrator

Award of Excellence
Reforma
Mexico City, Mexico
Jose Luis Barros, Illustrator; Carlos Medina, Designer; Alejo Najera, Section Designer; Hilda Garcia, Editor; Emilio Deheza, Art Director; Eduardo Danilo, Design Consultant

Award of Excellence
The Wall Street Journal
New York, NY
Cindy Shattuck, Art Director; David G. Klein, Illustrator

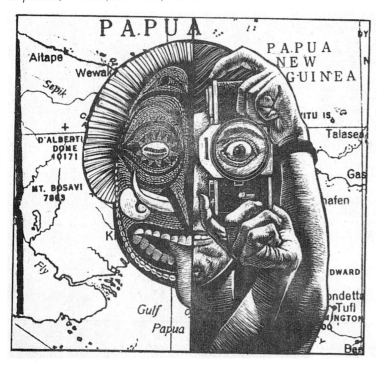

Award of Excellence
Wall Street Journal Reports
New York, NY
Nick Klein, Designer; Greg Leeds, Design Director; Brian Cronin, Illustrator

Award of Excellence
Wall Street Journal Reports
New York, NY
Nick Klein, Designer; Greg Leeds, Design Director/Designer; James Steinberg, Illustrator

Award of Excellence
The Anchorage Daily News
Anchorage, AK
Lance Lekander, Illustrator & Designer

Award of Excellence
The Anchorage Daily News
Anchorage, AK
Lance Lekander, Illustrator & Designer

Award of Excellence
The Anchorage Daily News
Anchorage, AK
Dee Boyles, Illustrator & Designer

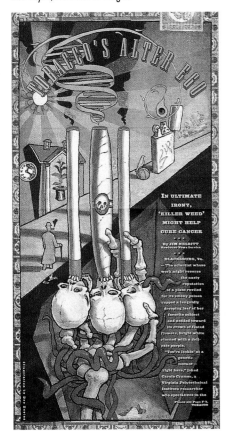

Silver
Dagens Nyheter
Stockholm, Sweden
Stina Wirsen, Illustrator

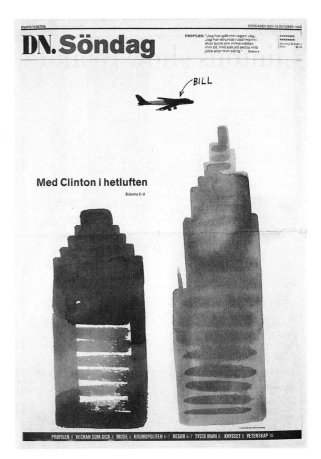

Silver
Dagens Nyheter
Stockholm, Sweden
Stina Wirsen, Illustrator; Kerstin Wigstrand, Layout

Silver
• Also an Award of Excellence for Features Portfolio
The Hartford Courant
Hartford, CT

Christopher Moore, Illustrator & Designer; Christian Potter Drury, Art Director

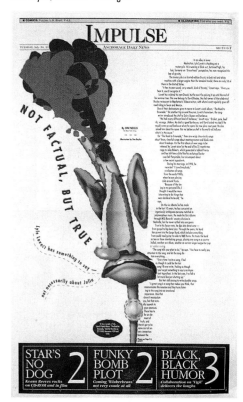

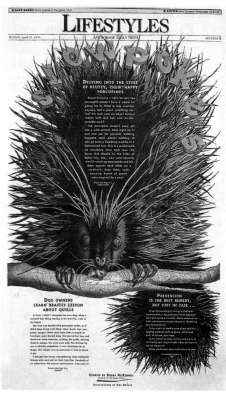

ENVIRONMENT

Silver
The Globe & Mail
Toronto, Canada

Kaspar DeLine, Art Director; Amanda Duffy, Illustrator; Robert Hough, Writer; David Clive, Editor

Award of Excellence
Dagens Nyheter
Stockholm, Sweden

Stina Wirsen, Illustrator

Award of Excellence
Dagens Nyheter
Stockholm, Sweden

Stina Wirsen, Illustrator; Peter Alenas, Designer

Silver
The Wichita Eagle
Wichita, KS
Tim Ladwig, Illustrator

Award of Excellence
The Boston Globe
Boston, MA
Catherine Aldrich, Art Director; Anthony Russo, Illustrator

Award of Excellence
El Mundo Del Siglo XXI
Madrid, Spain
Ricardo Martinez, Illustration Director

Award of Excellence
El Norte
Monterrey, Mexico

Arturo Rangel, Illustrator; Raul Braulio Martinez, Art
Director; Eduardo Danilo Ruiz, Design Consultant

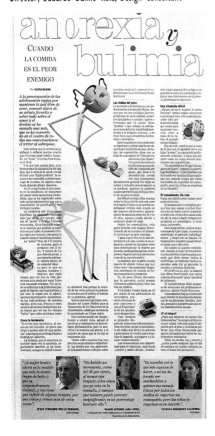

Award of Excellence
El Norte
Monterrey, Mexico

Arturo Rangel, Illustrator; Raul Braulio Martinez, Art Director;
Eduardo Danilo Ruiz, Design Consultant

Award of Excellence
The Globe & Mail/Report on Business
Toronto, Canada

Kaspar DeLine, Senior Art Director; Peter Ferguson, Illustrator;
Edward Kay, Writer; David Olive, Editor

Award of Excellence
The Montreal Gazette
Montreal, Canada

Jennifer Stowell, Illustrator; Gayle Grin, Feature Design
Editor; Gayle Grin, Designer; Iona Monahan, Fashion
Editor; Cecelia McGuire, Living Editor

Award of Excellence
La Revista
Madrid, Spain

Ana Juan, Illustrator; Rodrigo Sanchez, Art Director; Carmelo
Caderot, Design Director

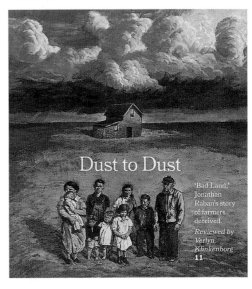

Award of Excellence
The New York Times
New York, NY

Steven Heller, Art Director; Wesley Bedrosian, Illustrator

Award of Excellence
The New York Times
New York, NY

Terry Allen, Illustrator; Linda Brewer, Art Director; Barbara Richer, Art Director

Award of Excellence
The New York Times Book Review
New York, NY

Steven Heller, Art Director; Andreas Ventura, Illustrator

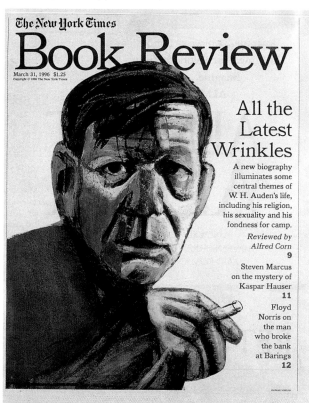

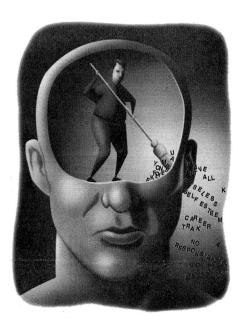

Award of Excellence
The New York Times
New York, NY

Janet Froelich, Art Director; Joel Cuyler, Art Director; Billy Sullivan, Artist

Award of Excellence
The New York Times Magazine
New York, NY

Janet Froelich, Art Director; Lisa Naftolin, Designer; Susan Dazzo, Designer; Daniel Adel, Illustrator

Award of Excellence
News & Record
Greensboro, NC

Tim Rickard, Illustrator

Award of Excellence
Pittsburgh Post-Gazette
Pittsburgh, PA

Stacy Innerst, Illustrator; Christopher Pett-Ridge, AME Graphics; Tracy Collins, Associate Editor/Graphics; Bill Pliske, Deputy Editor/Graphics; Anita Dufalla, Art Director

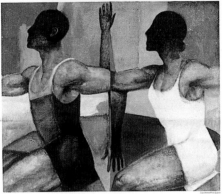

Award of Excellence
San Francisco Chronicle
San Francisco, CA
Ed Rachles, Graphics Designer

Award of Excellence
San Francisco Examiner
San Francisco, CA
Pat Sedlar, Illustrator/Designer; Kelly Frankeny, AME Design; Heidi Benson, Style Editor

Award of Excellence
NRC Handelsblad
Rotterdam, Netherlands
Karin Mathijsen Gerst, Design Editor; Ronald Blommestijn, Illustrator

Award of Excellence
San Francisco Examiner
San Francisco, CA
Don Asmussen, Illustrator; Kelly Frankeny, AME Design; Don McCartney, Designer; Jo Mancuso, Editor

Award of Excellence
The Seattle Times
Seattle, WA

Jeff Neumann, Illustrator/Designer

Award of Excellence
The Times-Picayune
New Orleans, LA

Kenneth Harrison, Illustrator

Award of Excellence
St. Paul Pioneer Press
St. Paul, MN

Kirk Lyttle, Graphic Artist

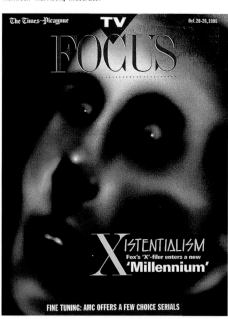

Silver
El Mundo
Madrid, Spain

Tono Benavides, Illustrator

En la playa. Con la imagen más sport. Top y pantalón corto de tejido elástico, de Gianni Versace. Sandalias, Isaac Mizrahi; gafas de sol, Piamonte; bolsa de plástico, Scooter; pañuelo, Dolce & Gabbana.

Gold
El Mundo
Madrid, Spain
Ana Juan, Illustrator

Cae la noche. Es el momento de bailar hasta la madrugada. Vestido con lentejuelas de plástico, sandalias de raso y pulsera; todo de Plein Sud.

Sueños de Verano

UN REPASO A LAS TENDENCIAS DE LA NUEVA TEMPORADA. DEL SPORT SESENTERO A LA ELEGANCIA URBANA, PASANDO POR EL BAÑO MÁS ATREVIDO. UN MANUAL DE ESTILO, INTERPRETADO POR LA ILUSTRADORA ANA JUAN.

Dibujos de ANA JUAN
Estilismo de MARIBEL DORADO

Ana Juan's pages in El Mundo won a Gold Medal for the beautiful marriage of content and illustration; it is an innovative way to use painting to interpret fashion.

Las páginas de Ana Juan en El Mundo se ganaron una Medalla de Oro por la hermosa unión de contenido e ilustración; es una manera novedosa de usar pintura para interpretar la moda.

Exotismo oriental. Con sabor a países lejanos. Vestido de raso, anillo, bolso de paja y alfileres para el pelo; todo de Scooter.

Silver
El Mundo
Madrid, Spain
Ulises Culebro, Illustrator

El cuervo de los cuentos de
Poe y el juego de la rayuela
de Cortázar, dos de los
semifinalistas

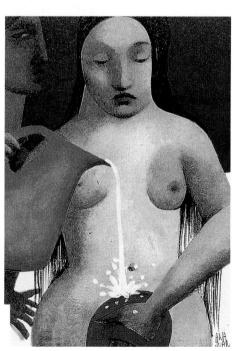

Silver
El Mundo Magazine
Madrid, Spain
Ana Juan, Illustrator

Just Say Bob

A Campaign Sketchbook

In which illustrator Steve Brodner, brush and tape recorder in hand, observes the Dole bandwagon in Washington and New Hampshire

Silver
The Washington Post
Washington, DC
Steve Brodner, Illustrator

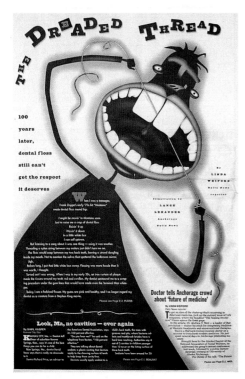

Award of Excellence
The Anchorage Daily News
Anchorage, AK
Lance Lekander, Illustrator & Designer

Award of Excellence
Berlingske Tidende
Copenhagen, Denmark
Lars Vegas Nielsen, Illustrator

Award of Excellence
• Also an Award of Excellence for Features Section
Berlingske Tidende
Copenhagen, Denmark
Lise Ronnebaek, Illustrator; Finn Vistisen, Mikael Hjorth, Sub-Editors; Flemming Flyvholm, Editor

Award of Excellence
The Anchorage Daily News
Anchorage, AK
Dee Boyles, Illustrator & Designer

Award of Excellence
El Mundo Del Siglo XXI
Madrid, Spain
Ulises Culebro, Illustrator

Award of Excellence
El Mundo
Madrid, Spain
Raul Arias, Illustrator

Award of Excellence
Berlingske Tidende
Copenhagen, Denmark
Jens Hage, Illustrator

Award of Excellence
El Mundo Del Siglo XXI
Madrid, Spain
Ulises Culebro, Illustrator

Award of Excellence
El Periodico de Catalunya/El Dominical
Barcelona, Spain
Martin Tognola, Illustrator

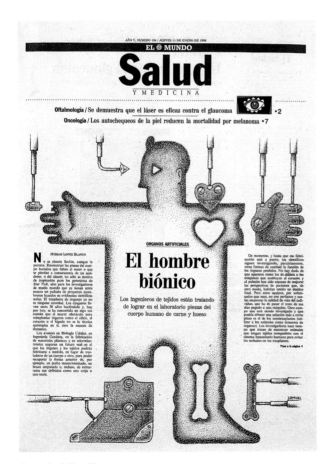

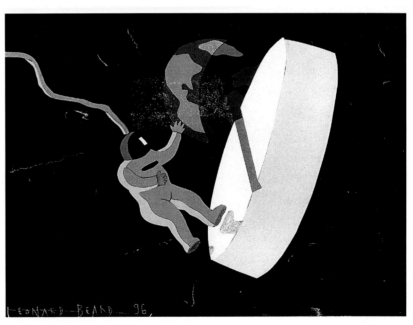

Award of Excellence
El Periodico de Catalunya/El Dominical
Barcelona, Spain
Leonard Beard, Illustrator

Award of Excellence
El Mundo Del Siglo XXI
Madrid, Spain
Samuel Velasco, Illustrator

Award of Excellence
Pittsburgh Post-Gazette
Pittsburgh, PA
Stacy Innerst, Illustrator

Award of Excellence
The Los Angeles Times/Orange County Edition
Costa Mesa, CA
Val B. Mina, Artist

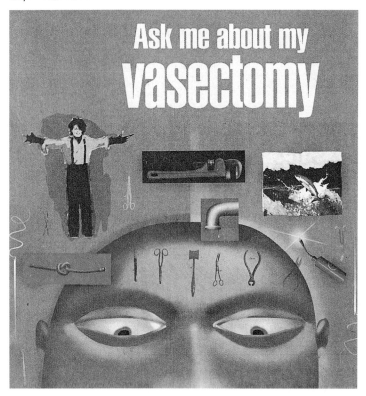

Award of Excellence
Pradillo
Madrid, Spain
Ana Juan, Illustrator

Silver
• Also an Award of Excellence for Color Illustration
The New York Times Book Review
New York, NY

Julien Allen, Illustrator; Steven Brodner, Illustrator; Bruce Strachan, Illustrator; Robert Grossman, Illustrator; C.F.. Payne, Illustrator; D.B. Johnson, Illustrator; Steven Heller, Art Director

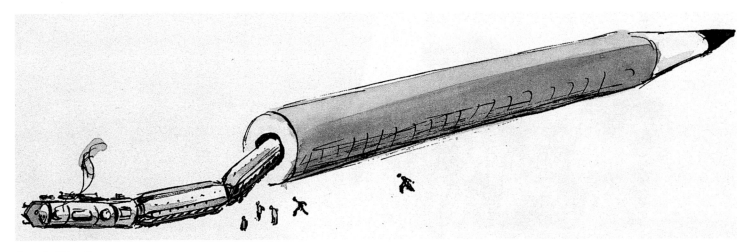

Award of Excellence
La Vanguardia
Barcelona, Spain

Carlos Perez de Rozas Arribas, Art Director; Rosa Mundet Poch, Chief of Design and Infographics; Emilio Alvarez, Section Designer; Antonia Soto, Designer; Mª Jose Oriol, Designer; Monica Caparros, Designer; Josep Mª Rius, Illustrator

Award of Excellence
The Boston Globe
Boston, MA

Rena Anderson Sokolow, Art Director & Designer; John Koch, Editor; High School Students, Illustrators

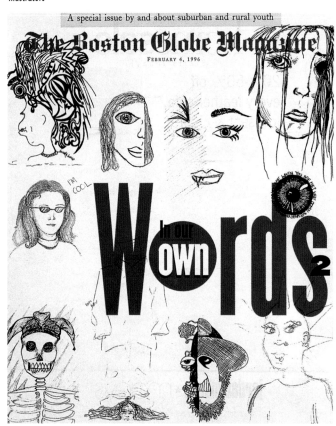

Award of Excellence
• Also an Award of Excellence for Magazine Special Section
The Philadelphia Inquirer Magazine
Philadelphia, PA

Christine Dunleavy, Art Director; Susan Syrnick, Asst. Art Director; Blair Drawson, William Low, Greg Clarke, Jeanne Berg, Joe Sorren, Herve Blondon; Artists

Award of Excellence
La Vanguardia
Barcelona, Spain

Carlos Perez de Rozas Arribas, Art Director; Rosa Mundet Poch, Chief of Design and Infographics; Emilio Alvarez, Section Designer; Antonio Soto, Designer; Ma Jose Oriol, Designer; Monica Caparros, Designer; Miguel Angel Gallardo, Illustrator

Award of Excellence
El Mundo
Madrid, Spain

Toño Benavides, Illustrator; Gorka Sampedro, Illustrator; Samuel Velasco, Illustrator; Raul Arias, Illustrator; Ulises Culebro, Illustrator; Ricardo Martínez, Illustrator

PHOTOJOURNALISM

Work represented in this category has to be staff-generated or first-use. Portfolio entries must have included six pieces of work in one of two divisions: Work by one photographer or work by more than one photographer. Staged or electronically manipulated photography must have been entered in the photo illustration division to be considered.

[SPOT NEWS]   [FEATURE]

[PHOTO STORY]

[PHOTO ILLUSTRATION]

[PORTFOLIO]

Silver
Press Democrat
Santa Rosa, CA
Annie Wells, Photographer;
John Metzger, Director of
Photography; Sharon
Roberts, AME Design

Silver
Providence Journal-Bulletin
Providence, RI
Steve Szydlowski, Photographer

Award of Excellence
Argus Leader
Sioux Falls, SD
Greg Latza, Photographer

Award of Excellence
The Ann Arbor News
Ann Arbor, MI
Stephanie Grace Lim, Photographer

Award of Excellence
The Columbian
Vancouver, WA
Dave Olson, Photographer

Award of Excellence
Denver Post
Denver, CO
Kent Meireis, Photographer

Award of Excellence
Newsday
Melville, NY
Audrey C. Tiernan, Photographer; Bob Eisner, Art Director & Designer

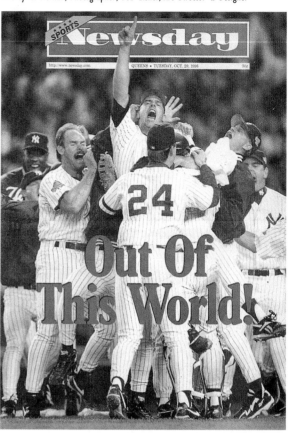

Award of Excellence
O Dia
Rio de Janeiro, Brazil
Leo Correa, Photographer

Award of Excellence
Providence Journal-Bulletin
Providence, RI
Kathy Borchers, Photographer

Award of Excellence
The Orlando Sentinel
Orlando, FL
Gary Bogdon, Senior Photographer; Joan Andrews, Associate Sports Editor

Award of Excellence
Portland Press Herald
Portland, ME
David A. Rodgers, Photographer

Award of Excellence
The Toronto Star
Toronto, Canada
Bernard Weil, Photographer

Award of Excellence
The Spokesman-Review
Spokane, WA
Colin Mulvany, Photographer

Award of Excellence
The Columbian
Vancouver, WA
Tom Boyd, Photographer

Silver
The New York Times Magazine
New York, NY
Janet Froelich, Art Director; Dan Winters, Photographer; Kathy Ryan, Photo Editor

Award of Excellence
Providence Journal-Bulletin
Providence, RI
John Freidah, Photographer

Award of Excellence
Contra Costa Times
Walnut Creek, CA
Karl Mondon, Photographer

USS CARL VINSON crew members hoist those phone lines Thursday upon returning to Alameda. Below, Brian Scronce of Concord hugs his kids, Brittani, 4, and Robert, 3.

Carrier returns from gulf duty

By ELIZABETH HAYES
Staff writer

ALAMEDA — Absolutely no sailors aboard the USS Carl Vinson protested that their six-month deployment was too short — especially new fathers who cradled their babies for the first time Thursday.

Several minutes before 9 a.m. came the call to "man the rails." Sailors clad in dress blues ran to line the periphery of the flight deck. Moments later, the Vinson glided under the banner-bedecked Golden Gate Bridge, as "Another One Bites the Dust" played over loudspeakers.

It was the Vinson's final homecoming to the Bay Area. It will shift home ports to Bremerton, Wash., in mid-January.

As it docked at Alameda Naval Air Station, a band played and family members hoisted signs and hollered. Sailors peered into binoculars trying to find loved ones. As they streamed ashore — the 51 new fathers first — wives jumped and screamed, some looking nervous, others shedding tears of joy.

While the new dads may have seen baby pictures, it was not the same as holding them.

"This is too awesome," said Mike Ferro, holding his 4-month-old daughter, Francesca Lynne, who contentedly sucked on a pacifier.

Ferro, whose wife is from Concord, videotaped himself reading stories before his daughter's birth so she later could get to know him in his absence.

The Vinson sailed May 14, heading across the Pacific on the first leg of WestPac '96. The 5,900-member crew stopped in Japan, Hong Kong and Singapore, then sailed through the Indian Ocean to the Persian Gulf at the beginning of July. There they remained for three months — the hardest stretch, several sailors said.

The heat was oppressive, and the carrier stayed out of sight of land for 60 days.

"You lost 10 pounds," said Seaman Anthony Silas.

The Vinson joined Operations Desert Strike and Southern Watch, providing deterrence and patrol and enforcing the expanded no-fly zone in southern Iraq. F-14D Tomcats from Air Wing 14 on the Vinson escorted Air Force B-52 bombers as they traveled the length of the gulf.

But by all accounts, the stint went well.

Please see VINSON, Back Page

Award of Excellence
Contra Costa Times
Walnut Creek, CA
Dan Rosenstrauch, Photographer

Award of Excellence
The New York Times
New York, NY
Janet Froelich, Art Director & Designer; Burk Uzzie, Photographer; Kathy Ryan, Photo Editor

Award of Excellence
The New York Times Magazine
New York, NY
Janet Froelich, Art Director; Susan Dazzo, Designer; Gentl & Hyers, Photographer; Kathy Ryan, Photo Editor

Award of Excellence
The New York Times Magazine
New York, NY
Michaelangelo DiBattista, Photographer; Janet Froelich, Art Director; Joel Cuyler, Designer; Elizabeth Stewart, Stylist

Award of Excellence
The Spokesman-Review
Spokane, WA
Colin Mulvany, Photographer

Award of Excellence
The Los Angeles Times/Orange County Edition
Costa Mesa, CA
Don Tormey, Senior Photo Editor; Kevin Bronson, Designer; Glenn Koenig, Photographer

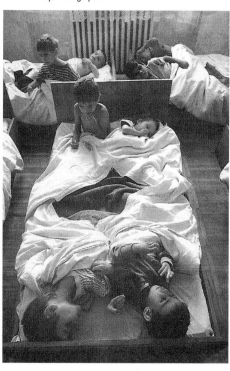

Award of Excellence
San Jose Mercury News
San Jose, CA
Geri Migielicz, Photographer

Award of Excellence
The Spokesman-Review
Spokane, WA
Colin Mulvany, Photographer

Award of Excellence
The Wichita Eagle
Wichita, KS
Randy Tobias, Photographer

THE MAGAZINE OF SOUTH *Florida* • MARCH 24, 1996

SUNSHINE

Once there was a rich man who dressed his simians in sailor suits and treated them like his own children. He created a foundation to care for the animals, and then he died. Now some say Mr. Mannheimer's monkeys are in peril.

MONKEY BUSINESS

Award of Excellence
Sun-Sentinel
Fort Lauderdale, FL
Greg Carannante, Art Director; Susan Stocker, Photographer

Award of Excellence
Pittsburgh Post-Gazette
Pittsburgh, PA
John Beale, Photographer; Jim Mendenhall, Photo Editor; Curt Chandler, Director of Photography; Christopher Pett-Ridge, AME Graphics; Wendy Warner, Page Designer

El Pais Semanal was given a Gold Medal for the lyrical combination of the images and the words "A Castro lo hicimos entre todos..."

El País Semanal recibió una Medalla de Oro por la combinación lírica de imágenes y las palabras "A Castro lo hicimos entre todos..."

**Gold
El Pais
Semanal**
Madrid, Spain
David Garcia, Art Director; Eugenio Gonzalez, Design Director; Maria Paz Domingo, Designer; Gustavo Sanchez, Designer; Francis Giacobetti, Photographer; Alex Martinez, Editor

FIDEL CASTRO

Don Quijote de La Habana

Recientemente he conocido a una dama del exilio cubano cuyos antepasados llegaron a la isla sólo 50 años después del conquistador Diego de Velázquez, en el siglo XVI. Sus grandes posesiones en la provincia de Camagüey y sus palacetes en el Venado de La Habana fueron incautados por la Revolución. Como es lógico, odia a Castro. Pero esta dama que ha sido educada en los mejores colegios de Europa tiene su escala de odios bien organizada. En primer lugar odia a Fulgencio Batista, el responsable de todo, según ella. Aquel tirano arro-jaba a sus enemigos a los tiburones directamente desde el Morro y fue el primero en permitirse el lujo de bombardear un pueblo abierto, aparte de fusilar a mansalva a miles de adversarios políticos contra los cañaverales. Sin esa crueldad la revolución castrista no se hubiera dado. En segundo lugar, esta distinguida dama odia a Mas Canosa, un fanático del exilio de Miami con antecedentes turbios, que se mueve entre la ambición personal y la venganza. La dama opina que si un día Mas Canosa lograra la presidencia de Cuba sería a costa de un baño de sangre, algo que no podría soportar. Sólo en tercer lugar el odio de la dama está reservado para Fidel Castro, un loco, visionario e hijo de papá, causante de su destierro. Tal vez esta dama tiene razón. La figura de Castro no puede ser analizada sin aquel pasado de terror y sin la incertidumbre de un futuro sangriento. En medio está el camino hacia la democracia sin violencia, que ella desea para Cuba dentro de la oposición moderada, que debe hacerse desde el interior. Acuciado o acosado en medio de este cami- *(continúa en página 47)*

TEXTO: MANUEL VICENT
FOTOGRAFÍA: FRANCIS GIACOBETTI

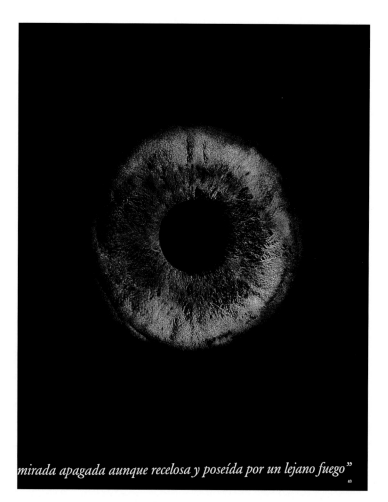

"...mirada apagada aunque recelosa y poseída por un lejano fuego"

"A Castro lo hicimos entre todos. Todos aquellos que en los años sesenta quisieron cambiar la miseria social por una feliz utopía"

Award of Excellence
The Los Angeles Times/Orange County Edition
Costa Mesa, CA

Gail Fisher, Photographer & Photo Editor; Colin Crawford, Director of Photography; Chuck Nigash, Designer

BAER: Bringing Hope, Health to Guatemala

'When she thinks of God, she doesn't look up, she looks sideways.'

BETH

Award of Excellence
The Los Angeles Times/Orange County Edition
Costa Mesa, CA

Gail Fisher, Photographer; Colin Crawford, Director/Photography; Chuck Nigash, Designer

"PEOPLE ARTICULATE THE MEANING IN THEIR LIVES IN DIFFERENT WAYS."

IT'S THE SEASON

to share

Fort Pierce couple 'do their best' to take care of four grandchildren

OCEANS of TROUBLE
ARE THE WORLD'S FISHERIES DOOMED?

Way of life threatened along with Gulf's vast bounty

The ocean is under siege.

Award of Excellence
Palm Beach Post
West Palm Beach, FL

Xin Liu, Photographer; Mark Edelson, Photo Editor; Sarah Franquet, Designer; Jan Tuckwood, Associate Editor

Award of Excellence
• Also an Award of Excellence for Single-subject Series

The Times-Picayune
New Orleans, LA

George Berke, Design Director; Tim Morris, Project Director; Doug Parker, Photo Ed.; Ted Jackson, Photographer; Paul Fresty, Graphics Ed.; James O'Byrne, Sunday Ed.; Emmett Mayer III; Angela Hill, Erica Bynum, Kenneth Harrison, Artist

Multiple Personalities

Everyone in this picture has two things in common. First, they are all wearing sweaters by Giorgio Armani, who served up the best knitwear collection for fall. And second, they are all John Leguizamo, the actor who created Mambo Mouth and Spic-o-Rama and who is truly a multiple of sex.

After dinner, Kasey bathes Mariah in the kitchen sink and prepares her for bed.

Kasey's life is consumed by daily chores and her baby. She mows lawns for money while her friends graduate from high school.

Kasey hugs her best friend, Michelle Choquett, at Michelle's graduation. Kasey has at least another year of school left.

Cutting grass to earn money for expenses, Kasey keeps Mariah in sight.

A RAPIDLY CHANGING SOCIETY

An emergency room health worker in Freeport's hospital in Tembagapura changes bandages for an Amungme child whose hut in the village of Tsinga caught fire; all his relatives were killed. Freeport airlifted the injured boy from Tsinga to the 50-bed hospital.

Ten years ago, this area was a jungle. Today, it's taking on the character of a modern American suburb, with gently curved streets, tract houses and even satellite dishes dotting the yards. Freeport built the town to handle the influx of mine workers from other parts of Indonesia.

Thousands of tribesmen looking for jobs are drawn to the coastal area of Irian Jaya. But not all of them can find work at the Freeport mine, so many squat on Karaka Island, where they catch fish and sell it to Freeport.

A man lifts a sack of vegetables to be loaded onto a Freeport truck, as women wait to sell their produce at the Kwamkilama vegetable market near Timika. Freeport buys vegetables from local growers every Tuesday and Friday to feed employees of the mine.

A motorcycle taxi zooms down a street in Timika, the epicenter of the development boom sparked by Freeport's gold and copper mine. A fire in the background boils tar to be used to pave a road in the expanding town.

Photos by
TYRONE
TURNER
Staff photographer

Inside: Ann Landers ... Miss Manners ... Liz Smith ... People & Places ... Horoscope ... Movie Guide ... Comics ... Television

TODAY
THE SUN

June 12, 1996   Section E

WEDNESDAY

BSO concerts come back with a bang

Fireworks will punctuate the night at the Baltimore Symphony's Oregon Ridge series. Get ready for Summer MusicFest '96 too. (Page 3a)

More Inside

Miss Manners: Used handkerchiefs pose a dilemma for a gentleman. (Page 3a)

Index

Comics	6a
Crossword	6a
Horoscope	4a
Jumble	6a
Movies	3a
Television	6a

In Brief

Anxious girls come up short

CHICAGO — With beauties like Cindy Crawford as role models, adolescent girls have enough to be anxious about. But new comes word that anxiety itself actually keeps girls from reaching so-petuoded stature. Researchers found that anxiety may stunt girls' growth.

Anxious girls may grow up to be as much as 2 inches shorter than non-anxious girls, said Dr. Daniel Pine, lead author of a study in this month's issue of the journal *Pediatrics*.

Anxious girls were about twice as likely as non-anxious girls to be under 5-foot-4 as adults, he said yesterday.

The authors theorize that anxiety inhibits the body's production of growth hormone. Pine said more research is needed to confirm their hypothesis.

Associated Press

DAYS of the Dinosaurs

■ **Music:** *Once thought to be extinct, the Sex Pistols, REO Speedwagon, Jethro Tull, Lynyrd Skynyrd and Frampton come alive at the box office in a summer of gray, onstage and in the crowd. T-Rex, anyone?*

By J.D. CONSIDINE
SUN POP MUSIC CRITIC

They said rock and roll would never die, but who ever imagined it would lead to the Summer of the Living Dead?

Look through the listings for the local amphitheaters, and you'll find plenty of the year's hottest acts —

assuming the year in question is 1978. And while that may be good news for classic rock aficionados, there haven't been this many dinosaurs walking the earth since the Jurassic Period.

How bad is it?

At the Merriweather Post Pavilion in Columbia, the summer got under way Sunday with a double bill of Styx and Kansas, while upcoming shows include such cutting-edge acts as the Moody Blues (tomorrow); Chicago with Crosby, Stills and Nash (Friday); Boston with Cheap Trick (Aug. 6); Lynyrd Skynyrd with the Doobie Brothers (Aug. 7); and Jethro Tull with Emerson, Lake and Palmer (Aug. 23).

Pier Six is representing the '70s with War, the Average White Band (June 17) and Night Birth (July 20), Gladys Knight (July 26), and Little Feat with Dr. John (Aug. 24). A couple of shows there go even further back in time, what with double bills like Jerry Lee Lewis and Little Richard (June 20) or Frankie Valli & the Four Seasons and the Four Tops (July 12).

Meanwhile, down in Bristow, Va., even the newly-built Nissan Pavilion is attracting its share of oldies. In addition to its own dates with the Moody Blues (June 12) and the Boston/Cheap Trick pairing (Aug. 4), Nissan will be host to REO Speedwagon with Foreigner and Peter Frampton (July 17), Steely Dan (July 21), and the Steve Miller Band with Pat Benatar (Aug 2). —

Add in the fact that the two most-hyped tours hit — [See Music, 5a]

PHOTO ILLUSTRATION BY JERRY JACKSON/SUN STAFF

Award of Excellence
Portland Press Herald
Portland, ME
David A. Rodgers, Photographer

Award of Excellence
The San Diego Union-Tribune
San Diego, CA
Anita Arambula, Art Director, Illustrator & Designer; Amy Stirnkorb, Designer

Award of Excellence
The Philadelphia Inquirer Magazine
Philadelphia, PA
Christine Dunleavy, Art Director; Susan Syrnick, Assistant Art Director & Designer; Michael Bryant, Photographer

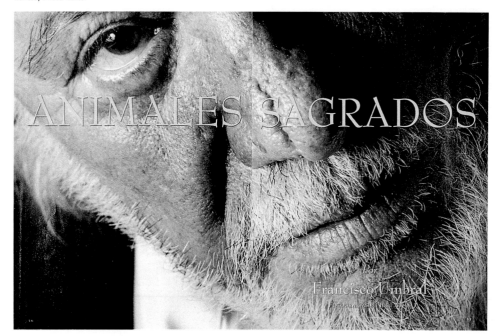

Award of Excellence
The Los Angeles Times/Orange County Edition
Costa Mesa, CA
Gail Fisher, Photographer/Photo Editor; Colin Crawford, Director/Photography; Chuck Nigash, Designer

Award of Excellence
The Boston Globe
Boston, MA
Lane Turner, Photographer; Catherine Aldrich, Art Director

Award of Excellence
Press Democrat
Santa Rosa, CA
Annie Wells, Photographer; John Metzger, Director of Photography; Sharon Roberts, AME Design

Award of Excellence
Palm Beach Post
West Palm Beach, FL
Xin Liu, Photographer; Mark Edelson, Photo Editor

Award of Excellence
Providence Journal-Bulletin
Providence, RI
Mary Beth Meehan, Photographer

Award of Excellence
The Spokesman-Review
Spokane, WA
Colin Mulvany, Photographer

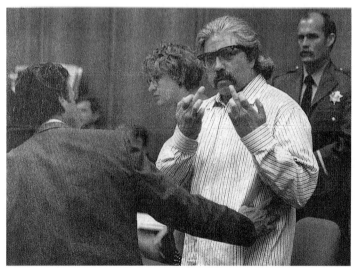

Award of Excellence
Press Democrat
Santa Rosa, CA

John Burgess, Photographer; Kent Porter, Photographer; Chad Surmick, Photographer; Annie Wells, Photographer; Peter DaSilva, Photographer; John Metzger, Director of Photography; Sharon Roberts, AME Design

Award of Excellence
The Register-Guard
Eugene, OR
Andy Nelson, Photographer

INFORMATIONAL GRAPHICS

Included in this category were charted information, graphs, diagrams and maps with or without the use of illustration or photography. Portfolios must have included six pieces of work entered in one of two divisions: Work by one artist, work by more than one artist.

[BREAKING NEWS]

[BLACK & WHITE AND/OR ONE COLOR]

[TWO OR MORE COLORS]

[PORTFOLIO]

Award of Excellence
Clarin
Buenos Aires, Argentina

Hector Ceballos, Artist; Andrea Tozzini, Artist; Jaime Serra, Graphics Editor

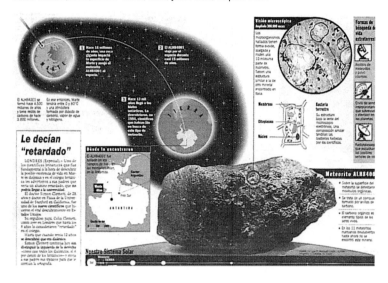

Award of Excellence
Clarin
Buenos Aires, Argentina

Alejandro Tumas, Artist; Gerardo Morel, Artist

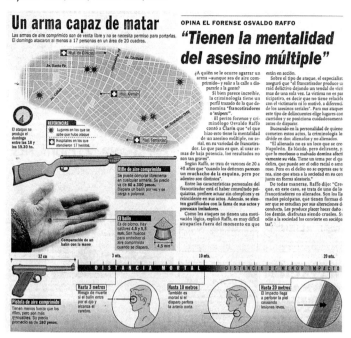

Award of Excellence
El Mundo Del Siglo XXI
Madrid, Spain

Modesto J. Carrasco, Infographic Artist;
Ramon Rodriguiez, Infographic Artist;
Dina Sanchez, Infographic Artist

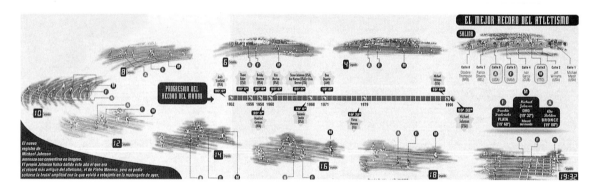

Award of Excellence
Clarin
Buenos Aires, Argentina

Staff

Award of Excellence
Clarin
Buenos Aires, Argentina

Alejandro Tumas, Artist; Jaime Serra, Graphics Editor

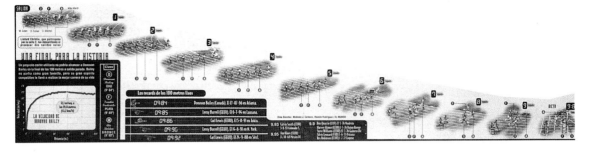

Award of Excellence
El Mundo Del Siglo XXI
Madrid, Spain

Dina Sanchez, Infographic Artist; Modesto J. Carrasco, Infographic artist; Ramon Rodriguez, Infographic artist

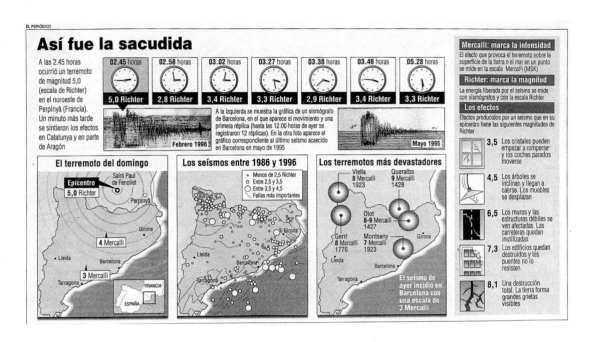

Award of Excellence
El Periodico de Catalunya
Barcelona, Spain

Jordi Catala, Author/Editor; Alex R. Fischer, Author

Award of Excellence
El Mundo Deportivo
Barcelona, Spain

Vanessa Mauri, Designer

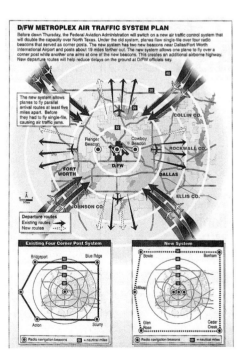

Award of Excellence
The Dallas Morning News
Dallas, TX

W. Matt Pinkney, Artist/Illustrator

Award of Excellence
The Dallas Morning News
Dallas, TX

Chris Morris, Artist/Designer; W. Matt Pinkney, Artist/Designer; Lon Tweeten, Artist/Designer; Laurie Joseph, Assistant Art Director; Kathleen Vincent, Art Director

Award of Excellence
The New York Times
New York, NY

Joe Ward, Graphics Editor

In the Zone,
Out of the Park

Juan Gonzalez's 3-run homer in Game 1 propelled the
Rangers to a victory over David Cone. Cone tried to come
inside on Gonzalez but the ball stayed out over the plate, and
then went out over the fence. Last night, Andy Pettitte made
the same mistake, allowing the Ranger slugger to see too good
a pitch – twice. Gonzalez accounted for all the Rangers' four
runs in his first two at-bats. Pettitte and then Mariano Rivera
finally managed to keep the ball out of his power zone. By his
fifth at-bat, the Yankees had learned their lesson. They
intentionally walked him. When he came up in extra innings it
was his turn to make adjustments.

Gonzalez's strike zone.

FOX

① Strike ① Ball Result

FIRST AT-BAT	SECOND AT-BAT	THIRD AT-BAT	FOURTH AT-BAT	SIXTH AT-BAT
MISTAKE I	**MISTAKE II**	**LESSON LEARNED I**	**LESSON LEARNED II**	**ADJUSTMENT TIME**
Gonzalez lays off a high inside fastball but Pettitte's next pitch finds too much of the plate and is rapped down the left field line.	With two men on, Pettitte's first pitch is in the dirt. Again his second pitch is too fat and is crushed to left.	Pettitte finally stays away from Gonzalez's power, getting him to chase three outside pitches.	Rivera's two pitches in the strike zone are kept away from Gonzalez. His inside pitch is off the plate.	Yanks get away with another pitch in the heart of the plate that is hit far, but foul. Gonzalez, knowing he will be pitched away, goes with it and grounds a single to right.
Home Run	3-run homer	Popup to first	Grounder to short	Single to right

Award of Excellence
El Periodico de Catalunya
Barcelona, Spain

Jordi Catala, Author/Editor; Ricard Gracia, Author

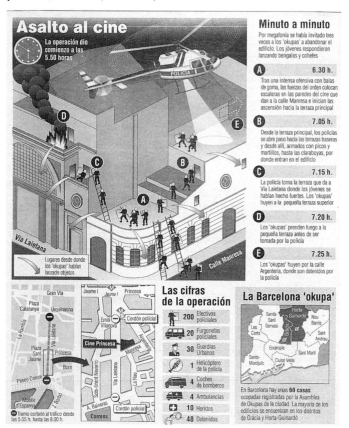

Award of Excellence
Marca
Madrid, Spain

Jose Juan Gamez, Design Director; Cesar Galera, Graphic Artist

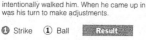
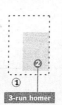
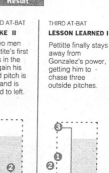
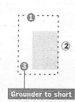

Award of Excellence
El Pais
Madrid, Spain

Gustavo Hermoso, Photographer

Award of Excellence
The News & Observer
Raleigh, NC

Nam Nguyen, Illustrator; Tom Mosier, Illustrator; Ken Mowry, Illustrator and Graphic Dir.; Marcus Walton, Reporter; Lynette Mitchell, Reporter; David Pickel, AME/Presentation

Award of Excellence
The New York Times
New York, NY

Tim Oliver, Designer; Patrick Lyons, Graphics Editor; Dylan McClain, Graphics Editor

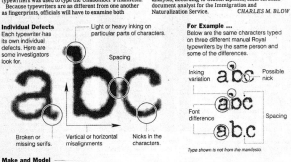

Award of Excellence
The New York Times
New York, NY

Charles M. Blow, Graphics Director

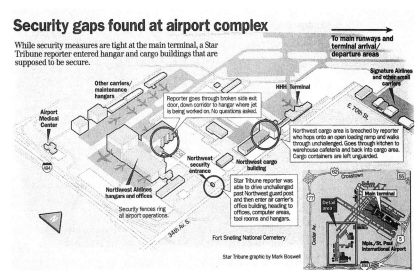

Award of Excellence
Star Tribune
Minneapolis, MN

Mark Boswell, Staff Artist; Ray Grumney, News Graphics Editor

Award of Excellence
USA Today
Arlington, VA

Staff

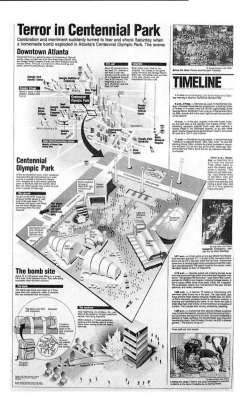

Award of Excellence
USA Today
Arlington, VA

Grant Jerding, Graphic Artist; John Siniff, Graphics Editor; Paul Hoversten, Reporter; Dash Parham, Graphics Director; Bob Reynolds, Graphics Editor; Mick Calvacca, Graphics Editor; Richard Curtis, ME/Graphics & Photo

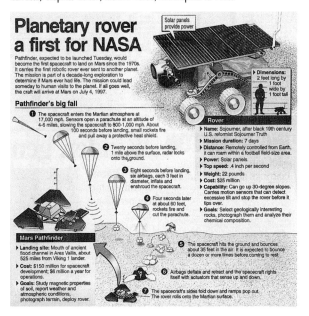

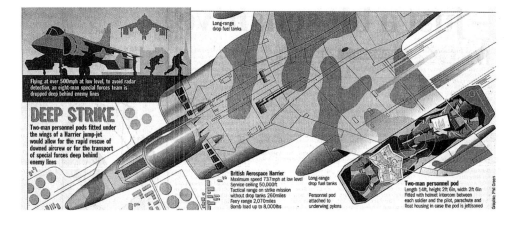

Award of Excellence
The Sunday Telegraph
London, England

Phillip Green, Graphics Editor

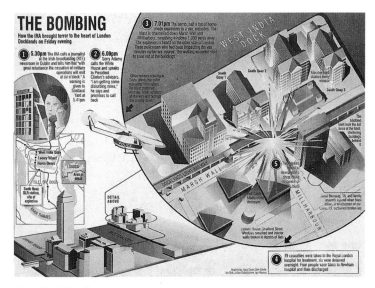

Award of Excellence
The Sunday Telegraph
London, England

Phillip Green, Graphics Editor; Katie Murray, Graphic Artist; Bob Williams, Illustrator

Award of Excellence
The Sunday Times
London, England

Gary Cook, Graphics Editor; John Smith, Artist; Ian Bott, Artist; Julian Osbaldstone, Artist; Ian Moores, Artist

Award of Excellence
Chicago Tribune
Chicago, IL

Stacy Sweat, Graphics Editor; Therese Shechter, Associate Graphics Editor; Nancy I.Z. Reese, Associate Graphics Editor; Celeste Bernard, Graphics Coordinator; Steve Layton, Graphic Artist; Steven Duenes, Graphic Artist; Scott Holingue, Graphic Artist; Lara Weber, Graphics Coordinator

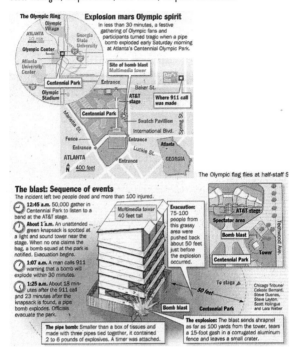

Award of Excellence
Chicago Tribune
Chicago, IL

Steve Layton, Graphic Artist; Steven Duenes, Graphic Artist; Melissa Nagy, Graphics Coordinator; Nancy I.Z. Reese, Associate Graphics Editor

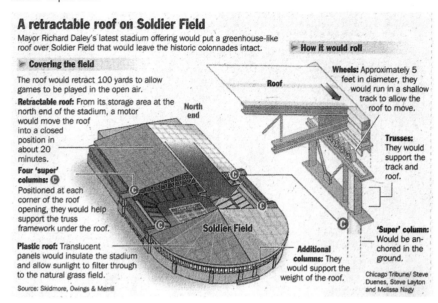

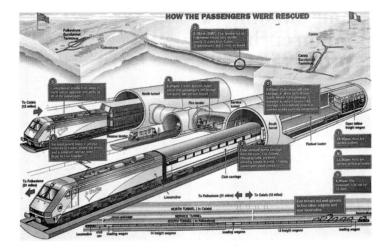

Award of Excellence
Daily Telegraph
London, England

Alan Gilliland, Graphics Editor; Richard Burgess, Deputy Graphics Editor; Vivian Kent, Graphic Artist; Glenn Swann, Graphic Artist

Award of Excellence
El Mundo Deportivo
Barcelona, Spain

Quique Belil, Designer

Award of Excellence
Expansión
Madrid, Spain

José Juan Gámez, Design Director; Pablo Ma Ramírez, Graphic Artist; Blanca Serrano, Graphic Artist; Juan Ferreira, Graphic Artist

Award of Excellence
Expressen
Stockholm, Sweden

Stefan Rothmaier, Graphics; Goran Forsberg, Graphics Editor; Christian Holmen, Researcher; Thomas Mattsson, Researcher

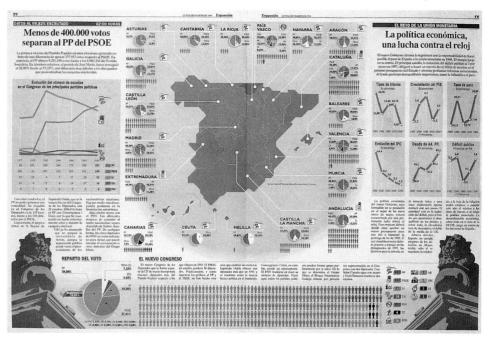

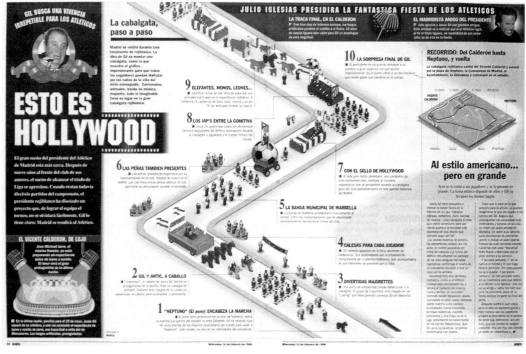

Award of Excellence
Marca
Madrid, Spain
Staff

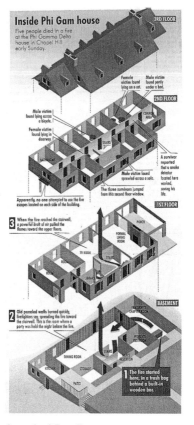

Award of Excellence
News & Observer
Raleigh, NC

Charles Apple, Illustrator & Reporter; Joby Warrick, James Shiffer, Reporters; Ken Mowry, Graphics Director; David Pickel, AME Presentation

Award of Excellence
The Times
London, England
Geoffrey Sims; John Lawson; Tony Garrett

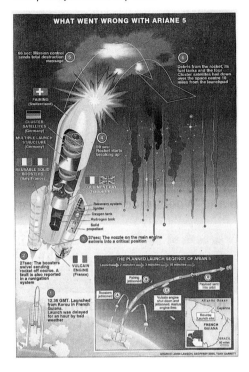

Award of Excellence
The Times
London, England
Geoffrey Sims; Tony Garrett; David Hart; Laura Sylvester; Helen Smithson

Experts claim multiple failures in safety systems

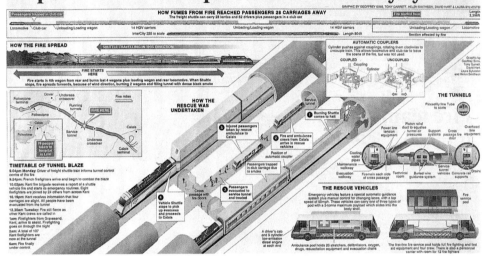

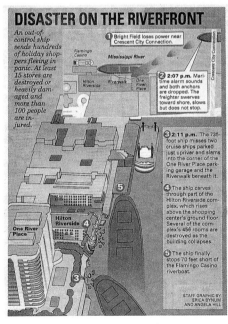

Award of Excellence
The Times-Picayune
New Orleans, LA
Angela Hill, Graphics Editor; Erica B. Bynum, Graphic Artist;
George Berke, Design Director; James O'Byrne, Sunday Editor

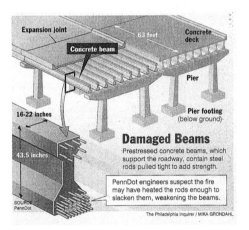

Award of Excellence
The Philadelphia Inquirer
Philadelphia, PA
David Milne, AME Design; Bill Marsh, Design Director; Mika
Grondahl, Graphic Artist; Gayle Sims, Graphics Editor

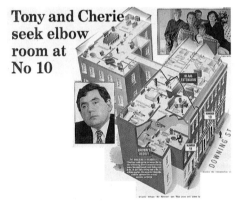

Award of Excellence
The Sunday Times
London, England
Gary Cook, Graphics Editor

Award of Excellence
• Also an Award of Excellence for Breaking News Graphics
Clarin
Buenos Aires, Argentina

Anibal Ces, Artist; Lucas Varela, Artist; Jaime Serra, Graphics Ed.

Award of Excellence
• Also an Award of Excellence for Breaking News Graphics
The New York Times
New York, NY

Charles M. Blow, Graphics Director; Graphics Staff

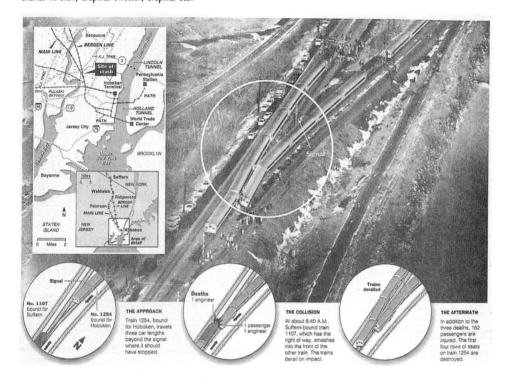

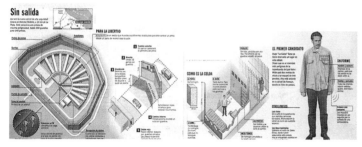

Award of Excellence
Clarin
Buenos Aires, Argentina

Alejandro Tumas, Artist; Jaime Serra, Graphics Editor

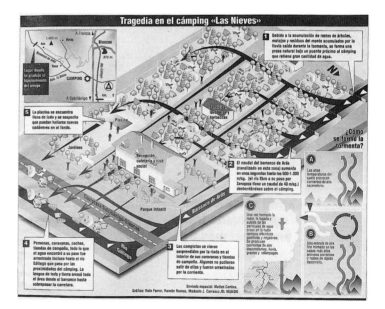

Award of Excellence
El Mundo
Madrid, Spain

Modesto Carrasco, Graphic Journalist; Dina Sánchez, Graphic Journalist; Chema Matía, Graphic Journalist; Ramón Rodríguez, Graphic Journalist; Matías Cortina, Graphic Journalist; Ramón Ramos, Graphic Journalist; Rafael Ferrer, Graphic Journalist; Juancho Cruz; Graphic Journalist

Silver
Clarin
Buenos Aires, Argentina
Bianki, Artist; Jaime Serra, Graphics Editor

EL LARGO CAMINO QUE TOMA UN PROYECTO EN HOLLYWOOD HASTA TRANSFORMARSE EN PELICULA

Cómo una simple idea puede
TERMINAR EN EXITO

Las idas y vueltas de los proyectos involucran desde actores hasta banqueros.

Así se llega al "The End"

Silver
The New York Times
New York, NY
Archie Tse, Graphics Editor

The Flow of Time

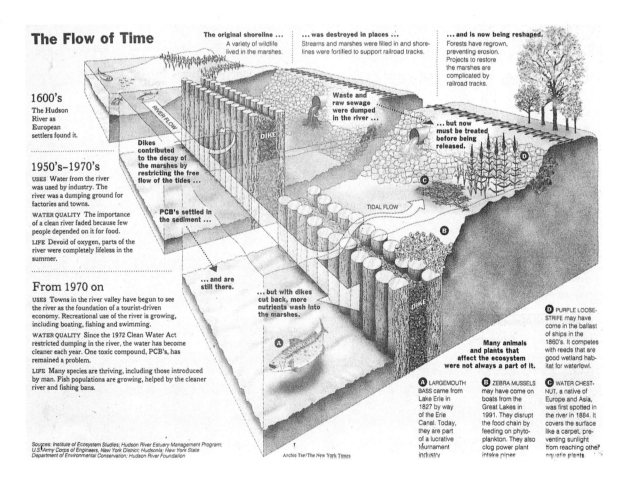

The original shoreline ...
A variety of wildlife lived in the marshes.

... was destroyed in places ...
Streams and marshes were filled in and shorelines were fortified to support railroad tracks.

... and is now being reshaped.
Forests have regrown, preventing erosion. Projects to restore the marshes are complicated by railroad tracks.

1600's
The Hudson River as European settlers found it.

1950's–1970's
USES Water from the river was used by industry. The river was a dumping ground for factories and towns.

WATER QUALITY The importance of a clean river faded because few people depended on it for food.

LIFE Devoid of oxygen, parts of the river were completely lifeless in the summer.

From 1970 on
USES Towns in the river valley have begun to see the river as the foundation of a tourist-driven economy. Recreational use of the river is growing, including boating, fishing and swimming.

WATER QUALITY Since the 1972 Clean Water Act restricted dumping in the river, the water has become cleaner each year. One toxic compound, PCB's, has remained a problem.

LIFE Many species are thriving, including those introduced by man. Fish populations are growing, helped by the cleaner river and fishing bans.

Dikes contributed to the decay of the marshes by restricting the free flow of the tides ...

PCB's settled in the sediment ...

Waste and raw sewage were dumped in the river ...

... but now must be treated before being released.

... and are still there.

... but with dikes cut back, more nutrients wash into the marshes.

RIVER FLOW

TIDAL FLOW

Many animals and plants that affect the ecosystem were not always a part of it.

A LARGEMOUTH BASS came from Lake Erie in 1827 by way of the Erie Canal. Today, they are part of a lucrative tournament industry

B ZEBRA MUSSELS may have come on boats from the Great Lakes in 1991. They disrupt the food chain by feeding on phytoplankton. They also clog power plant intake pipes

C WATER CHESTNUT, a native of Europe and Asia, was first spotted in the river in 1884. It covers the surface like a carpet, preventing sunlight from reaching other aquatic plants.

D PURPLE LOOSESTRIFE may have come in the ballast of ships in the 1860's. It competes with reeds that are good wetland habitat for waterfowl.

Sources: Institute of Ecosystem Studies; Hudson River Estuary Management Program; U.S. Army Corps of Engineers, New York District; Hudsonia; New York State Department of Environmental Conservation; Hudson River Foundation

Archie Tse/The New York Times

Silver
San Francisco Chronicle
San Francisco, CA

Steve Kearsley, Graphic Artist

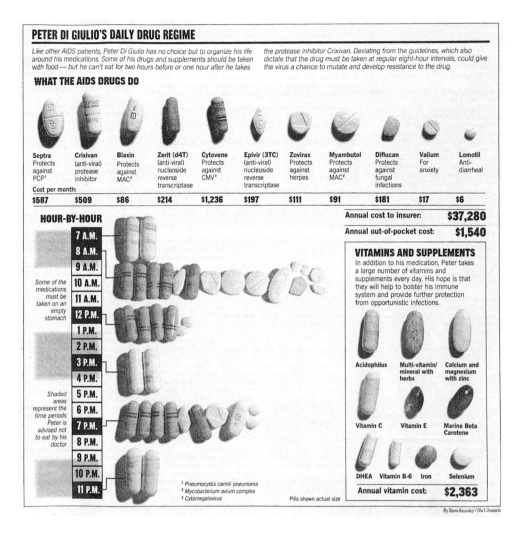

PETER DI GIULIO'S DAILY DRUG REGIME

Like other AIDS patients, Peter Di Giulio has no choice but to organize his life around his medications. Some of his drugs and supplements should be taken with food — but he can't eat for two hours before or one hour after he takes the protease inhibitor Crixivan. Deviating from the guidelines, which also dictate that the drug must be taken at regular eight-hour intervals, could give the virus a chance to mutate and develop resistance to the drug.

WHAT THE AIDS DRUGS DO

Septra	Crixivan	Biaxin	Zerit (d4T)	Cytovene	Epivir (3TC)	Zovirax	Myambutol	Diflucan	Valium	Lomotil
Protects against PCP[1]	(anti-viral) protease inhibitor	Protects against MAC[2]	(anti-viral) nucleoside reverse transcriptase	Protects against CMV[3]	(anti-viral) nucleoside reverse transcriptase	Protects against herpes	Protects against MAC[2]	Protects against fungal infections	For anxiety	Anti-diarrheal

Cost per month:

$587	$509	$86	$214	$1,236	$197	$111	$91	$181	$17	$6

HOUR-BY-HOUR

7 A.M.
8 A.M.
9 A.M.
10 A.M.
11 A.M.
12 P.M.
1 P.M.
2 P.M.
3 P.M.
4 P.M.
5 P.M.
6 P.M.
7 P.M.
8 P.M.
9 P.M.
10 P.M.
11 P.M.

Some of the medications must be taken on an empty stomach

Shaded areas represent the time periods Peter is advised not to eat by his doctor

Annual cost to insurer:	**$37,280**
Annual out-of-pocket cost:	**$1,540**

VITAMINS AND SUPPLEMENTS

In addition to his medication, Peter takes a large number of vitamins and supplements every day. His hope is that they will help to bolster his immune system and provide further protection from opportunistic infections.

Acidophilus / Multi-vitamin/mineral with herbs / Calcium and magnesium with zinc

Vitamin C / Vitamin E / Marine Beta Carotene

DHEA / Vitamin B-6 / Iron / Selenium

Annual vitamin cost:	**$2,363**

[1] Pneumocystis carinii pneumonia
[2] Mycobacterium avium complex
[3] Cytomegalovirus

Pills shown actual size

By Steve Kearsley / The Chronicle

Silver
The New York Times
New York, NY

Charles M. Blow, Graphics Editor/Illustrator; Michael Valenti, Art Director

Calving of Right Whales Faces New Threats

Heavy Traffic Near Nursery

Pregnant Eubalaena glacialis females migrate to a calving area near war game sites and busy naval and commercial shipping lanes. The map on the left shows the migration route and the one on the right shows sightings of living (●) and dead (○) whales.

ROUTE

NOVA SCOTIA (Canada)

Stellwagen Bank

Bulls and other cows

Brunswick

Mothers with calves

N.Y.

Kings Bay Naval Base

GEORGIA

FLORIDA

Pregnant Females

GA

Gray's Reef

ATLANTIC OCEAN

Area of detail

FLA

Mayport Naval Station

SIGHTINGS
From Dec. 9, 1995 to Feb. 29, 1996

DEAD WHALES
Represented by open circles. Arrows indicate drift direction.

Critical habitat

31°

These lines represent the survey flyovers.

Gunnery range

12 MILES

80°30'

A Species Fails to Recover

Despite measures to protect it, the North Atlantic right whale, once the "right" whale to hunt for blubber, has failed to thrive. Calving has surged this year, but there have a record number of deaths. Possible explanations include ship collisions, entanglement in fishing gear and habitat decline in feeding areas.

By WILLIAM J. BROAD

N OW, in early springtime, is when female northern right whales and their newborns migrate northward from calving grounds off Florida and Georgia to around Cape Cod, Mass., taking about a month for the journey. It has been a good season for baby making among the northern rights. Scientists have sighted 20 calves, a record after years of falling counts. Only 320 or so of the behemoths now ply the North Atlantic, and a high rate of reproduction is seen as critical to the comeback of these big mammals, once hunted to near extinction and now the most endangered of the great whales.

But despite more than a half century of protection, as well as sustained Federal and private conservation ef-

Dangers include heavy ship traffic and gun practice.

forts, the 55-foot, black and gray whales are failing to rally and their population remains dangerously low, baffling scientists and alarming environmentalists.

Six whales have died so far this year, including three calves, the highest number of deaths on record for so short a period. Part of the problem is that the lumbering giants swim through one of the nation's busiest sea lanes for commercial shipping and naval maneuvers; at times getting hit. Other whales get entangled in fishing gear.

But scientists say the roots of the problem go beyond such incidents and are increasingly a grim mystery, prompting a redoubling of protective efforts and detective work.

"We don't know what's going on," Dr. Scott D. Kraus, chief scientist at the New England Aquarium in Boston, the main research group working to save the animal, said in an interview. "It gets nerve-racking."

Environmental groups, including Greenpeace and the International Wildlife Coalition, recently contended that Navy war games off Georgia and Florida with five-inch guns and 500-pound bombs were probably responsible for many of the recent deaths.

But scientists, while happy to question Navy practices, often say that

Continued on Page C11

Sources: National Oceanic and Atmospheric Administration; New England Aquarium

Charles M. Blow/The New York Times

Award of Excellence
Detroit Free Press
Detroit, MI

Rick Nease, Illustrator; Laura Varon Brown, Graphics Director; Pat Chargot, Reporter

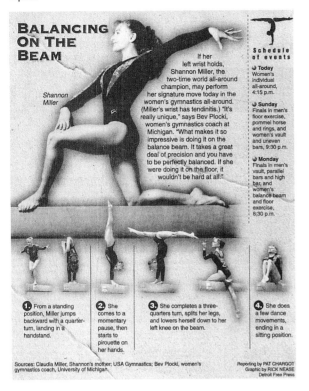

Award of Excellence
The Detroit News
Detroit, MI

Dale Peskin, Deputy ME; Chris Kozlowski, Design/Graphics Editor; Chris Willis, Assistant Graphics Editor; Tim Summers, Graphic Artist; Karen Van Antwerp, Graphic Researcher; Howard Lovy, Reporter; Shanna Flowers, Assistant City Editor

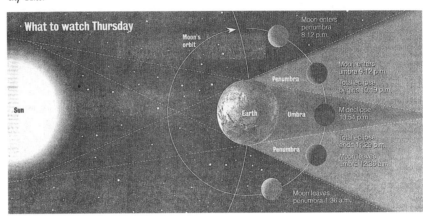

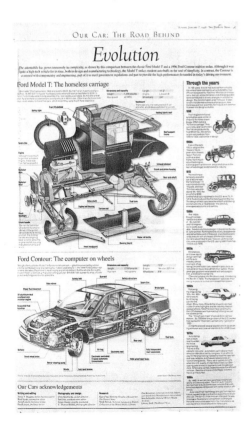

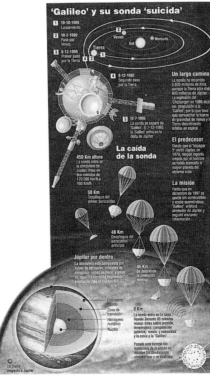

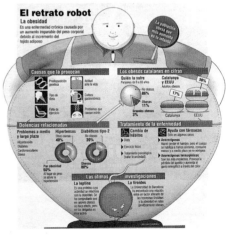

Award of Excellence
El Periodico de Catalunya
Barcelona, Spain

Cristina Claverol, Author; Jordi Catala, Infografic Editor

Award of Excellence
The Detroit News
Detroit, MI

Dale Peskin, Deputy ME; Chris Kozlowski, Design /Graphics Director; Jamee Tanner, Graphic Artist

Award of Excellence
El Periodico de Catalunya
Barcelona, Spain

Cristina Claverol, Author; Jordi Catala, Infographic editor

Award of Excellence
The New York Times
New York, NY

Charles Blow, Graphics Director; Staff

Searching for Debris and Remains in the Everglades

Investigators searching for debris and human remains at the site of a ValuJet DC-9 crash in the Everglades near Miami are encountering a number of unusual obstacles. Here is a look at the search process.

THE SEARCH PROCEDURES

Making a Grid
A grid is made of the area and it is searched in sectors.

Search Teams
Teams of five searchers wade shoulder-to-shoulder through the water in 20 minute intervals, probing the bottom.

Armed Escort
An escort, riding on an airboat with an automatic weapon, looks for alligators.

THE SEARCHERS' GEAR

First Layer
TYVEK SUITS Protect the wearers from dangerous substances like jet fuel.

GLOVES Taped on.

Second Layer
RUBBER SUIT Put on over the Tyvek suit.

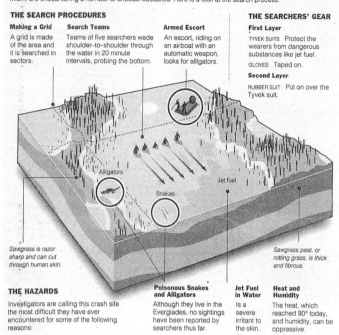

Sawgrass is razor sharp and can cut through human skin.

Alligators

Snakes

Jet fuel

Sawgrass peat, or rotting grass, is thick and fibrous.

THE HAZARDS

Investigators are calling this crash site the most difficult they have ever encountered for some of the following reasons:

Poisonous Snakes and Alligators
Although they live in the Everglades, no sightings have been reported by searchers thus far.

Jet Fuel in Water
Is a severe irritant to the skin.

Heat and Humidity
The heat, which reached 90° today, and humidity, can be oppressive.

Source: National Transportation Safety Board, Florida Game and Freshwater Fish Commission, Pennsylvania State University

---

Award of Excellence
The New York Times
New York, NY

Archie Tse, Graphics Editor; Al Granberg, Illustrator

Changes Beneath the Surface

Many of the significant innovations that the Transit Authority will incorporate into its next fleet of subway cars will go unseen by riders. Some of those changes, shown here on the shell of one of the Transit Authority's test trains, were specified this spring in a report to potential manufacturers.

AIR-CONDITIONING
Today, fixing a broken air conditioner — the most common summer breakdown — can mean taking the car out of service for days because parts are in the ceiling and floor. The new trains will be cooled by a one-piece unit, which can be replaced in less than two hours.

INTERCAR CONNECTORS
On most current trains, there are no wires connecting the cars. Instead, electrical commands for braking and door-opening travel from car to car through spring-mounted metal pins at the ends of the cars that press against one another. The pins are a chronic source of trouble because they often stick. The new cars will be hard-wired together, in sets of three, four or five, eliminating most pins.

OPERATOR'S CAB
Each group of three to five cars will have just two cabs, rather than the current one or two per car. That means less equipment to maintain and more room for passenger seats. Cab crews will allow the crew to see at a glance what is working and what isn't.

DATA PORT
Each car will have a data port in its side, allowing workers to plug in laptop computers to see how all parts of the car are working and the car's maintenance history.

DOORS
Instead of being pushed and pulled by levers, which break frequently, the doors on the new trains will be controlled by a screw mechanism that uses fewer parts.

CONTROLLERS
Under each of today's cars is a controller, a box about eight feet long and two feet wide, filled with dozens of mechanical switches that regulate everything from acceleration to air-conditioning. It will be replaced by a much smaller box with a couple of circuit boards, eliminating hundreds of moving parts and a lot of weight.

The Subway Train of Tomorrow

Sleeker, Smoother and (the T.A. Hopes) Easier to Maintain

By RICHARD PÉREZ-PEÑA

A revolution is being planned for the subway system, but when it arrives, it will remain mostly invisible.

In the next few months, the Transit Authority plans to buy a new generation of trains. Some changes will be obvious, like electronic message boards and recorded announcements, but for the most part, the subway car of the future will look much like the one of the present. The advances will be hidden under the trains' steel skins.

Internally, almost every mechanism will have been fundamentally altered, from the motors that drive the train to the air-conditioning system to the gadgets that open and close the doors, each with an eye toward making it cheaper to operate, less likely to break down, and easier to fix if it does. In many cases, bulky workings based on technology half a century old or more will be replaced by computer circuitry. Computer touch-screens will tell train crews and repair workers in an instant what is working and what isn't — even whether there is a half-inch obstruction between the halves of a door that looks closed.

Almost four years ago, two high-tech test trains began riding the underground rails on the A and No. 2 lines, giving the Transit Authority a chance to try out some of its most ambitious plans. In terms of technology, the test train were to the trains built in the 1980's what a calculator is to an abacus. With technology preceding space since 1992, the trains that are scheduled to begin arriving at the end of 1998 will be more like the supercomputers.

The test trains created quite a buzz when they were new, with features like wider doors to make entry and exit easier, roomier seats and speakers on the outside of each car. But little was said about the more profound changes in the innards of the trains — changes that will be even greater in the new model.

The Transit Authority released in the spring the first detailed description of what it hoped to include in the new trains, as part of an effort to interest potential manufacturers.

"We went through everything we could think of, we rack everyone's wish list and we went in it really carefully to see what we could do and what we couldn't," said Joseph E. Hofmann, the Transit Authority's senior vice president in charge of subways.

The guiding principle has been to eliminate the most common causes of breakdowns, often by doing away with moving parts. "The failure points, the moving

Continued on Page 42

WHEEL TRUCK
With motors and other parts getting smaller, more machinery can fit between the wheels, so the metal undercarriages will be smaller and lighter. This will allow easier access to the wheels for repairs.

BRAKES
To slow the train, the motors apply resistance instead of power and become electric generators. At present, the energy they generate is dissipated as heat through grids under the train, making a blast of hot air as a train slows. On new trains, the excess power will be pumped back into the third rail, cutting energy consumption by 25 percent.

SUSPENSION
Current cars ride on heavy steel springs. The new ones will also have air bags, and possibly steel and rubber domes, for a smoother ride and less wear on the car.

MOTORS
The new trains will use alternating current rather than direct current. AC motors are smaller, lighter and have fewer moving parts, so they need less maintenance. They are more powerful, which means fewer motors per train to maintain. They also are much less than DC motors, which means fewer fixes. Only in the last decade has technology made it easy to control AC motors, and to convert the DC power supplied by the third rail.

Sources: Metropolitan Transit Authority, Kawasaki Rail Car Inc.   Al Granberg and Archie Tse/The New York Times

---

Award of Excellence
The New York Times
New York, NY

Archie Tse, Graphics Editor; C. B. Williams, Artist

Much has improved ...   ... but one problem persists

Award of Excellence
The New York Times
New York, NY

Joe Ward, Graphics Editor; Carol Fabricatore, Illustrator

**IN HER OWN WORDS
SHANNON MILLER**

"There's not enough time to think about all the things I need to do for the whole routine. I practice it so many times that my body knows what to do automatically."

"I concentrate on running real hard and keeping my arms straight for the block. The block is the most difficult part, I have to get enough height for the flipping and spinning I have to do."

:05.3 THE LANDING   :04.6 THE BLOCK   :04.2 THE ROUNDOFF   :03.1 THE SPRINT   START

8 STICKING IT
As she comes out of her final flips and turns, Miller brings her hands down to her sides to stabilize her body, and bends her knees to absorb the impact. Her body is bent slightly backward as she lands, but her momentum carries her upright. She tries to stop on a dime, avoiding any extra steps after she lands.

7 HEAD OVER HEELS
While she is twisting, she keeps her body rigidly straight – called a layout – and flips head over heels like a tumbling knife 1½ times.

6 DO THE TWISTS
After she leaves the horse, she pulls her arms toward her left shoulder, causing her body to begin twisting. She will twist 1½ times.

5 RICOCHET
When she hits the horse, her tremendous momentum is ricocheted skyward – called the block – to allow for the height needed to perform the difficult twists and turns of the routine.

4 BLIND FAITH
From the springboard, Miller performs the most dangerous segment of the routine when she reaches back blindly for the horse, concentrating on keeping her arms straight, trusting that she will hit somewhere on the 12-inch surface.

3 ABOUT FACE
She takes a skip or hurdle step from her right foot back to her right foot and raises her hands over her head. This stretches her body and starts it turning for her round-off – a cartwheel that takes her to the springboard and leaves her with her back to the horse.

2 ON HER MARK
Because rushes of adrenaline in competition can cause the athletes to be off stride, gymnasts often place chalk marks near the end of the runway to point out where their hands should land for the cartwheel. All the marks can cause confusion, so Miller uses a mark halfway down the runway to make sure she is on the right foot at the right time.

1 THE KEYS
Miller visualizes her routine and concentrates on a few key elements which mark: get good speed; reach for the horse with straight arms; pull arms down for landing.

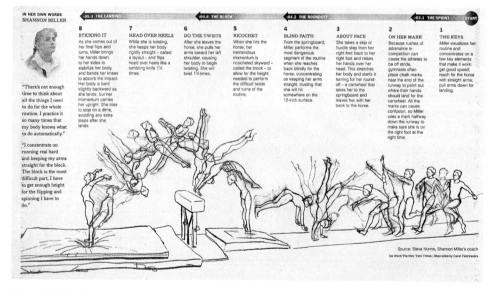

Source: Steve Nunno, Shannon Miller's coach
Joe Ward/The New York Times; Illustration by Carol Fabricatore

---

Salvaging Flight 800: The Divers' Task

Scores of divers are aiding in the salvage of T.W.A. Flight 800. Tethered, or "hard-hat," divers, shown here, work in the main debris field and have several missions: looking for bodies, charting the location of debris and helping collect wreckage. Scuba divers, whose maximum dive time is about 10 minutes, work outside the main field, plotting and retrieving debris.

Topside control
On deck, a "console" crew regulates air supply and keeps in constant verbal communication with divers. The crew can also send down a remote-controlled camera to monitor operations and videotape the wreckage.

Umbilical lifeline
Each diver is tethered to the deck of the ship by a long umbilical assembly, which contains an air-supply hose and a communications cable.

The tether also keeps the diver in constant physical touch with the ship – if he is injured, or becomes trapped or entangled in wreckage, he can be pulled up to safety. It also serves as a backup signaling system if electronic communications fail – divers use a tugging "language," in which a set number of tugs signals trouble or a need for air.

Visibility
Divers can see about 15 feet in front of them at the bottom in good weather, but as they move debris, sand clouds the area. They use hand-held flashlights, and additional lights can be attached to their helmets.

Hazards
• Jagged metal edges and twisted wires in the wreckage
• Entanglement of tethers in the wreckage
• Pressurized parts of the plane, like parts of the landing gear, that may suddenly give way and shoot projectiles
• Hypothermia, with water temperature near 40° at this depth
• The bends – a result of too-rapid decompression that can cause severe pain and lead to unconsciousness

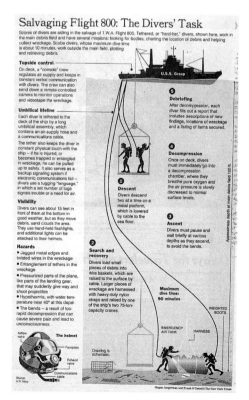

U.S.S. Grasp

6 Debriefing
After decompression, each diver fills out a report that includes descriptions of new findings, locations of wreckage and a listing of items secured.

4 Decompression
Once on deck, divers must immediately go into a decompression chamber, where they breathe pure oxygen and the air pressure is slowly decreased to normal surface levels.

1 Descent
Divers descend two at a time on a metal platform, which is lowered by cable to the sea floor.

3 Ascent
Divers must pause and wait briefly at various depths as they ascend, to avoid the bends.

2 Search and recovery
Divers load small pieces of debris into wire baskets, which are raised to the surface by cable. Larger pieces of wreckage are harnessed with heavy-duty nylon straps and raised by one of the ship's two 75-ton-capacity cranes.

Maximum dive time: 90 minutes

Approximate depth at main debris field 120 ft.

WEIGHTED BOOTS

EMERGENCY AIR TANK   HARNESS

The helmet
Faceplate

Exhaust valve

Airflow valve

Communications cable

Source U.S. Navy

Drawing is schematic.

Megan Jaegerman and Frank O'Connell/The New York Times

Award of Excellence
• Also an Award of Excellence for Informational Graphics Portfolio
The New York Times
New York, NY

Frank O'Connell, Illustrator; Megan Jaegerman, Graphics Editor

Award of Excellence
The New York Times
New York, NY
Megan Jaegerman, Graphics Editor & Illustrator

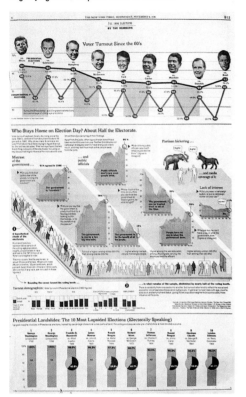

Award of Excellence
The New York Times
New York, NY
John Papasian, Artist

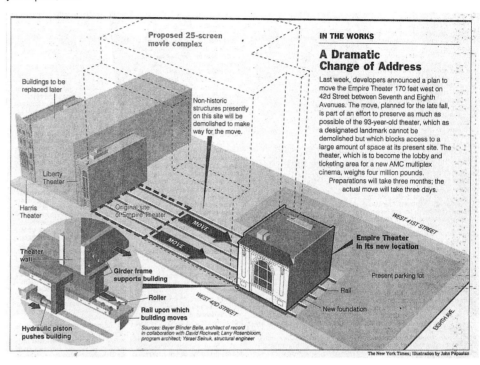

Award of Excellence
The New York Times
New York, NY
Charles M. Blow, Graphics Editor/Illustrator; Michael Valenti, Art Director

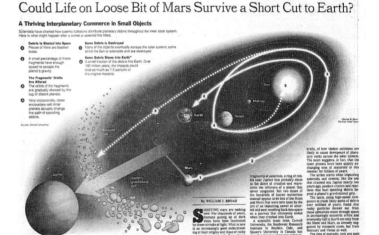

Award of Excellence
The New York Times
New York, NY
Archie Tse, Graphics Editor/Illustrator

Award of Excellence
The Orange County Register
Santa Ana, CA

Paul Carbo, Illustrator; Tia Lai, Art Director

Award of Excellence
The New York Times
New York, NY

Nigel Holmes, Illustrator; Michael Valenti, Art Director

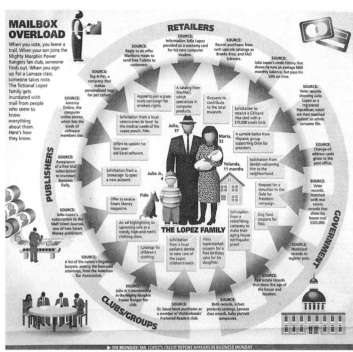

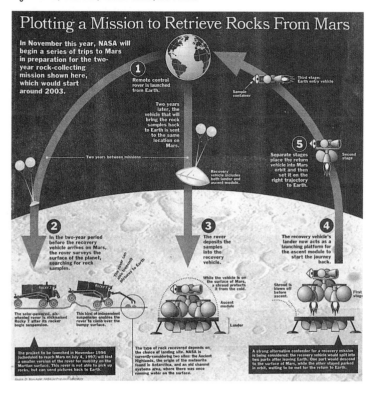

Award of Excellence
The Orange County Register
Santa Ana, CA

Paul Carbo, Illustrator; Tia Lai, Art Director; Chris Boucly,
Graphics Reporter

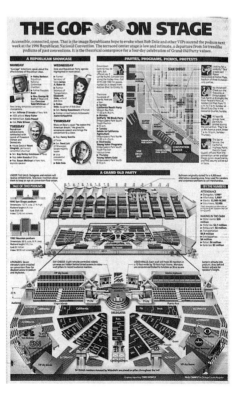

Award of Excellence
The Orange County Register
Santa Ana, CA

Paul Carbo, Illustrator; Tia Lai, Art Director; Chris Boucly,
Graphics Reporter

Award of Excellence
The New York Times
New York, NY

Patrick Lyons, Graphics Editor; Joe Zeff, Designer

Award of Excellence
The Star-Ledger
Newark, NJ

Andre Malok, Graphics Reporter; Robert Britt,
Graphics Editor

The digital revolution

A new world of technology in television broadcasting is fast approaching. Television and the computer manufacturers are in a battle for consumer dollars in the digital home entertainment industry.

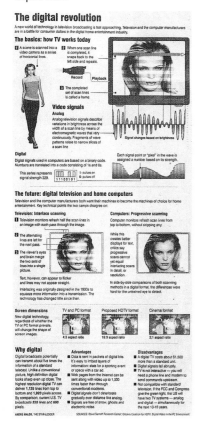

Award of Excellence
The Albuquerque Journal
Albuquerque, NM

Carol Cooperrider, Illustrator; Mary Schuver, Designer; George Gibson,
Graphics Coordinator; Annemarie Neff, Assistant Design Director; Joe Kirby,
Design Director; Carolyn Flynn, AME Photo and Design

Award of Excellence
Star-Ledger
Newark, NJ

Andre Malok, Graphics Reporter; Jim Pathe, Photographer;
Kevin Whitmer, Sports Editor; Robert Britt, Graphics Editor

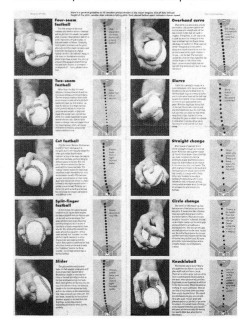

Award of Excellence
Star Tribune
Minneapolis, MN

Jane Friedmann, News Graphic Artist; Ray Grumney, News Graphic Director; Tom Sweeney, Photographer; Jay Weiner, Staff Writer;
Kevin Diaz, Staff Writer

Award of Excellence
Asbury Park Press
Neptune, NJ

Andrew Prendimano, Art and Photo Director; Ed Gabel, Artist;
Harris Siegel, ME Design & Photography

El Mundo Del Siglo XXI Magazine was awarded a Gold Medal for superb storytelling power in its four-page history of the Olympiadas Del Siglo XX from 1900–1992. Great attention to detail in use of graphics and copy.

La Revista El Mundo Del Siglo XXI se ganó una Medalla de Oro por la magnífica narrativa en su historia en cuatro páginas de los Juegos Olímpicos Del Siglo XX desde 1900 hasta 1992. Se presta mucha atención a los detalles en el uso de gráficas y copia.

Gold
El Mundo Del Siglo XXI Magazine
Madrid, Spain

Ramón Rodríguez, Graphic Journalist; Dina Sánchez, Graphic Journalist; Juancho Cruz, Graphic Journalist; Chema Matía, Graphic Journalist

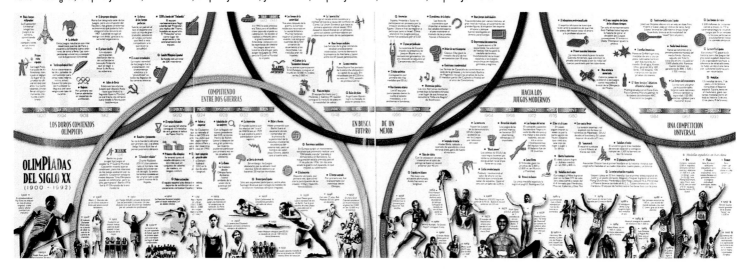

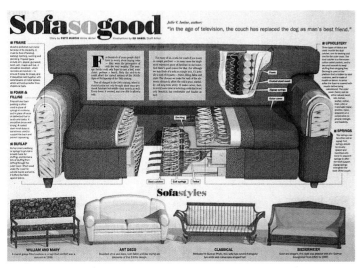

Award of Excellence
Asbury Park Press
Neptune, NJ

Ed Gabel, Artist; Amy Catalano, Designer; Andrew Prendimano, Art & Photo Director; Harris Siegel, ME Design & Photography

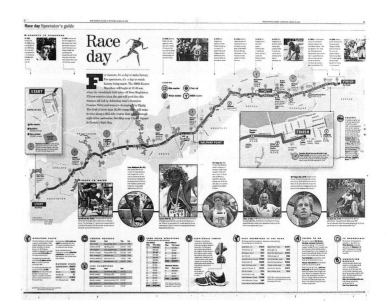

Award of Excellence
The Boston Globe
Boston, MA

Neil C. Pinchin, Designer

Award of Excellence
Chicago Tribune
Chicago, IL

Stephen Ravenscraft, Artist; Terry Volpp, Graphics Coordinator; David Jahntz, Artist; Nancy I.Z. Reese, Associate Graphics Editor; Therese Shechter, Associate Graphics Editor; Stacy Sweat, Graphics Director

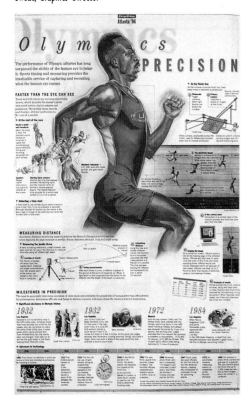

Award of Excellence
Clarin
Buenos Aires, Argentina
Jaime Serra, Graphics Editor

Award of Excellence
The Chicago Tribune
Chicago, IL

Steve Layton, Graphic Artist; Jeanie Adams, Assistant Picture Editor; Stacy Sweat, Graphics Editor; John Crewdson, Senior Writer

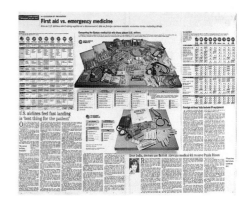

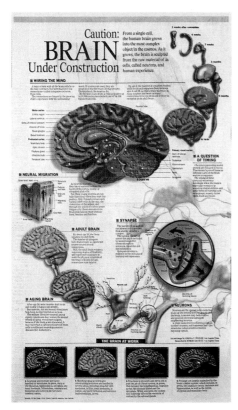

Award of Excellence
The Los Angeles Times
Los Angeles, CA
Lorena Iniguez, News Graphic Artist/Designer

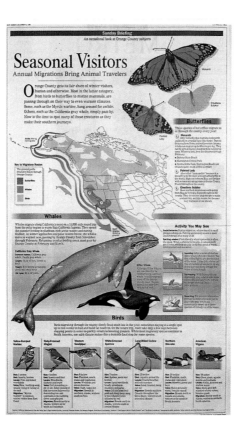

Award of Excellence
The Los Angeles Times/Orange County Edition
Costa Mesa, CA
Doris Shields, Artist/Researcher; April Jackson, Researcher

Award of Excellence
Expansión
Madrid, Spain

Jose Juan Gamez, Design Director; Bianca Serrano, Graphic Artist

Award of Excellence
The Oregonian
Portland, OR

Steve Cowden, Artist/Illustrator

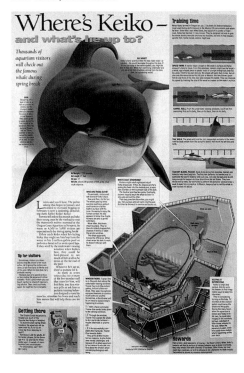

Award of Excellence
Reforma
Mexico City, Mexico

Juan Jesus Cortes, Illustrator; Roberto Gutierrez, Section Designer; Jaime Rubio, Editor; Ernesto Carrillo, Graphics Editor; Emilio Deheza, Art Director; Eduardo Danilo, Design Consultant

Award of Excellence
The San Diego Union-Tribune
San Diego, CA

Paul Horn, Graphics Journalist

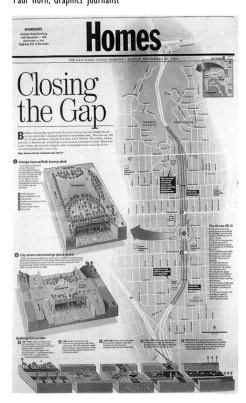

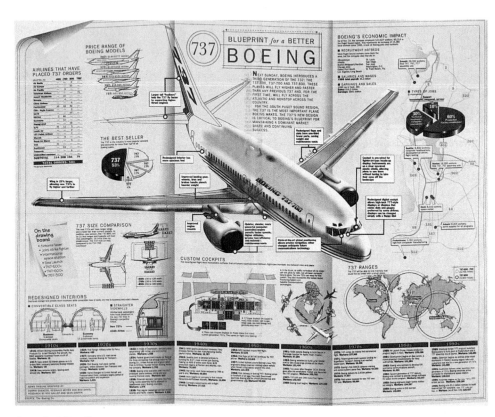

Award of Excellence
News Tribune
Tacoma, WA

Roy Gallop, Graphic Artist & Researcher; Derrik Quenzer, Graphic Artist; Boo Davis, Graphic Artist; Sean Griffin, Reporter & Researcher; Reggie Myers, Art Director

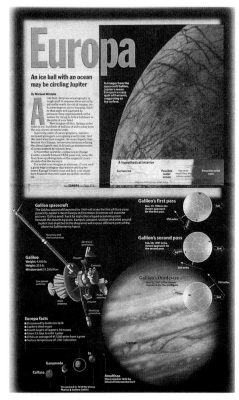

Award of Excellence
The San Diego Union-Tribune
San Diego, CA

Mark Nowlin, Graphics Journalist

Award of Excellence
St. Petersburg Times
St. Petersburg, FL

Cristina Martinez, Artist

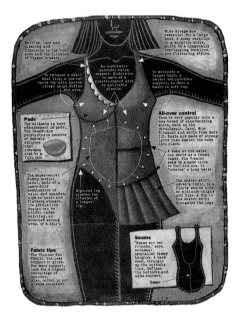

Award of Excellence
Star Tribune
Minneapolis, MN

Sid Jablonski, Graphics Designer; Ron Shara, Staff Writer; Mike Blahnik, Sport Team Leader; Tim Wheatley, Sports Section Coordinator; Ray Grumney, News Graphics Editor; Anders Ramberg, Design Director

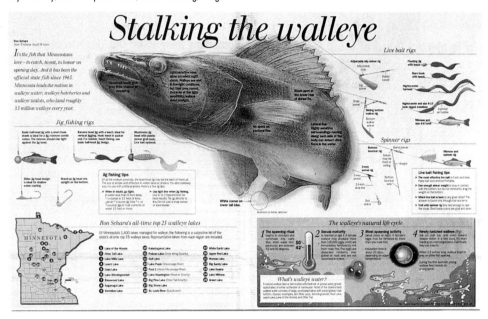

Award of Excellence
Chicago Tribune
Chicago, IL

Steven Duenes, Graphic Artist

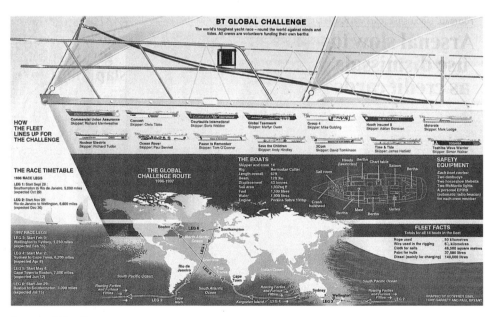

Award of Excellence
The Times
London, England

Geoffrey Sims; Tony Garrett; Paul Bryant

Award of Excellence
El Mundo Del Siglo XXI
Madrid, Spain
Dina Sanchez, Graphic Journalist

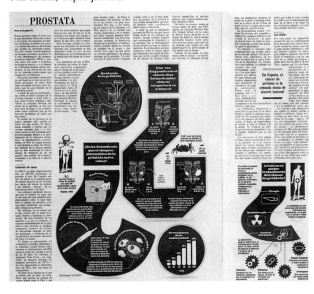

Award of Excellence
El Mundo
Madrid, Spain
Rafael Estrada, Graphic Journalist

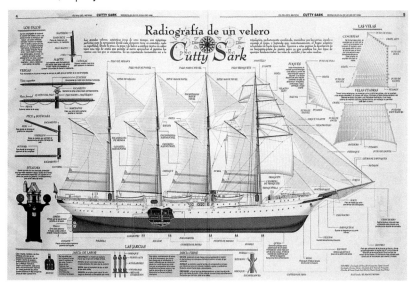

Award of Excellence
El Mundo Del Siglo XXI
Madrid, Spain
Modesto J. Carrasco, Graphic Journalist

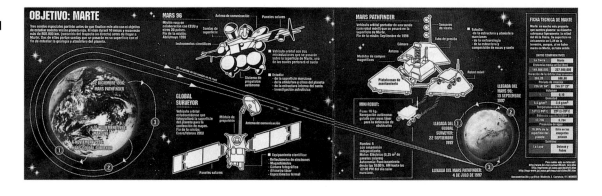

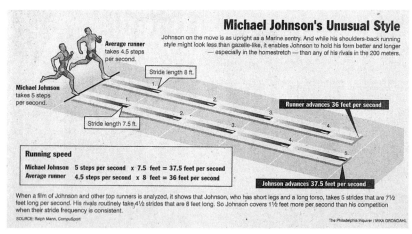

Award of Excellence
The Philadelphia Inquirer
Philadelphia, PA
Mika Grondahl, Graphic Artist

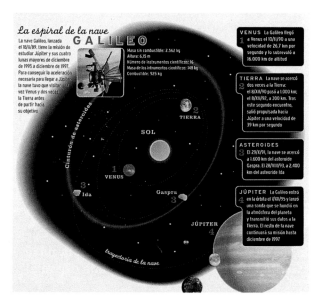

Award of Excellence
La Vanguardia
Barcelona, Spain
Angels Soler Birosta, Illustrator

Silver
El Mundo Del Siglo XXI
Madrid, Spain

Mario Tascon, Designer; Marcos Balfagon, Illustrator; Dina Sanchez, Modesto J. Carrasco, Ramon Ramos, Francisco Alvarez, Graphic Journalists; Rafael Ferrer, Editor

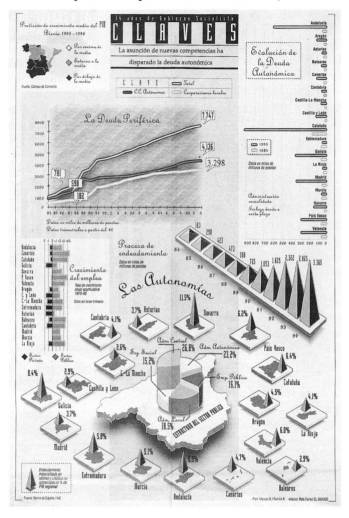

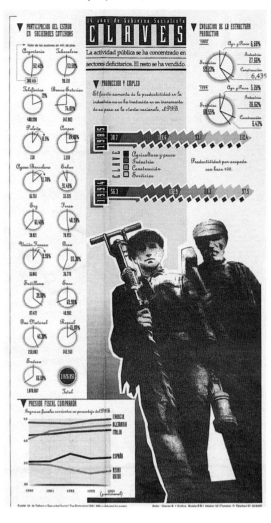

Award of Excellence
The Philadelphia Inquirer
Philadelphia, PA

Cynthia Greer, Graphic Artist

Award of Excellence
• Also an Award of Excellence for Features Other Page
El Mundo
Madrid, Spain

Mario Tascón, Graphic Journalist; Rafael Ferrer, Graphic Journalist; Juan Santiuste, Illustrator; Eva M. Chaparro, Text

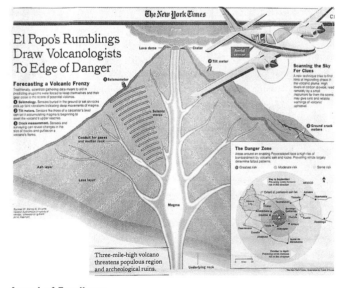

Award of Excellence
The New York Times
New York, NY

Frank O'Connell, Illustrator

Award of Excellence
El Mundo
Madrid, Spain

Mario Tascón, Designer; Marcos Balfagón, Illustrator; Dina Sánchez, Graphic Journalist; Modesto J. Carrasco, Graphic Journalist; Ramón Ramos, Graphic Journalist; Francisco Alvarez, Graphic Journalist; Rafael Ferrer, Editor

Award of Excellence
El Mundo
Madrid, Spain

Ramon Ramos, Graphics Journalist; Dina Sanchez, Graphics Journalist; Chema Matia, Graphics Journalist; Modesto J. Carrasco, Graphic Journalist; Gorka Sampedro, Graphics Journalist; Rafael Estrada, Graphics Journalist; Juancho Cruz, Graphic Journalist

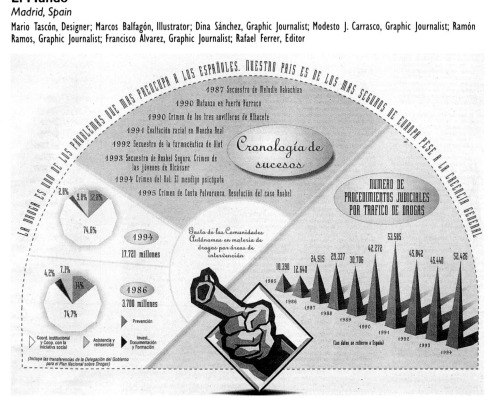

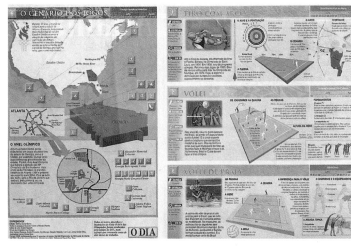

Award of Excellence
O Dia
Rio de Janeiro, Brazil

Ary Moraes, Graphic & Illustration Director; Janey Costa Silva, Graphic Artist; Ary Moraes, Graphic Artist; Aloisio Vilanova, Graphic Artist; Andre Provedel, Graphic Artist; Claudio Roberto, Graphic Artist; Ivan Luiz, Graphic Artist

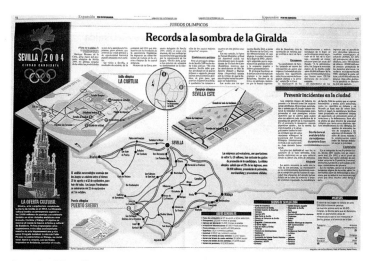

Award of Excellence
Expansión
Madrid, Spain

José Juan Gamáz, Design Director; Pablo Ma Ramírez, Graphics Artist; Blanca Serrano, Graphics Artist; Nacho de Haro, Graphics Artist; Ramón Franco, Graphics Artist; Mar Domingo, Graphics Artist; Diego Amrambillet, Graphics Artist; Juan D. Ferreira; Graphics Artist

MISCELLANEOUS

Entries that did not fit in one of the 21 categories in this competition could be included here. Also included are redesigns and reprints. Brief biographies of the 21 judges who had to make the tough decisions for the 18th Edition follow the reprints. Finally, every effort was made to provide a complete, correct index of winning publications and the names of the individuals responsible as listed on the entry forms.

[REDESIGN]

[REPRINTS]

[JUDGES]

[INDEX]

Award of Excellence
The Budapest Sun
Budapest, Hungary

Reuben J. Stern, Editor & Art Director; Anita Altman, Style Editor; Greg Horowitz, Production Manager; Jim Michaels, Editor & Publisher

Before

After

Before

After

Award of Excellence
El Pais Semanal
Madrid, Spain

David García, Art Director; Eugenio González, Design Director; María Paz Domingo, Designer; Gustavo Sánchez, Designer; Isabel Benito, Designer; Alex Martínez, Chief Editor

Award of Excellence
The Star-Ledger
Newark, NJ

Jim Willse, Editor; Chris Buckley, Feature Design Editor; Robert Britt, Graphics Editor; Charles Cooper, ME Production; George Frederick, AME/Design

Before

After

Award of Excellence
Asbury Park Press
Neptune, NJ

Harris Siegel, ME Design & Photography; Amy Catalano, Designer; Andrew Prendimano, Art & Photo Director

Before

After

Before

After

Award of Excellence
Duluth News-Tribune
Duluth, MN

Lewis H. Leung, Designer; Deborah Withey, Designer/Redesign Director; Pat McIlheran, Design Coordinator; Vicki Gowler, Executive Editor; Staff

Award of Excellence
Duluth News-Tribune
Duluth, MN

Lewis H. Leung, Designer; Deborah Withey, Designer/Redesign Director; Pat McIlheran, Design Coordinator; Vicki Gowler, Executive Editor

Before

After

Award of Excellence
The Albuquerque Journal
Albuquerque, NM

Mary Schuver, Designer; Isabel Sanchez, Assistant Metro Editor; Annemarie Neff, Assistant Design Director; Joe Kirby, Design Director; Carolyn Flynn, AME/Photo and Design

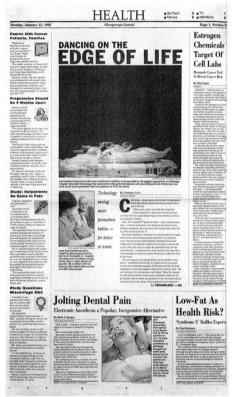

Before

After

Before

After

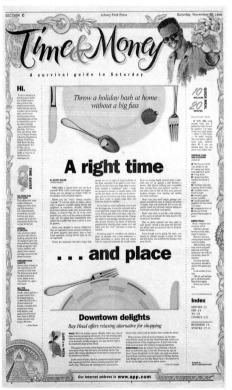

Award of Excellence
Asbury Park Press
Neptune, NJ

Harry Ziegler, ME/Lifestyles; Andrew Prendimano, Art & Photo Director; Harris Siegel, ME Design & Photography; Jacie Chun, Illustrator; Stacey Bersani, Editor

Award of Excellence
The Boston Globe
Boston, MA

Natalie Diffloth, Art Director & Designer; Neil C. Pinchin, Art Director

Before

After

The Budapest Sun
Budapest, Hungary
Reuben J. Stern, Art Director; Anita Altman, Style Editor; Greg Horowitz, Production Manager; Kriszta Tóth, Assistant Style Editor

Award of Excellence
Oregon Daily Emerald
Eugene, OR
Steven Asbury, Editor-in-Chief & Designer

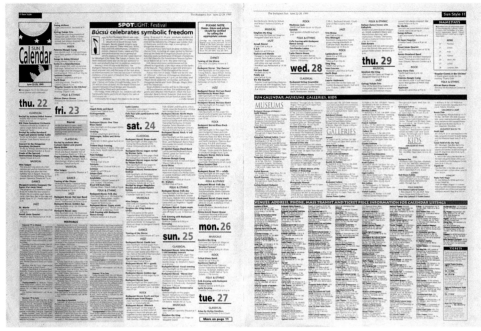

Before

Before

After

After

Award of Excellence
The Oregonian
Portland, OR
Tim Harrower, Researcher/Writer/Designer

Award of Excellence
La Vanguardia
Barcelona, Spain
Carlos Perez de Rozas Arribas, Art Director; Rosa Mundet Poch, Chief of Design and Infographics; Salvador Alimbau, Designer; Rosa Anechina, Infographic Designer; Albert Fernandez, Infographic Designer

Award of Excellence
The Times-Picayune
New Orleans, LA
G. Andrew Boyd, Photographer; Chuck Cook, Photographer; Thom Scott, Photographer; Jennifer Zdon, Photographer; John McCusker, Photographer; Dinah Rogers, Asst Photo Ed; Staci Andrews, Designer

Award of Excellence
Newsday
Melville, NY
Ned Levine, Project Art Director; Bill Zimmerman, Editor; Peggy Brown, Writer; Steve Geiger, Comics Artist; Bob Eisner, Director of Editorial Design; Myna Georgiou, Researcher

Award of Excellence
The Globe & Mail
Toronto, Canada
Michael Gregg, Executive Art Director; Eric Nelson, Art Director News

CANADA'S NATIONAL NEWSPAPER

THE GLOBE AND MAIL

©1996 — 153rd Year — $1.60 plus GST at retailers in Greater Toronto — Toronto, Saturday, September 21, 1996 — Sun, cloud, isolated showers. High near 22. Details, map, E3.

Leaves from a reader's notebook: Alberto Manguel's sensual History of Reading. Story, C26. *(TRACY COX)*

Award of Excellence
Indianapolis Star & News
Indianapolis, IN
John Scott, Artist; John Bigelow, Artist

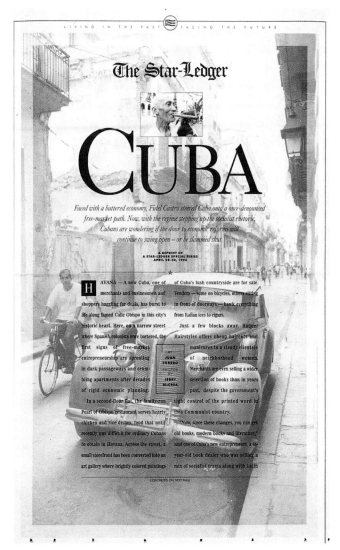

Award of Excellence
The Star-Ledger
Newark, NJ
Pablo Colon, Designer; Peter Ambush, Graphics; Chris Buckley, Art Director; George Frederick, AME Design; Arnold Braeske, Section Editor; Pim Van Hemmen, Photo Editor; Christopher P. Collins, Photo Editor; Jerry McCrea; Photographer

Best-designed newspaper judges

This group of five judges was looking only at the competition's overall design category, studying newspapers as a whole. They determined the top overall newspapers for information and design presentation in all 20 categories of the competition in three circulation sizes. These newspapers have the distinction of being the World's Best-Designed Newspapers.

Jueces de los Periódicos Mejor Diseñados

El primer grupo de cinco jueces sólo estaba juzgando la categoría de diseño general de la competencia, estudiando a los periódicos en su totalidad. Tomaron determinaciones de los mejores periódicos en general, en cuanto a información y diseño de presentación, en todas las 20 categorías de la competencia, en tres tamaños de circulación. Estos periódicos se distinguen por ser los Periódicos Mejor Diseñados del Mundo.

John Muller has recently returned to El Mundo (Madrid, Spain) after being executive editor of El Universal (Venezuela) where he was responsible for its redesign which was completed in November 1996. He has been a correspondent for newspapers, magazines and radio.

• • •

John Muller ha regresado hace poco a El Mundo (Madrid, España), después de haber trabajado como editor ejecutivo de El Universal (Venezuela), donde fue responsable del rediseño que acaba de completarse en noviembre de 1996. Ha sido corresponsal de varios periódicos, revistas y radio.

• • • • •

Jennie Buckner has been the editor of The Charlotte Observer since 1993. Before joining the newspaper she was vice president/news for Knight-Ridder, Inc. She has worked for the San Jose Mercury News and the Detroit Free Press in a number of editing positions.

Jennie Buckner ha sido editora de The Charlotte Observer desde 1993. Antes de trabajar para este periódico, fue Vicepresidenta de Noticias de Knight-Ridder, Inc. Antes de eso, trabajó para el San Jose Mercury News y el Detroit Free Press, ocupando una serie de posiciones editoriales.

Valerie Bender is features editor at The Fresno Bee where she went in 1996 after spending four years at The News Journal, Wilmington, Del., as managing editor and assistant managing editor. She spent 11 years at the Fort Lauderdale Sun-Sentinel where she became deputy managing editor for overall design and photography. Before becoming involved in design she was a reporter, layout editor and desk chief.

• • •

Valerie Bender es editora de crónicas especiales de The Fresno Bee, donde comenzó a trabajar en 1996 después de trabajar cuatro años en el The News Journal, Wilmington, Delaware, como editora gerente. Trabajó 11 años en el Fort Lauderdale Sun-Sentinel, en donde trabajó como editora y sub-gerente de diseño general y fotografía. Antes de comenzar a trabajar en diseño, trabajó como reportera, editora de compaginación y jefa de redacción.

• • • • •

Ray Ollwerther es editor ejecutivo del Asbury Park Press (en New Jersey) y Vicepresidente de Noticias del Press y The Home News & Tribune, con un personal total combinado de 370 empleados. Comenzó a trabajar para el Press en 1972 como reportero, editor de noche y en proyectos como editor gerente, antes de asumir el cargo de editor ejecutivo en 1988.

Ole Munk is graphic designer and newspaper consultant and partner in the design company Ribergård & Munk Graphic Design. Since 1993, he has worked on design and infographic projects with a number of Scandinavian newspapers and magazines. He was editor of the SND/S journal Aviserat from 1994 to 1995 and is educated as an architect.

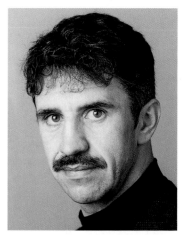

Ole Munk es un diseñador gráfico y consultor de periódicos, así como socio de la compañía de diseño Ribergard & Munk Graphic Design. Desde 1993 ha trabajado en proyectos de diseño e infografía con una serie de periódicos y revistas escandinavas. Fue editor de la revista Aviserat del SND/S de 1994 a 1995, y su educación formal fue como arquitecto.

Ray Ollwerther is executive editor of the Asbury Park Press (N.J.) and vice president/news for the Press and The Home News & Tribune, with a combined staff of 370. He joined the Press in 1972, serving as reporter, night suburban editor and assistant managing editor/projects before becoming executive editor in 1988.

General competition judges

This group of 16 judges was organized much as in past competitions: three groups of five judges with a "floater judge" to solve conflicts and act as a backup to the three groups.

Jueces de la competencia general

El grupo de dieciséis jueces se organizó básicamente de la misma manera que en competencias anteriores: tres grupos de cinco jueces con un "juez flotante" para resolver conflictos y servir de suplente para los tres grupos.

· · · · ·

Pegie Stark Adam is a faculty associate in visual journalism at The Poynter Institute for Media Studies, St. Petersburg, Fla., where she was graphics and design director from 1991 to 1995. She has been a graphics editor at The Detroit News, graphics director at the Detroit Free Press and art editor/design at the St. Petersburg Times. She has written and designed books on design and color and has worked on newspaper design projects in the U.S., Canada and England.

Pegie Stark Adam es profesora asociada en periodismo visual de The Poynter Institute for Media Studies, en San Petersburgo, Florida, donde fue directora gráfica y de diseño entre 1991 y 1995. Ha sido editora gráfica de The Detroit News, directora gráfica del Detroit Free Press y editora de arte y diseño del St. Petersburg Times. Ha redactado y diseñado libros acerca de diseño y color, y ha trabajado en proyectos de diseño de periódicos en los EE.UU., Canadá e Inglaterra.

Kelly Frankeny is assistant managing editor/design at the San Francisco Examiner where she oversees the art and photo department and the overall design for the newspaper and the Sunday magazine. Before joining the Examiner she was a graphics artist and assistant art director for the Dallas Times Herald. She has received many awards from SND and other organizations. Her newspaper has been named the "World's Best-Designed Newspaper" every year since 1994.

· · ·

Kelly Frankeny es Directora Gerente de Diseño del San Francisco Examiner, donde está a cargo del departamento de arte y fotografía así como del diseño general del periódico y el dominical. Antes de comenzar a trabajar en el Examiner, trabajó como artista gráfica y asistente al director de arte del Dallas Times Herald. Ha recibido muchos premios del SND así como otras organizaciones. Su periódico ha sido nombrado Periódico Mejor Diseñado del Mundo desde que se creó este premio en 1994.

Kevin Dolan is assistant news editor at The Santa Fe New Mexican where he has been since 1993. Before that, he was news editor of the Daily Republic in Fairfield, Calif.

· · ·

Kevin Dolan es sub-director de noticias de The Santa Fe New Mexican, donde ha trabajado desde 1993. Anteriormente fue editor de noticias de The Daily Republic en Fairfield, California.

Christopher Kozlowski is assistant managing editor/design & graphics at The Detroit News where he is responsible for the presentation of the newspaper. He has worked at The News since 1993. He also worked at North Hills (Pa.) News Record, Lansing (Mich.) State Journal and The News-Sentinel (Ind.).

· · ·

Christopher Kozlowski es Director Gerente de Diseño y Gráficas de The Detroit News, donde es responsable de la presentación del periódico. Ha trabajado en este periódico desde 1993. También trabajó en News Record de North Hills, State Journal de Lansing y The News Sentinel.

Kelly Doe is art director of the Washington Post Magazine where she has been for six years. Previously she spent time in New York at Mirabella Magazine and in California at Hippocrates Magazine and The San Jose Mercury News. Her work has received numerous publication design awards from SND as well as other organizations. Other projects include work for The San Jose Institute of Contemporary Art, The San Francisco Art Institute and The San Jose Public Art Commission.

Kelly Doe es directora de arte del Washington Post Magazine, donde ha trabajado ya durante seis años. Anteriormente trabajó por un tiempo en Nueva York, en Mirabella Magazine, y en California en Hippocrates Magazine y en The San Jose Mercury News. Su trabajo ha recibido numerosos premios de diseño de publicaciones de SND, así como de otras organizaciones. Otros proyectos incluyen trabajo que ha hecho para el Instituto de Arte Contemporáneo de San Jose, el Instituto de Arte de San Francisco y la Comisión de Arte Público de San Jose.

Bryan Monroe is assistant managing editor at the San Jose (Calif.) Mercury News where he is in charge of the news desk and photo, art, design and systems departments. In 1992, he engineered a major redesign of the News. Before arriving at the News in 1991, he was assistant director for Knight-Ridder, Inc.'s project targeting readers age 25 to 43. A well-known speaker at many newspaper conferences, he has won numerous awards from SND and other news-related organizations.

Bryan Monroe es Editor Gerente del San Jose Mercury News en California, donde está a cargo de los departamentos de noticias y foto, arte, diseño y sistemas. En 1992 ideó un rediseño de gran envergadura del San Jose Mercury News. Antes de comenzar a trabajar para este periódico en 1991, fue asistente del director para un proyecto de Knight-Ridder, Inc. cuya audiencia deseada eran lectores entre los 25 y los 43 años de edad. Es un orador muy conocido en muchas conferencias periodísticas y ha ganado numerosos premios de SND, así como de otras organizaciones noticiosas.

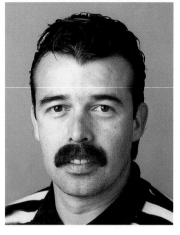

Raul Martinez is art director of El Norte (Mexico) where he leads a design staff of more than 70.

• • •

Raúl Martínez es director de arte de El Norte (México), donde es jefe de un personal de diseño con más de 70 empleados.

Janet Michaud began designing sports at The Boston Globe in 1996. Before joining The Globe, she was a news designer and night layout editor at the Asbury Park Press in New Jersey and a designer at the Utica Observer-Dispatch in upstate New York.

• • •

Janet Michaud comenzó a diseñar en la sección de deportes de The Boston Globe en 1986. Antes de comenzar a trabajar en The Globe trabajó como diseñadora de noticias y editora nocturna de compaginación del Asbury Park Press en New Jersey y como diseñadora en el Utica Observer-Dispatch en el estado de Nueva York.

Duncan Mil is art director at Graphic News (London). In 1971, he joined the Sunday Times in London and from 1976 to 1988 he was a freelancer for the British national press. In 1991, he founded his own international graphics service.

Duncan Mil es director de arte de Graphic News (Londres). En 1971 comenzó a trabajar para el Sunday Times en Londres y desde 1976 hasta 1988 trabajó como contratista independiente para la prensa nacional británica. En 1991 fundó su propio servicio internacional de artes gráficas.

Neal Pattison is assistant managing editor at the Seattle Post-Intelligencer (Wash.) and SND president. Prior to joining the newspaper he was managing editor at the Albuquerque Tribune. He has been a designer, reporter and editor at newspapers with circulations ranging from 3,500 to 400,000.

Dash Parham is director of graphics at USA TODAY. Prior to this position, he was art director for nine years. Before joining the newspaper, he worked as art director for various advertising agencies and design firms in the Washington, D.C. area. He teaches publication design at Howard University's School of Communications. He has won numerous awards from SND, Communication Arts and other journalism organizations.

Dash Parham es director de artes gráficas de USA TODAY. Antes de ocupar este puesto ya había sido director de arte durante nueve años. Antes de comenzar a trabajar para este periódico trabajó como director de arte en varias agencias publicitarias y compañías de diseño en el área de Washington, D.C. Enseña diseño de publicaciones en la Facultad de Comunicación de Howard University. Se ha ganado numerosos premios de SND, Communication Arts y otras organizaciones periodísticas.

• • • • •

Neal Pattison es Editor Gerente del Seattle Post-Intelligencer (en Washington) y Presidente de SND. Antes de comenzar a trabajar en este periódico fue Editor Gerente del Albuquerque Tribune en Nueva México. Ha sido diseñador, reportero y editor de periódicos con circulaciones de entre 3.500 y 400.000 ejemplares.

Reginald Myers is art director at the News Tribune in Tacoma, Wash. Prior to joining that newspaper he was a staff artist at The Miami News and The Miami Herald. He has won numerous SND awards and shared a Pulitzer Prize for Public Service while an artist at The Herald.

• • •

Reginald Myers es director de arte del News Tribune, en Tacoma, Washington. Antes de comenzar a trabajar en este periódico fue miembro del personal artístico de The Miami News y The Miami Herald. Se ha ganado numerosos premios de SND, y compartió un Premio Pulitzer de Servicio Público mientras era artista de The Herald.

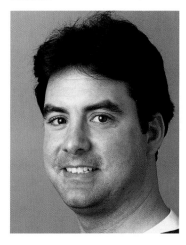

Michael Price is the creator of the journalism graphics degree at Ball State University in Muncie, Ind. A former art director, he has been a faculty fellow at National Geographic magazine and is the 1997 fellow at The Philadelphia Inquirer. Graphics adviser to The Ball State Daily News, he was Ball State's 1996 Teacher of the Year.

Joe Zeff is associate art director at Time magazine. Before joining Time, he was the first presentation editor at The New York Times for its business and metro sections. He has worked at the Detroit Free Press and Pittsburgh Post-Gazette. He has won numerous awards for his work in design and has lectured internationally about the creative possibilities for content-driven design.

Joe Zeff es director asociado de arte de la revista Time. Antes de comenzar a trabajar para Time, fue el primer editor de presentación de la secciones metropolitana y de negocios de The New York Times. También trabajó en el Detroit Free Press y el Pittsburg Post-Gazette. Se ha ganado numerosos premios por su trabajo en diseño y ha dictado cátedra internacionalmente acerca de las posibilidades creativas del diseño en base al contenido.

• • • • •

Michael Price es el creador del título en gráficas para el periodismo en la Universidad de Ball State, en Mundie, Indiana. Anteriormente director de arte, ha sido colegiado docente de la revista National Geographic y lo es actualmente de The Philadelphia Inquirer. Asesor de artes gráficas de The Ball State Daily News, ha salido Profesor del Año 1996 de Ball State.

Michel Samson is assistant managing editor at Le Soleil (Quebec) where he is chief of the news desk primarily responsible for page A-one design. He coordinates the news graphic team in producing feature pages, magazine pages and informational graphics. He has worked as a reporter, editor and designer at five newspapers since 1966 and teaches news design at Laval University's Communication Department.

• • •

Michael Samson es Editor Gerente de Le Soleil (Quebec), donde es jefe de noticias, principalmente responsable del diseño de la página A-1. Está a cargo de coordinar el equipo de artes gráficas para noticias en la producción de páginas de crónicas, revistas y gráficas informativas. Ha trabajado como reportero, editor y diseñador en cinco periódicos desde 1966. Enseña diseño de noticias en el Departamento de Comunicaciones de la Universidad de Laval.

Warren Watson is executive editor of the Kennebec Journal and Central Maine Morning Sentinel. He was formerly managing editior/operations and associate publisher for the Portland (Maine) Press Herald and graphics editor of the St. Petersburg Times. He is a frequent speaker on design and contributor to industry periodicals. He founded the SND's Selling by Design program in 1993.

Warren Watson es editor ejecutivo del Kennebec Journal y del Central Maine Morning Sentinel. Anteriormente fue Editor Gerente de Operaciones y Asociado de Publicación del Portland Press Herald (en Maine), así como editor gráfico del St. Petersburg Times. Es orador frecuente sobre el tema de diseño y contribuye mucho a las revistas del ramo periodístico. Fundó el programa Selling by Design (Vendiendo Mediante Diseño) de SND en 1993.

By Person's Name

By Publication's Name